MICROPROCESSOR-BASED PROCESS CONTROL

MICROPROCESSOR-BASED PROCESS CONTROL

CURTIS D. JOHNSON
University of Houston

PRENTICE-HALL, INC., *Englewood Cliffs, New Jersey 07632*

Library of Congress Cataloging in Publication Data

Johnson, Curtis D. (date)
  Microprocessor-based process control.

  Includes index.
  1. Process control.   2. Microprocessors.   I. Title
TS156.8.J628   1984   629.8'95   83-17832
ISBN   0-13-580654-2

Editorial/production supervision and
  interior design: *Rosalie Herion*
Cover design: *20/20 Services, Inc., Mark Berghash*
Manufacturing buyer: *Anthony Caruso*

Printed in the United States of America

10   9   8   7   6   5   4   3   2   1

ISBN   0-13-580654-2

Prentice-Hall International, Inc., *London*
Prentice-Hall of Australia Pty. Limited, *Sydney*
Editora Prentice-Hall do Brasil, Ltda., *Rio de Janeiro*
Prentice-Hall Canada Inc., *Toronto*
Prentice-Hall of India Private Limited, *New Delhi*
Prentice-Hall of Japan, Inc., *Tokyo*
Prentice-Hall of Southeast Asia Pte. Ltd., *Singapore*
Whitehall Books Limited, *Wellington, New Zealand*

CONTENTS

PREFACE

Applications of microprocessors have expanded throughout modern society and will continue to do so to the limits of imagination. Visible applications such as home and small business computers are really only the tip of the iceberg. The microprocessor is an integral part of internal equipment in a vast assortment of applications. Process control is one such application. In process control the application of microprocessors occurs everywhere, from the intelligent acquisition of data to on-site controllers, which take the control operations away from a centralized control room and place it at the site.

The purpose of this text is to present the essential and practical aspects of microprocessor applications to control and in particular to process control. This text is practical in that concern is not for the analysis of control system operation but rather for the design of hardware and software, which can provide the mechanism of control. The tuning of such control systems and topics such as stability and optimal control analysis are not treated in this text.

Texts on the application of microprocessors too often spend much of their space on the microprocessor itself. This text instead assumes that the reader has already learned the basics of microprocessor hardware and assembly language. The design of the text has been structured, however, so that such a course could be taken in parallel, as a co-requisite. Details of the computer are not needed until the third chapter. The math prerequisite is algebra, and it is assumed that the reader also has had a course in digital electronics. Prior knowledge of control systems is not required. It should be understood, however, that this text presents the computer hardware and software "machinery" needed for control. There would certainly be much more to learn before a control system could be designed and tuned for optimum and stable operation.

In any text involving microprocessors there is always the question of which microprocessor to use. This text is not really *about* microprocessors; rather, it covers the application of microprocessor-based computers. Thus an attempt has been made to present the algorithms independent of a particular microprocessor, using general flowcharts of algorithms. As specific examples, the common 8080 and 6800 mnemonic codes have also been presented.

Chapter 1 is an overview of control systems for process control, summarizing the general concepts so that the reader can put in perspective the remaining material. Chapter 2 presents the essential features of analog data acquisition, including transducers as well as a brief treatment of analog signal conditioning. Op amps are presented as the basic tool for such signal conditioning. Chapters 3 and 4 present the hardware and software of data acquisition and initial processing, including the ADC and DAC along with basic software processes such as linearization and sampling consequences. Chapter 5 covers control operations associated with discrete-state systems. Such systems are perhaps more common than continuous-state control systems normally are thought to be. Chapter 6 presents the software required for continuous-state control systems using proportional, integral (reset), and derivative (rate) algorithms. In all cases the software is presented as both a flowchart and a sample code in either 8080 or 6800 mnemonics. The flowcharts can be used as a guide to expressing the algorithms in any microprocessor code.

I am indebted to many people and organizations for this text. In particular I wish to recognize the Institut National D'Electricité et D'Electronique (INELEC) in Algeria, where the idea and framework of this book were developed. In addition, I must thank the Nippon Electric Company (NEC) and Designer Software, without whose computer and word-processing software the text could never have been written in as timely a fashion. Of course, the patience of my wife Helene Blake and son Greg were required throughout.

CURTIS D. JOHNSON

MICROPROCESSOR-BASED PROCESS CONTROL

CHAPTER 1

INTRODUCTION TO CONTROL SYSTEMS

☐ ☐ ☐ ☐ ☐ ☐ ☐ ☐ ☐ ☐ ☐ ☐ ☐

☐ ☐ ☐ ☐ ☐ ☐ ☐ ☐ ☐ ☐ ☐ ☐ ☐

☐ ☐ ☐ ☐ ☐ ☐ ☐ ☐ ☐ ☐ ☐ ☐ ☐

OBJECTIVES

The overall goal of this chapter is to gain a general idea of process control and how it is accomplished. After studying this chapter and doing the problems at the end of the chapter, you will be able to:

1. Explain the purpose of process control.
2. Draw a block diagram of a process control loop and explain the function of each part of the loop.
3. Describe how the performance of a process control loop is evaluated.
4. Give a description of four modes of control.
5. Describe analog control system configurations.
6. Describe digital control system configurations.

1-1   DEFINITION OF PROCESS CONTROL

In the industrial world, the word *process* refers to an interacting set of operations that lead to the manufacture or development of some product. In the chemical industry, *process* means the operations necessary to take an assemblage of raw materials and cause them to react in some prescribed fashion to produce a desired end product, such as gasoline. In the food industry, *process* means to take raw materials and operate on them in such a manner that an edible product results. In each case, and in all other cases in the process industries, the end product *must have certain specified properties*, which depend on the conditions of the reactions and operations that produce them. The word *control* is used to describe the steps necessary to assure that the conditions produce the correct properties in the product. There are many ways to achieve this control of the process, but certain general features can be identified, and this will be done in this section.

1-1.1   The Process

In a very general sense a process can be described by an equation. Suppose we let a product be *defined* by a set of properties, P_1, P_2, . . . , P_n. Each of these properties must have a certain value for the product to be correct. Examples of properties are things like color, density, chemical composition, and size. The value of the properties obviously depends on the conditions that exist during the manufacturing process, and in some cases they may depend on each other. If the set of variables, v_1, v_2, . . . , v_m is all the things on which the properties depend, then an equation can be written for each property:

$$P_i = F(v_1, v_2, \ldots, v_m, t) \tag{1-1}$$

where P_i = the ith property

t = time.

This equation simply states that P_i is a *function* of all the variables in the parentheses. The variables may be quantities like temperature, pressure, flow rate, and rotational rate. Notice that the time, t, has been included in this equation. This is an important thing for you to remember: *Process control is a time-based concept.* The objective is to maintain a property at some specified value *in time* as the manufacturing process proceeds.

Controlled Variables.   To produce a product with the specified properties, some or all the variables in Eq. (1-1) must be maintained at specific values. For example, if a process produces crackers, one property is cracker color. Clearly, the oven temperature is a variable that must be maintained at a specific value to assure this property. Not all the variables in a process need to be controlled; indeed some cannot be controlled. For example, the ambient outside air temperature may affect some property, but clearly it cannot be controlled. In such a case some other variable must be used to compensate. When the value of a variable is controlled, the result is that

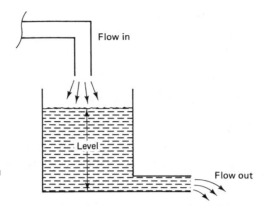

FIG. 1-1   This self-regulating system will adopt a level for which flow in equals flow out.

the value is maintained at or near a specified quantity. In this sense the value of the variable is *regulated*.

In general, many of the variables on which a property depends must be controlled to assure the property has the specified value. In the cracker example, other variables affect the cracker color, such as conveyor speed, proportion of ingredients, and humidity. In general, then, many variables may need to be regulated or controlled to assure one property.

Self-regulation.   Some of the variables in a process may exhibit the property of *self-regulation*, whereby they will *naturally* maintain a certain value under normal conditions. As an example, consider the level of liquid in a tank as shown in Fig. 1-1. The rate of flow out depends on the level. For a given rate of flow into the tank, the level will rise until the flow out matches the flow in. The level then remains fixed. Of course, if the conditions change, such as the flow in increasing, then the level will change, so it is not really regulated. On the other hand, unless the flow in exceeds some critical value, the tank will never overflow.

1-1.2   The Control

The formal relationship given in Eq. (1-1) shows that control of variables is necessary to maintain the properties of the product within specification. It does not say anything about how such control is to be accomplished. To control the property, it is necessary to regulate the values of one or more variables.

Control Strategy.   To understand the strategy used for regulation or control of a variable, it is helpful to consider the following equation:

$$v_j = G(v_1, v_2, \ldots, v_c, \ldots, v_m, t) \qquad (1\text{-}2)$$

This equation shows that the value of a variable, v_j, actually depends on many other variables in the process, and also on time. This is not hard to see; for example, the oven temperature in our cracker color example clearly depends on many variables, such as conveyor speed, number of crackers in the oven, air currents in the oven,

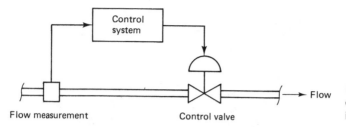

FIG. 1-2 This flow control is an example of single-variable independent control.

heater current, and perhaps even outside ambient air temperature. The other variables in Eq. (1-2) represent these quantities. To regulate the value of v_j, the following strategy can be used:

1. Select one variable in Eq. (1-2) to be a *controlling* variable. This will be a variable that affects the value of v_j *and* that we can change. For the oven problem, this could be the heater current. In Eq. (1-2) the controlling variable has been labeled as v_c.
2. Make a *measurement* of the controlled variable, v_j, to determine its present value.
3. *Compare* the measured value of the controlled variable with the desired value for maintenance of the product property. The desired value is called the *set point* of the controlled variable.
4. *Determine* a change in the controlling variable that will correct any deviation, or *error*, of the controlled variable from the set point.
5. *Feed back* this changed value of the controlling variable to the process to create a correction to the controlled variable.

If this procedure is repeated from steps 2 through 5 on a regular basis, the result is regulation of the variable in time. Furthermore, if such a procedure is set up for *all* the variables on which *all* the product properties depend, the result is called *process control*. The study of process control is the study of how the preceding steps can be accomplished. In this text, methods using microprocessor-based computers to accomplish process control will be presented.

Single-Variable Control.　In many instances in the process industries, a variable can be placed under a control strategy that is independent of other critical process variables. For example, in Fig. 1-2 the flow rate of liquid through a pipe can be regulated by varying the opening of a valve in response to a measurement of flow rate, in accordance with the strategy outlined previously. Whereas the flow rate depends *implicitly* on many other variables, such as liquid temperature and pressure, it is quite possible to control the flow rate without interacting with these variables. The system "stands alone" and is called a single-variable control system.

Multivariable Control.　In many of the complex manufacturing processes of the modern world, a high degree of interaction exists among the variables of the process. In such systems a variation of one variable will have consequences on the

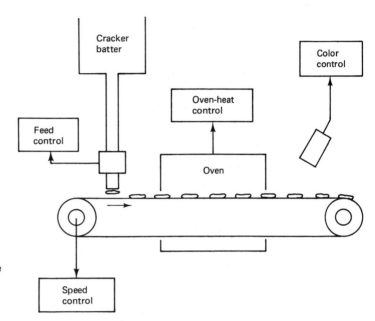

FIG. 1-3 A multivariable interactive control system may have many control systems, such as this cracker-baking example.

values of many other variables, and the control process must account for this interaction in the control strategy. This is a multivariable control system. An example is given in Fig. 1-3, where it is clear that, for example, changes in the rate of cracker batter feed cannot be made arbitrarily without also changing the conveyor speed, and perhaps the oven temperature, if the cracker baking is to be controlled. Multivariable control is often most difficult to accomplish. The introduction of computers into the control system has made the job of multivariable control much more manageable.

1-1.3 Process Control Loop

In the previous section, two important concepts involved in control were presented. The first is the idea that a sequential, *repetitive* procedure is followed to accomplish the control. The second is the introduction of the term *feedback* to describe the last step in the strategy, wherein a correction was fed back to the process in the form of changes in the controlling variable, v_c. A pictorial presentation of these concepts helps in understanding how the control system works. In Fig. 1-4 a *block diagram* of a

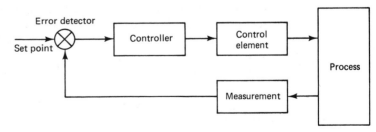

FIG. 1-4 This is a block diagram of a general process control loop.

process control loop is presented for the case of single-variable control. Each block represents one part of the control strategy listed previously.

Process.   The process block represents the overall process. All the properties and variables that constitute the manufacturing or production process are a part of this block. The block is drawn, however, to draw attention to only one variable, the controlled variable and the variables on which its value depends, as given by Eq. (1-2).

Measurement.   The measurement block represents whatever operations are necessary to determine the present value of the controlled variable. The output of this block is a *measured indication* of the controlled variable expressed in some other form, such as voltage, current, or a digital signal.

Error Detector.   The operation of comparison of the measured controlled variable to the desired value, the set point, is performed by the error detector. The output is the difference between the measured value and the set-point value. When using computers in control systems, you will see that this is usually accomplished in software.

Controller.   The next block is the part of the loop that determines the changes in the controlling variable that are needed to correct errors in the controlled variable. This block represents the "brains" of the control system. The output of this block will be a signal, called the *feedback signal*, that will change the value of the controlling variable in the process and thereby the controlled variable, via Eq. (1-2). In traditional analog control systems, the controller is essentially an analog computer. When using the microprocessor-based computer, you will see that the controller function is performed using software.

Control Element.   The final block in the control loop is the part that converts the signal from the controller into actual variations in the controlling variable. In practice, the final control element is *part of the process* itself, as it must be to bring about changes in the process variables.

1-1.4   The Control Dilemma

The rest of this chapter and much of this text will be devoted to an in-depth study of the details of process control, using microprocessor-based computers to provide the controller function. Now, however, before starting a study of the details of the problem, you should pause to consider the overall picture of what process control is trying to accomplish and how well this can be done.

The objective of process control is the desire to maintain some process variable at a specific value (or perhaps a set of such variables, but let's just concentrate on one). The strategy used is to make measurements of the variable, and if they deviate from the correct values, action to correct the error is taken. *Therefore*, to regulate the value, *it must be allowed to change!* There must be an error before action can be initiated to eliminate the error. So the dilemma of process control is that error-free control is impossible. The task of process control is thus to keep the error as small as possible.

The last question to be considered is the cause of controlled variable errors. If all the variables on which the controlled variable depends are known and fixed, no control is necessary since the value of the controlled variable will not change. In fact, however, in all cases where control is used (and therefore necessary) there will be variables *that are not under control.* It is the spontaneous variation or fluctuations of these variables that will cause errors in the controlled variable and necessitate a control system for regulation.

1-2 PERFORMANCE OF CONTROL SYSTEMS

It has been pointed out that *perfect* regulation of a process variable by process control is not possible. This gives rise to the question, then, of how to determine that the process control system is working. How much error is allowable? In general, the question of measuring the performance of a process control loop is of great importance to the process and also to the design of the control system itself. In this section the problem of *evaluation* of process control loop performance will be considered.

1-2.1 Error

The deviation between the actual value of a controlled variable and the set point is called the *error.* The error is what process control is all about, and so it is very important to have a clear idea of the meaning of this term. Error may be represented in the following ways.

Variable Value.   In some cases the error may be represented in terms of the actual variable under control. For example, if a temperature set point is 230°C and the measured value is 220°C, the error is − 10°C. In most cases this is not very meaningful since it is difficult to determine if this is good or bad.

Percent of Set Point.   Another possible representation of error is in terms of the percent of that error relative to the set point itself. In the previous temperature example, the error would be represented as

$$\frac{(-10)}{(230)} \times 100 = -4.4\%$$

Again, this representation is not often used because it is difficult to interpret the numbers in realistic terms.

Percent of Range.   The most common type of error representation depends on prior determination of a range of values of the controlled variable. Then the error is expressed as a fraction or percent of the controlled variable range. To use this method, it is necessary to select the range of controlled variables within which control is to be exercised. Let v_{max} be the maximum value of the controlled variable within the range of control and v_{min} be the minimum. Then the error is defined as

$$e_p = 100 \times \frac{v - v_{sp}}{v_{max} - v_{min}} \tag{1-3}$$

where v_{sp} = controlled variable set point. One reason that this representation of error is preferred is that it relates error to the range over which control is desired. For example, for the temperature problem Ex. 1-1 illustrates that the $-10°C$ value can mean very different things depending on the intended *range* of control.

EXAMPLE 1-1   Calculate the error expressed as percent of range for the case of a 230°C set point and a $-10°C$ error for a 100° to 300°C range and for a 205° to 255°C range.

Solution: Equation (1-3) will give the result in both cases with the only difference being in the denominator. In either case, $v - v_{sp} = -10°C$.
For the first case the error is found easily, since $v_{max} - v_{min} = 300 - 100 = 200°C$. Thus, $e_p = 100 \times (-10/200) = -5\%$ error.
For the second case, $v_{max} - v_{min} = 255 - 205 = 50°C$. Thus, $e_p = 100 \times (-10/50) = -20\%$ error!

This example shows that a given error can have vastly different meaning depending on the target control range of the control system for the controlled variable. Certainly, in the second case a $-10°C$ error is more significant and the percent of range error shows this. In analog control systems, error is virtually always expressed as percent of range because variables are always expressed in fixed ranges of current, pressure, or voltage. In digital computer control systems, this is no longer really necessary, so absolute values of a variable can be used. Nevertheless, fraction of range is still often used because interpretation of the parameters of the control system is easier.

Generally, a control system is designed with some *allowable* error in the controlled variable. If the error is within this value, the variable is considered controlled.

1-2.2 Steady-State Response

Suppose a control loop is designed to regulate a process variable. *Without* the control loop the value of the variable may "wander" over long time scales owing to random or periodic variations of some other variable on which it is dependent. With the control loop intact and operating, this long-term variation will be greatly diminished in amplitude. There will be some residual error, as necessary to activate the control process outlined in the strategy, but this can be kept very small. Curve 1 of Fig. 1-5 shows an example of room temperature that varies in a periodic fashion over a 24-hour period because of the influence of ambient external temperature. With the control loop operating and the room temperature the controlled variable, these variations are reduced to a small fraction of the uncontrolled variation, as shown in curve 2 of Fig. 1-5. Such operation of a control system is referred to as the *steady-state response* of the control system.

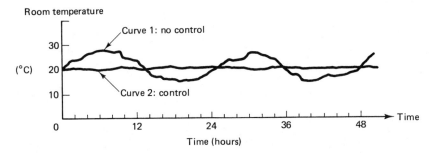

FIG. 1-5   This graph illustrates how a control system prevents large variation of the controlled variable.

Steady-state response is measured by the *residual error* between the actual value
of the controlled variable and the set point. It is not unreasonable to expect the residual errors of steady-state response to be kept below a few percent of the range in
many cases.

1-2.3   Transient Response

In many cases a variable on which the controlled variable depends will experience a
sudden or *discontinuous* change in its value, usually from external influences beyond
the control of the system. This will cause a corresponding discontinuous error in the
controlled variable, and the control system must try to correct for this effect. A condition such as this is called a *transient*, and the corresponding response of the control
loop to correct for the condition is called the *transient response* of the control loop.
In the room temperature example, a transient might be the sudden opening of a door,
thereby causing a sudden change in room temperature conditions. Protecting against
transients is one of the most difficult tasks of the control loop. Transient response is
characterized in two forms, underdamped and overdamped.

Underdamped.   In this case the response of the control system to a transient
error is such as to cause the controlled variable to *oscillate* about the set point, eventu-
ally settling back to the residual error. This is shown in Fig. 1-6. It is assumed that a

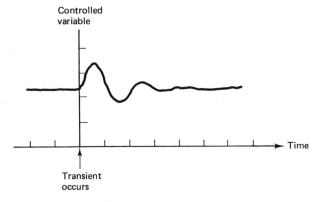

FIG. 1-6   This is underdamped
transient response. Notice that
oscillations about the set point
occur.

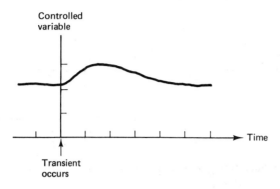

FIG. 1-7 In overdamped response to a transient, no oscillation occurs, but it may take much longer to return to the set point.

transient occurred at $t = 0$, and the resulting excursions of the controlled variable are as shown. You should realize that *without* the control system the excursions would have been much worse!

Overdamped.   Another possible result of a transient in the process is a variation of the controlled variable as shown in Fig. 1-7. Notice that the variable executes *no* oscillations about the set point.

Transient responses are called "responses of the control system" because they are not just reflections of the process, but also of the control system used to regulate variables in the process. Proper design and adjustment of the control system can *create* overdamped or underdamped response and even instability, as will be shown later.

1-2.4   Measures of Control

Given the definition of error and the types of response of the control system to external influences, how do we specify how well the control loop is doing its job? There are a number of measures of control that help decide how well the control loop is working or how it should be adjusted to work.

Residual Error.   One measure is simply to note the time-averaged residual error in the system. Since this is usually expressed in percent of range, it is important to interpret the number in terms of the narrowness of the range of control.

Dynamic Error.   The dynamic error is specified by examination of the transient response of the system to a given transient error input. Figure 1-8a shows how the dynamic response is specified for underdamped systems, and Fig. 1-8b shows the dynamic response for overdamped systems. Notice that the *maximum error* that results from the transient is significant, as well as the *duration* of the deviation from acceptable error levels. In the underdamped case the period or frequency of the resulting oscillation is also measured and reported. The control loop will be working best when adjusted such that the duration and maximum error are both *minimized* for some given transient input. Duration is measured from the time the controlled

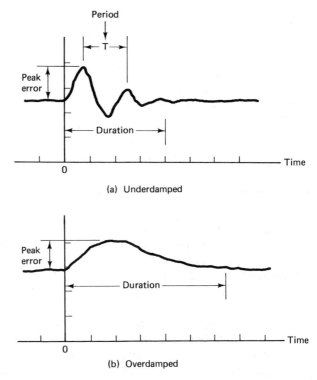

Period

|←T→|

Peak
error

|←— Duration —→|

0   Time

(a) Underdamped

Peak
error

|←—— Duration ——→|

0   Time

(b) Overdamped

FIG. 1-8 These graphs illustrate the parameters used to measure the transient response of a control system.

variable exceeds the allowable error specification to the time when it again remains within specification.

The use of computers in the control system has enabled the development of "self-adjusting" or "self-adapting" control systems. These systems can make measurements of their own responses, evaluate the responses, and make adjustments of their operating parameters to improve performance. All this is accomplished under programmed instructions.

1-2.5   Control System Instability

When considering the issue of instability in control systems, it is important to note that the statement is not made that the "process" is unstable, but rather the control system is. This is because in many cases the *instability* is *caused by the control system* and is not part of the natural response of the process that is under control.

Instability.   Two types of instabilities occur in process control installations. In both cases the definition of the instability is *growth without limit*. This means that the value of the variable, presumably under regulation, will suddenly begin to grow in value, without limit. Practically, something will finally terminate the growth, but often with serious results, like a shutdown of the process or even an explosion. Figure 1-9 shows the two types of growth without limit that occur. In one case the value of

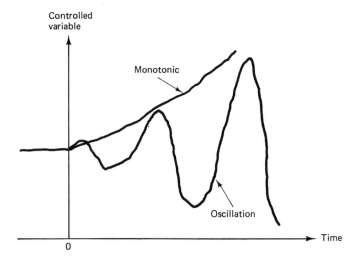

FIG. 1-9 There are two types of instability; one exhibits oscillations about the set point and one does not.

the variable simply begins to increase as a function of time. This is referred to as *monotonic* instability. In the other case the value of the variable begins to oscillate with growing amplitude as a function of time. This is called *oscillating* instability. Actually, the first type of instability is usually due to a *failure* of the control system to function, whereas the second is usually *caused* by the control system.

Monotonic Instability. Monotonic instabilities occur when a process variable *without* self-regulation is not subjected to control. Perhaps a control system has experienced a failure. Figure 1-10 shows an example in the case of a control system to regulate liquid level by adjusting input flow rate with a valve. If the system fails, with the valve open for example, then the level will simply increase, without limit, until the tank overflows. Generally, protections are built in to control systems to warn of conditions such as this. The protections are called *alarms*.

Oscillating Instability. Oscillating instability in a control system installation is generally caused by incorrect matching of the control system to the process.

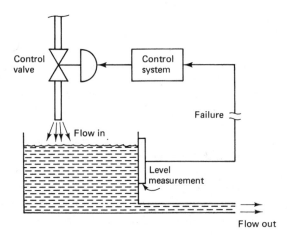

FIG. 1-10 This system would exhibit monotonic instability since the tank will simply overflow owing to the failure.

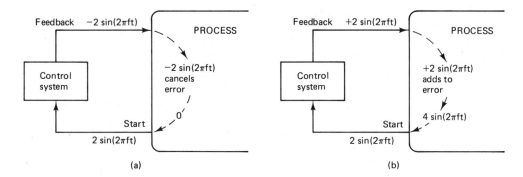

FIG. 1-11   When the feedback tends to aid the error, the oscillation type of instability may occur as shown in the second case.

The control system begins to *amplify* an error of some critical frequency instead of driving its value to zero. This is because of the *feedback* aspect of the control system. To illustrate this, consider the diagram of Fig. 1-11. It has been assumed that some small oscillation error of frequency, *f*, has occurred in the controlled variable. Normally, the control system would be expected to correct this by feeding back a signal of some proportional value, *but of opposite sign*. Thus, if the error were $2 \sin (2\pi ft)$, the expected feedback would ideally be something like $-2 \sin (2\pi ft)$, which has a 180° phase shift. Then the result would be zero and the error would be eliminated, as illustrated by Fig. 1-11a. However, in some cases, due to incorrect design of the control system, there is an additional *phase shift* of the error in being processed by the control system such that the signal that comes back is shifted by an additional 180°. Then the feedback to the process would be $+2 \sin (2\pi ft)$, and the error is actually increased in magnitude! This effect is illustrated in Fig. 1-11b. All control systems experience variations in net gain and phase shift as a function of frequency. It is very important to study these variations very carefully to assure that an instability condition such as this cannot occur.

It is interesting that instability is as much a part of computer process control systems as traditional analog systems. This is in part because the strategy of control is the same in either case, and it is the strategy that can create instability.

1-3 METHODS OF CONTROL

The previous sections have given a description of the basic principles of process control and control systems. In this section the procedures or methods that are used to *accomplish* regulation of a process variable will be explained. No details of the actual control system need be given in order to explain just what the control system must do to regulate the value of some variable. Of course, the ultimate goal of this text is to show the details of how process control is accomplished using microprocessor-based computers. What will be presented in this section will be the procedures used for any control system configuration, whether electronic, pneumatic, or digital computer.

1-3.1 Transfer Functions

To specify the methods of control, it will be necessary to describe the process control system in mathematical terms. In general, this is done by treating each block of the control system, as shown in Fig. 1-4, as an operational unit that "operates" on the input to produce a specific output. The operation performed by a block is described by a *transfer function*, which simply specifies how the output is related to the input.

Measurement. The transfer function of the measurement block tells how the measured indication of the controlled variable is related to the variable itself:

$$v_m = T(v, t) \tag{1-4}$$

where v_m = measured indication of variable

      v = controlled variable

and where T stands for the transfer function operation. In Ch. 2 a number of different measurement systems will be discussed and the transfer functions given. In general, the function will be *nonlinear*, which means that a plot of v_m versus v will *not* be a straight line. The form of the output can be of many different types, depending on the method used to make the measurement. Usually, the output will be a voltage or current. Often, for example, the measurement originates with a variation of resistance of some device as the measured variable changes; this is then changed to a voltage or current. The time dependence is usually a *lag* between the measurement block output and the actual moment of measurement. Figure 1-12 presents as an example the transfer function of a temperature-measurement device, a thermocouple, which produces a voltage as a function of temperature. One of the first steps in using computers in process control will be to convert the measurement information into *digital format*.

Error Detector. The error detector inputs the set point and measured variable and outputs the difference. The transfer function can be formally stated in terms of the difference between the controlled variable and the set point:

$$e = v - v_{sp} \tag{1-5}$$

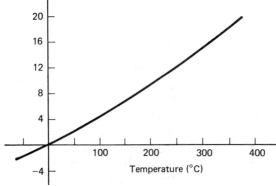

FIG. 1-12 This thermocouple transfer function shows how voltage is produced as a function of temperature. Is it linear?

where e = error expressed in terms of the measured variable. In actual practice, the error will be expressed as percent of range, as defined by Eq. (1-3). Thus, an important consideration of the control system is to define the range over which the control will be exercised. Once the minimum and maximum have been established, Eq. (1-3) can be used to specify the error as a percent of range.

Controller.   The transfer function of the controller is determined by how the proper feedback response is to be derived. In the next section a number of different controller responses are considered. In general, the response of the controller can be written

$$c = C(e, t) \qquad (1-6)$$

where c = output signal to the final control element. This function can take on many forms. If an error occurs in a controlled variable, this block must determine what kind of corrective action to take. Suppose the cracker oven temperature is too low; then the oven must be heated. But how? Should it be heated slowly, very fast, maximum heat, or gradual buildup? These issues are decided by the controller. The controller is a *computer* that accepts the error input and performs certain "programmed" calculations to determine the proper output. Historically, this was done by analog "pneumatic" computers, then by analog electronic computers, and finally by digital electronic computers. Recent advances in microelectronics have brought about a growing application of microprocessor-based computers to process control. A study of this application is the objective of this text.

Final Control Element.   The final control element has a transfer function that tells how the controller output signal is converted into an actual variation of the controlling variable. In general, the final control operation may be a high-energy operation, such as operating a massive pipeline valve. The transfer generally shows some lags because the operation involves changes in the process itself. The transfer function may be written

$$v_c = F(c, t) \qquad (1-7)$$

Process.   The process transfer function, as given by Eq. (1-2), relates the controlled variable to the controlling variable, time, and the other variables in the process. In general, the process transfer function is not known, although certain assumptions can be made about its characteristics to aid in the design and use of a control system.

1-3.2 Controller Action

All the transfer functions that determine the characteristics of the control loop are fixed by selection of equipment, except the controller. The controller transfer function is *selected* to provide the best possible control and, of course, stability. The various types of controller transfer functions are referred to as the *modes* or *action* of the

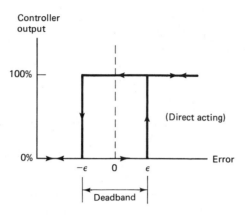

FIG. 1-13 The ON/OFF or two-position controller can have only two outputs, 0% or 100% in this case. Notice the deadband or hysteresis.

controller. In this section, four common types of controller action will be presented and discussed: ON/OFF, proportional control, integral, and derivative. These same modes can be found in all configurations of control system design. The presentation will be aided by graphs that show the relationship between the controller output, c, and error input, e. The controller output is commonly expressed as a 0% to 100% signal. The error will be expressed as a percent of range.

ON/OFF. One of the most common, and simplest, modes of controller action is the ON/OFF or *two-position* mode. This mode, which is illustrated in Fig. 1-13, has a transfer function with only two possible output states, 0% or 100%. As Fig. 1-13 shows, if the error rises above a certain critical value, the output changes from 0% to 100%. If the error decreases, it must fall *below* zero before the output drops from 100% back to 0%. Thus, there is a *deadband* around zero error within which no change in controller output will occur. Most simple control systems, such as room air-conditioners, work by an ON/OFF mode. The controlled variable *will always oscillate* in such a system, with a frequency that increases with decreasing width of the deadband. In equation form, the mode is defined by

$$c = \begin{cases} 0\% & e < -\epsilon \\ 100\% & e > +\epsilon \end{cases} \tag{1-8}$$

where ϵ = one-half the deadband.

EXAMPLE 1-2 An ON/OFF control system will be used to control temperature. The set point is 80°C and the deadband is 6°C. When the controller output is ON, the system cools at -1°C per minute (min), and when the output is OFF, the system heats at $+4$°C/min. Graph the temperature versus time. What is the period of the oscillation?

Solution: To construct the graph, let us assume the controller output is ON and that the temperature is at the set point. Then the system is cooling at -1°C/min. When the temperature reaches $80 - 3 = 77$°C, the controller output will switch to OFF and the system will heat at $+4$°C/min. Then when the temperature reaches $80 + 3 = 83$°C, the control-

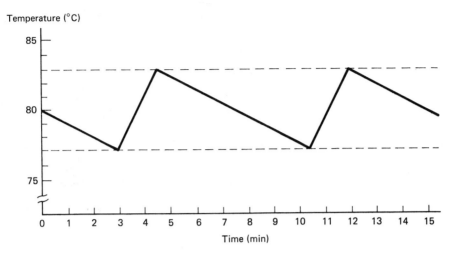

FIG. 1-14   This is the solution to Ex. 1-2.

ler output will become ON and cooling starts again. This sequence is plotted in Fig. 1-14. From the graph the period is easily seen to be 7.5 min.

In practical applications of ON/OFF control, there will be some undershoot and overshoot at the switching points, causing variations in period from that predicted, as in Ex. 1-2. In this mode the amount of allowable error is determined by the size of the deadband and the degree of undershoot and overshoot. Example 1-2 illustrates the natural oscillation of systems under ON/OFF control.

Proportional Control Mode.   The proportional mode is how one usually assumes that a control system should work. In this mode the output of the controller is simply *proportional* to the error itself. If the error is large, the feedback correction is large, and if the error gets smaller, the feedback correction gets smaller proportionally. The relationship between the two is determined by a constant called the *proportional gain*. In equation form, the mode is

$$c_P = K_P e_p + c_0 \tag{1-9}$$

where c_P = controller output in percent

$\quad K_P$ = proportional gain in percent of output/percent of error

$\quad e_p$ = error in percent of range

$\quad c_0$ = output with zero error.

The graph of this mode is shown in Fig. 1-15 for two different values of gain. Note that there is a *saturation* value of error when the output reaches 100%, since further increases in error do not produce further increases in output. This same effect occurs when the output drops to 0%. The error band within which the output is between 0% and 100% is called the *proportional band*. The higher the gain is, the smaller the proportional band.

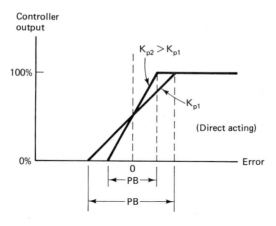

FIG. 1-15 In the proportional mode the output can vary smoothly over a range depending on the error magnitude and gain. Larger gain means smaller range of variation.

EXAMPLE 1-3   A control system is to control pressure from 120 pounds per square inch (psi) to 240 psi with a 180-psi set point. If the proportional gain is 2.5%/% and the zero error output is 65%, write the controller equation. What is the proportional band?

Solution: First it will be necessary to express the error in terms of percentage of range. Using Eq. (1-3), this becomes

$$e_p = 100 \, \frac{p - 180}{240 - 120} = 0.833(p - 180)$$

The equation for the proportional controller mode or action is now simply obtained from Eq. (1-9):

$$c_P = 2.5e_p + 65$$

The proportional band is found by finding the range of error over which the output

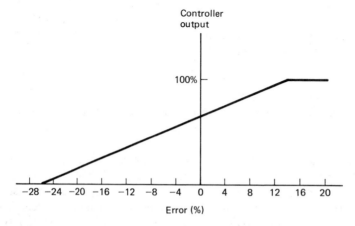

FIG. 1-16 This is the controller response of Ex. 1-3.

spans 0% to 100%. Using the controller equation, the output is 0 when $0 = 2.5e_{p0} + 65$ or at $e_{p0} = -26\%$. The output is 100% when $100 = 2.5e_{p100} + 65$ or at $e_{p100} = +14\%$. The proportional band is thus given by a range of -26% to $+14\%$, or 40%. This is shown in Fig. 1-16. In terms of pressure, we use the percent of range equation to find the pressures for which the output is 0% and 100%.

This is easily found to be 148.8 psi for 0% and 196.8 psi at 100%, or a pressure range of 48 psi. So even though the stated range of control is to be 120 to 240 psi, due to saturation of the controller ouput, the actual range is 148.8 to 196.8 psi.

Offset Error.   One problem with the proportional mode is the fact that the zero error controller ouput, c_0, is a fixed number. The value of c_0 is initially selected to give the proper, error-free value of the controlled variable under assumed values of all other pertinent process variables. Transient variations of these other variables, which will cause the controlled variable to change, are corrected by variations of the value of c according to the proportional mode equation. However, if one of these process variables experiences a *permanent* change, which is called a *load change*, a change in the value of c to support zero error would also be required. The proportional mode cannot provide this correction. In such a case it is necessary for the system to support a fixed error such that the sum of $K_P e_p$ and c_0 will equal the new required value of controlled variable output.

Integral Mode.   Another mode or action often used in the control system is based upon the *history* of error that has occurred in the controlled variable. This is also called *reset* action. The proportional mode determines a feedback that is based on what the error *is* at a particular instant. The integral mode determines a feedback based on what the history of the error has been. It is thus possible that the error may be zero at some instant and yet the controller is feeding back a correction because of a history of errors in the process.

From a physical point of view, the integral mode term is calculated by finding the *net area* under the error curve versus time, up to the time at which the feedback is to occur. Actual controller output is then found by multiplying this area by a constant called the *integral gain*. Thus

$$c_I(t) = K_I A_e(t) + c_I(0) \tag{1-10}$$

where $c_I(t)$ = controller output for integral mode (%) at time t

$\quad K_I$ = integral mode gain [% per (%-time)]

$\quad A_e(t)$ = net area of error versus time (%-time) calculated at time t from $t = 0$

$\quad c_I0)$ = controller output at $t = 0$

$\quad$ time = whatever time unit is appropriate (second, minute, hour).

To see how this works, consider Ex. 1-4.

EXAMPLE 1-4   Figure 1-17 shows the error as a function of time for a process under integral control. Find the controller output at 1, 2, 3, 4, 5, 6, and 7 min. The controller output at $t = 0$ is 55%. The integral gain is 2.5%/(%-min).

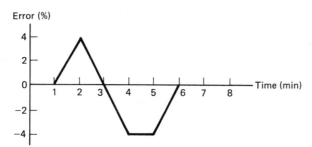

FIG. 1-17 This error will be used to evaluate integral-mode response in Ex. 1-4.

Solution: Equation (1-10) will give the controller output if areas are calculated at the appropriate times and multiplied by the integral gain.

At 1 minute: The area under the curve from 0 to 1 min is clearly *zero*; thus $A_e(1) = 0$ and therefore $c_I(1) = 55\%$.

At 2 minutes: The area under the curve from 1 to 2 min is the area of a triangle, one-half the base times the height. Thus $A_e(2) = \frac{1}{2}(1 \text{ min})(4\%) = 2\%\text{-min}$. The output is $c_I(2) = (2.5)(2) + 55\% = 60\%$.

At 3 minutes: The net area is now the sum of the triangle area found previously *plus* the area of the triangle from 2 to 3 min. This is the same area as the first; so $A_e(3) = 2 + 2 = 4\%\text{-min}$. Thus the output becomes $c_I(3) = (2.5)(4) + 55 = 10 + 55 = 65\%$.

At 4 minutes: Now we have a negative area, which we will subtract since we are finding the net area. From 3 to 4 min there is a triangle with a base of 1 min and a height ,of -4%. The *net* area is now $A_e(4) = \frac{1}{2}(1)(4) + \frac{1}{2}(1)(4) + \frac{1}{2}(1)(-4) = 2\%\text{-min}$. So the output is $c_I(4) = (2.5)(2) + 55 = 60\%$ again.

At 5 minutes: From 4 to 5 min the error is a constant -4%, so the additional area is simply $(1)(-4) = -4\%\text{-min}$. When combined with the area at $t = 4$, we get a net of $A_e(5) = -2\%$. Then the output becomes $c_I(5) = (2.5)(-2) + 55 = 50\%$.

At 6 minutes: From 5 to 6 min there is again a triangle of base 1 min and height -4%. So the additional area is $-2\%\text{-min}$. The net area is then $A_e(6) = -4\%$. The controller output becomes $c_I(6) = (2.5)(-4) + 55 = 45\%$.

At 7 minutes: Clearly, since the error is now zero, no new area is added and the output will remain at 45%.

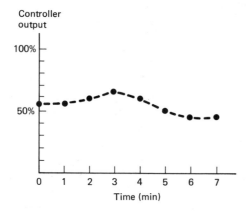

FIG. 1-18 The controller output of Ex. 1-4 is plotted here at eight points.

Figure 1-18 shows a line plot of the controller output as calculated here. The nonlinear curve results if points between integer minutes are calculated and plotted.

Example 1-4 illustrates how the controller ouput varies in response to the area of the error curve versus time, and not the error itself. Note that at the end the error is again zero, but the controller output is not what it started to be. It has been changed to a new setting of 45% for zero error. This is why the mode is called *reset* action, since it resets the zero error controller output.

The normal equation for an integral mode is written using integral calculus notation in the form

$$c_I(t) = K_I \int_0^t e_p(\tau) \, d\tau + c_I(0) \tag{1-11}$$

In using computers in control applications the form of the integral mode given in Eq. (1-10) is used, since an integral is found by a computer via area approaches anyway.

Reset Action.   Integral action provides a controller output that "floats" as a function of the error in time. Thus the value of controller output, with zero error, depends upon the history of error in the process. This means that the integral mode can provide for *automatic reset* of the zero error controller ouput to account for any process load change. This reset corrects the problem of offset error encountered when the proportional mode is used alone.

Derivative Mode.   The last mode or action to be considered in controller operation is based upon the *time rate of change of error.* In this case it is possible for the actual error to be zero, and yet derivative action would be creating a large controller response because the error is *changing*. Since it depends on the rate of change of error in time, the mode is often called *rate* action. The response of derivative action is not dependent on what the actual error is at a particular moment, but rather on the rate at which the error is changing at that moment. Figure 1-19 shows a case where the error is zero at some time but that, clearly, some adjustment of controller output is needed since the error is changing rapidly and will surely *not be zero* a moment later unless something is done.

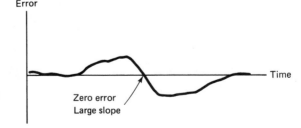

FIG. 1-19   For this case the error may be zero, but the derivative mode will respond to the rate of change instead, thus anticipating error.

The rate of change of error can be approximated by taking the difference between two values of error and dividing by the time between the two values:

$$c_D(t) = K_D \frac{e_p(t) - e_p(t_0)}{t - t_0} \tag{1-12}$$

where $c_D(t)$ = controller derivative output at time t (%)
   K_D = derivative gain [% per (%/time)]
   $e_p(t)$ = error at time t (%)
   $e_p(t_0)$ = error at time t_0 (%)
   time = appropriate unit of time (seconds, minute, hour).

The relation of Eq. (1-12) is really just the slope of the error time curve calculated between the error at time t and that at an earlier time t_0.

Notice that there is no controller output term corresponding to zero rate of change of error. Because of this, the derivative mode is never used alone since it will not respond to fixed error. It is always used in a composite fashion, as discussed later. Equation (1-12) is actually only an approximation of the derivative for smoothly varying error curves. As the time interval between t and t_0 gets smaller and smaller, the approximation gets better. In computer control this form of equation is used to approximate the derivative.

EXAMPLE 1-5   Given the error curve shown in Fig. 1-20, find the derivative controller contribution at $t = 5$ min if the previous sample was at 3 min. Compare this to the derivative if the previous sample was at 4 min and then at 4.5 min. The derivative gain is 5%/(%/min).

Solution: For the solution, Eq. (1-12) is used to find the derivative response under the given conditions. Thus, if the previous sample was at 3 min, the error is seen to be $+1\%$. Then the contribution is given by

$$c_D = \frac{(5)(2 - 1)}{5 - 3} = 2.5\%$$

If the previous sample was at 4 min, the value of the error is seen from Fig. 1-20 to be $+2\%$. The contribution is then

$$c_D = \frac{(5)(2 - 2)}{5 - 4} = 0\%!$$

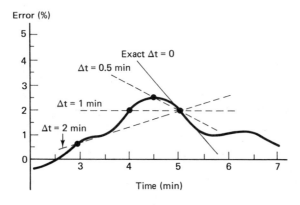

FIG. 1-20 This graph with Ex. 1-5 shows the critical effect of choosing a proper sample time.

If the previous sample was at 4.5 min, the value of the error is 2.5% and the derivative contribution is

$$c_D = \frac{(5)(2 - 2.5)}{5 - 4.5} = -5\%$$

These three estimates of the derivative (rate of change of error) at $t = 5$ are shown in Fig. 1-20. You can see that the last estimate is much more accurate than the first two.

Example 1-5 illustrates how much in error a derivative estimate can be owing to a poor choice of time between samples. It is for this reason that the rate action of a controller should only be used with great caution or serious control errors can result. Errors of the type in Ex. 1-5 can be avoided if the time between samples used to esti- mate the derivative is much less than the shortest time span over which the controlled variable is expected to make major changes. In Fig. 1-20 it is clear that considerable variation of the controlled variable error occurs in 2 min, less in 1 min, and in 0.5 min little gross change occurs.

The proper mathematical expression for the derivative mode, using the deriva- tive expression from calculus, is

$$c_D = K_D \frac{de_p}{dt} \tag{1-13}$$

Although Eq. (1-13) is the proper definition of derivative action in a controller, com- puter implementation uses Eq. (1-12). The principle reason is that data in digital com- puter control systems are available only on a sampled basis as stipulated in Eq. (1-12), whereas Eq. (1-13) requires data to be available continuously.

Composite Modes.   Actual implementation of controller action usually em- ploys combinations of the previous three modes. The most common combinations and their transfer function equations are as follows:

1. Proportional–integral (PI) mode:

$$c_{\mathrm{PI}} = K_P e_p + K_P K_I A_e \tag{1-14}$$

2. Proportional–derivative (PD) mode:

$$c_{\mathrm{PD}} = K_P e_p + K_P K_D \frac{e_p(t) - e_p(t_0)}{t - t_0} + c_0 \tag{1-15}$$

3. Proportional–integral–derivative (PID) mode or three-mode:

$$c_{\mathrm{PID}} = K_P e_p + K_P K_I A_e + K_P K_D \frac{e_p(t) - e_p(t_0)}{t - t_0} \tag{1-16}$$

Notice that the proportional gain appears in *every* term of the composite modes.

Direct and Reverse Action.   It should be mentioned that the reaction of a controller can be either direct or reverse. It is direct if a positive error produces a positive change in control ouput and negative if a positive error produces a negative change in output. The sign of K_P is positive for direct action and negative for reverse action.

1-4 CONTROL SYSTEM CONFIGURATIONS

The previous sections have shown the purpose and strategic methods that are used to perform process control. In this section the configurations of equipment and some details about actual process control loop operations will be given. Particular attention will be given to the use of computers to perform the required operations for control. First, however, the traditional analog approaches to process control will be covered.

1-4.1 Analog Process Control

The measurement function in process control converts *information* about the controlled variable into a signal. This signal is then used in the controller to determine a controller output signal. The controller output signal is then used to drive the final control element, which causes changes in the controlling variable. Analog process control refers to the type of signal carrier used and how it is related to the actual process variables.

Analog Relationship.   An analog relationship is said to exist between two variables if for every value of one variable there is a unique value of the other variable. This is easy to see in a graph of one variable versus the other. Figure 1-21 shows two types of analog relationships, linear and nonlinear. In both cases, for every value of v_1 there is a unique value of v_2 within the range over which they are defined. The linear relationship is characterized by a straight line, whereas the nonlinear relationship shows a curved line relating the two variables.

Analog Range.   The range of analog relationships between the controlled and controlling variable and the process signal carrier is easy to define. On the measurement side, a controlled variable is defined within a range of control, which in turn is used for error representation by the percent of range relation, Eq. (1-3). Whatever range is used in percent of range considerations is also used to define the analog range of the signal carrier. On the controlling variable side, you have seen that the

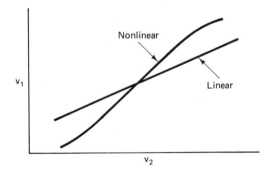

FIG. 1-21 When graphed, the difference between linear and nonlinear response is obvious.

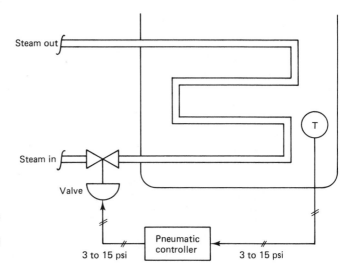

FIG. 1-22 In some cases an entire process control loop is pneumatic, such as in this temperature-control example.

controller action is defined by an output of 0% to 100%. Here 0% simply represents one extreme of possible controller action and 100% the opposite extreme. Thus the range of carrier signal with an analog relation to controlled variable is that defined by these two extremes.

Many different carriers have been used in the history of process control. Two carriers emerged finally as the most common ways of implementing analog process control. One uses a range of *air pressure* to represent the variables and is called a *pneumatic* process control system. The other uses a range of *electric current* to represent the variables and is called an *electronic* process control system.

Pneumatic. In pneumatic process control, all process variables are represented by the range of *3 to 15 pounds per square inch (psi)* of air pressure in a process signal pipe. This means that the controlled variable range has a minimum value represented by 3 psi and a maximum by 15 psi, and the controller output has 0% represented by 3 psi and 100% by 15 psi. A typical pure pneumatic process control loop is shown in Fig. 1-22. The system controls temperature (controlled variable) by variation of input steam using a valve (controlling variable). Measurement is made by a gas pressure thermometer, which converts temperature variation directly into pressure variation. The controller is a purely pneumatic analog computer. The final control element is a control valve actuated by the incoming pneumatic signal from the controller.

Electronic. A number of different electronic current ranges are used for process control, but one seems to predominate. In this case, process variables are represented by the range of 4 to 20 milliamperes (mA) of dc current. Thus the designed range of controlled variable has 4 mA as the minimum and 20 mA as the maximum. Likewise, the controller output is 4 mA for 0% and 20 mA for 100%. The

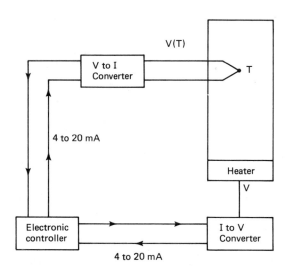

FIG. 1-23 Analog process control loops often use a current from 4 to 20 mA to represent all signals.

controller is an analog computer. In Fig. 1-23 an electronic process control loop is shown that regulates temperature in an oven. In this case a thermocouple converts temperature information into a voltage, which is conditioned so that the specified temperature range produces 4 to 20 mA. This signal is applied to the controller, which outputs a 4- to 20-mA signal to the heater control unit. In this case, 4 mA corresponds to the minimum heat input (not necessarily zero) and 20 mA to the maximum heat input.

Electronic–Pneumatic.   In modern practice it is quite common to see the electronic and pneumatic methods combined. One reason for this is that the 3- to 15-psi pneumatic signal is able to do more work than the 4- to 20-mA electric signal. For example, the pressure signal can drive a control valve directly, whereas the current signal would have to be amplified and conditioned to drive an electric motor connected to the valve. Also, in some cases a measurement is more easily made by a pneumatic process. In general, the *controller* function is easier to accomplish using

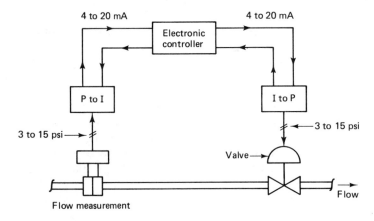

FIG. 1-24 To take advantage of the good characteristics of each, a combination of electronic and pneumatic is often used.

electronic techniques. A typical process control installation that uses both electronic and pneumatic systems is shown in Fig. 1-24 for controlling flow in a pipe. Note the use of *converters* to transform pressure signals to current signals, and vice versa.

1-4.2 Computer Support

The initial use of computers in process control was in support of the traditional analog system just described. This type of application of computers still exists since many industries use analog control systems and will no doubt continue to do so. Generally, the support activities are provided by large- or medium-scale computers.

Data Logging.   One of the first applications of computers in process control was for the rapid and efficient collection of data on process variables. The proper operation of a process industry depends on analysis of historical data generated during operations to determine more efficient and optimized operations for the process. In the past these data were recorded on strip-chart recorders and then laboriously analyzed by process engineers. A computer can be used to record these data automatically and then to analyze the data using preprogrammed instructions. This greatly improves the mechanism of tuning a process for maximum efficiency. Figure 1-25 shows a block diagram of how a data-logging system can be employed in a process control loop. Note the use of an *analog-to-digital converter* (ADC) to transform the analog measurement data into a digital format.

Supervisory Control.   The use of computers for data logging and analysis of the data led naturally to the decision that computers could be used to adjust the oper-

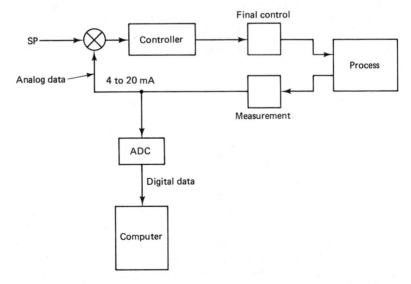

FIG. 1-25   In data logging, the computer samples measurement data via an analog-to-digital converter (ADC).

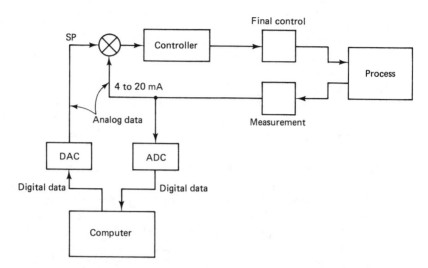

FIG. 1-26 Supervisory control lets the computer specify the set point by means of a digital-to-analog converter (DAC).

ation of a process control system automatically. In the previous case, after analysis of computer data by control and process engineers, a decision might be made to reset many loop set points for more optimum operation of the overall process. Under supervisory control the computer itself makes the set-point adjustments following programmed instructions. To perform supervisory control, it is only necessary to have the computer output set-point information back to the analog loop. This is done, as shown in Fig. 1-26, by adding a *digital-to-analog converter* (DAC) to the system of Fig. 1-25. This device converts the digital signal from the computer into a signal that can be used in the analog loop, such as a 4- to 20-mA current.

1-4.3   Direct Digital Control

Finally, we come to the major subject of this text, the use of a computer for the complete control function. This is called *direct digital control* (DDC) to emphasize that the analog features of the control system are no longer present. In most cases the digital control is provided by a digital computer, so this might as well be called direct computer control or computer process control. Nevertheless, the term DDC has come to be used to describe such an application.

In DDC the process control loop is still intact, but much has been replaced by software. Figure 1-27 shows the process control loop as implemented in DDC. Note the use of ADC and DAC to transform analog data to digital data, and vice versa. The measurement function and the final control operation remain, for the most part, analog in nature. The error detector and controller are now contained entirely within the software of the computer. In essence, it is found necessary to use the same control strategies adopted for historical analog process control, but now they are implemented via programs in the computer. Thus control will still be provided by propor-

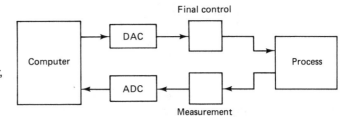

FIG. 1-27 Control using a computer, also called direct digital control, eliminates the analog control function.

tional, integral, and derivative action on the controlling variable error, but this will occur in computer instructions rather than electronic or pneumatic hardware.

The remainder of this text is devoted to a study of process control using microprocessor-based computers, except for some consideration of measurement in Chapter 2. It will be of value to summarize briefly the basic structure of computer control systems.

Hardware.   The equipment associated with the computer and its control system are referred to as the "hardware." This includes the microprocessor itself, as well as data-acquisition equipment, memory, and just about anything associated with the computer control operations. For the purposes of this text, the internal workings of the computer will not be considered. Instead the hardware considered will be that needed to make measurements, convert the data to a digital (binary) format, and input the data into the computer. The equipment for output is also considered.

Software.   Almost all the data processing from error detection to integration is done by programs written and executed by the computer during control operations. This is called the "software" associated with the control system. Study of software and how it is generated is very important to understanding computer control systems. Several chapters will be devoted to study of the software required for control. We will study the general math techniques or *algorithms* needed for control and then consider the problems faced when these algorithms are coded into microprocessor instructions.

Flowcharts.   Computer flowcharts will be used to show the structure of the algorithms needed for control. These charts can then be translated into detailed flowcharts and codes for the particular microprocessor employed in an application.

PROBLEMS

1-1   A food industry process produces potato chips. Construct a list of *properties* that would describe this product. For each property, construct a list of the set of *variables* on which the property depends.

1-2   From the set of variables deduced in Prob. 1-1, define which are or can be controlled.

1-3   A common home hot-water heater is an example of a controlled process. The properties are temperature, pressure, and hardness (mineral content). Which property is actually

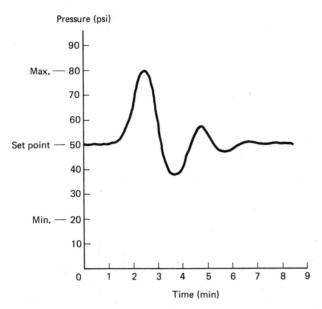

FIG. 1-28   This is the graph for Prob. 1-9.

controlled in the home? Make a list of the variables on which each property depends. Does the water temperature in the tank exhibit self-regulation? Why?

1-4 For the water temperature property of Prob. 1-3, identify how each step of the basic control strategy is accomplished.

1-5 Describe how the basic control strategy is applied to the following control environments: **(a)** maintaining speed in an automobile; **(b)** a room air-conditioning system; **(c)** adjusting water temperature when taking a shower.

1-6 Flow rate is controlled in a range of 25 cubic meters per hour (m^3/h) to 85 m^3/h. If the set point is 57 m^3/h, what is the percent of range errors for flows of 63 m^3/h and 0.5 m^3/min?

1-7 Suppose the percent of range error in Prob. 1-6 is 17%. What is the flow rate?

1-8 Temperature is controlled from 150°F to 330°F. The allowable error is ± 1.4°F. Express the allowable error in percent of range.

1-9 Figure 1-28 shows the transient response of a pressure control system. Is this overdamped or underdamped response? Find the duration, maximum error, and most negative error, expressed both as percent of range *and* in absolute units.

1-10 The transfer function of a liquid flow meter is given by

$$v = 0.027Q^2$$

where v = voltage output and Q = flow in gallons/minute. Is this a linear or nonlinear relationship? What is the output voltage for a flow of 7.6 gal/min? A voltage of 5.5 volts (V) represents what flow?

1-11 For the measurement system of Prob. 1-10, suppose the range of flow is 4.5 to 17.5 gal/min and the set point is 11 gal/min. If the flow is 15 gal/min, compare the error expressed as percent of range if calculated from flow and if calculated from voltage. Can you use error calculated from the voltage?

1-12 In an ON/OFF control system, ON provides a pressure increase of 3 psi/min and OFF provides a pressure decrease of -5 psi/min. The set point is 15 psi and the deadband is

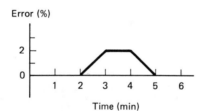

Error (%)

2

0

   1   2   3   4   5   6

Time (min)

FIG. 1-29 This error graph is for Probs. 1-15 through 1-17.

± 4.5 psi. The system starts at 0 pressure and ON. Plot the resulting curve of pressure versus time. What is the period of the oscillation?

1-13 Suppose the deadband in Prob. 1-12 is reduced to ± 2 psi. What is the period of oscillation?

1-14 A proportional controller is used to control level from 2.8 m to 6.5 m with a 3.7-m set point. The proportional gain is 5%/%, and no error produces an output of 54%. What is the controller equation? What output is produced by levels of 3.5 m and 4.0 m? What is the proportional band?

1-15 An integral-mode controller with a gain of 3.3%/(%-min) shows an error versus time as given in Fig. 1-29. Find the plot of controller output versus time. The controller ouput at $t = 0$ was 50%.

1-16 For the error curve of Fig. 1-29, find the output of a derivative control mode with a gain of 0.8%/(%/min) as a function of time.

1-17 A PID controller has a proportional gain of 5%/%, an integral gain of 1.5%/(%-min), and a derivative gain of 0.5%/(%/min). Write the controller equation if the output at $t = 0$ is 45%. Plot the controller output versus time if the error is as given in Fig. 1-29.

1-18 Draw a block diagram of how a computer would be used to provide DDC of water-heater temperature.

CHAPTER 2

MEASUREMENT AND SIGNAL CONDITIONING

OBJECTIVES

The basic purpose of this chapter is to study the analog procedures involved in taking measurements of process variables and conditioning the resulting signals. After studying this chapter and doing the problems at the end of the chapter, you will be able to:

1. Describe the three main elements of a measurement system.
2. Define three transducers for temperature measurement.
3. Define three transducers for displacement measurement.
4. Give a technical description of a strain gage.
5. Describe the general methods of measuring pressure and flow.
6. Explain the operation and use of a bridge circuit.
7. Explain how low- and high-pass filters can be constructed with resistors and capacitors.
8. Give the op-amp circuits for three amplifiers.
9. Explain the basic operations of analog transmitters.

2-1 INTRODUCTION

The general block diagram of a process control loop shows that one of the basic operations necessary to perform control is to make a *measurement* of the controlled variable. This operation is obviously necessary for either analog or digital control systems. Most variables that are controlled in industrial processes are analog, and it follows that the measurement function involves analog procedures. For microprocessor control systems, the variable must finally be expressed in a digital (binary) format, as will be described in Ch. 3, but often certain analog adjustments of the measurement signal must be made. In this chapter you will study typical analog procedures used in the measurement function. The general term *analog data acquisition* is used to describe the overall operations of converting controlled variable information into an analog form suitable for conversion to digital form.

2-1.1 Block Diagram

To understand the analog data-acquisition process, it is convenient to separate the system into the three distinct parts shown in Fig. 2-1: the transducer, signal conditioning, and transmitter.

Transducer.   The transducer is the part of the measurement system that initially converts the controlled variable into another form suitable for the next stage. In most cases, conversion will be from the actual variable into some form of electrical signal, although there is often an intermediate form, such as pneumatic. The transducer is often called the *primary element*, since it is the first operation of measurement. The transfer function of the transducer shows the relationship between the measured variable and the measurement signal.

Signal Conditioning.   This operation in the measurement function makes adjustments of the type and/or level of the measurement signal to provide compatibility with the next stage. For example, if a transducer produces a change in resistance versus temperature, then signal conditioning is used to convert the resistance change to voltage or current. In computer process control, signal conditioning is used to adjust the measurement signal to interface properly with the analog-to-digital conversion system.

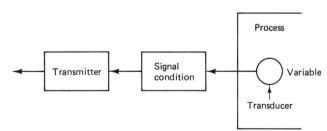

FIG. 2-1 The three basic elements of analog data acquisition are shown in this block diagram.

Transmitter.   The transmitter has the function of propagating measurement information from the site of measurement to the control room where the control function is to occur. If the control function is performed locally (i.e., at the site), there will be no transmitter. If there is a central control facility, it will be necessary to transmit all measurement signals to this facility. When this is done by an analog signal, usually a current, the transmitter converts measurement information into a properly scaled current. In some cases the signal is converted to a digital format at the measurement site and then transmitted as a serial bit stream.

2-1.2   Time Response

As noted previously, process control is a time-dependent operation, since the goal is to regulate the value of a variable *in time*. Because of this basic concern with time, the time response of every part of the process control loop is very important. In the case of the measurement function, the time response is indicated by the manner in which the output of the measurement system varies in time when the input varies in time. In general, the measurement operation is described by a transfer function as given by Eq. (1-4):

$$v_m = T(v, t) \tag{1-4}$$

What is needed at this point is a specification of the explicit forms of the time dependence in this equation.

To establish a formal and well-defined way to describe the time response of the measurement system, a specific situation is used. It is assumed that at a time, say

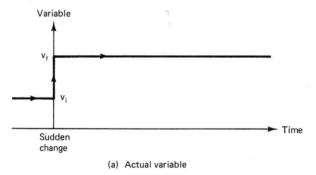

(a) Actual variable

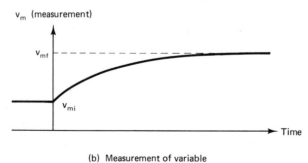

(b) Measurement of variable

FIG. 2-2 If an actual variable changes suddenly as in (a), the response of a first-order transducer will be as in (b).

$t = 0$, the measured variable makes a discontinuous change from one value to another. This is called a *step change* and is shown in Fig. 2-2a. Note that, at $t = 0$, the measured variable changed from an initial value, v_i, to a final value, v_f. The corresponding measured indications, as defined by Eq. (1-4), are assumed to be v_{mi} and v_{mf}. Two principal types of time response are found in measurement systems.

First-Order Time Response.   The most common type of time response is called the first-order time response, or *first-order lag*. It is characterized by the fact that the measured indication lags behind rapid changes in the measured variable. In the standard case illustrated in Fig. 2-2a, this response is illustrated by Fig. 2-2b and is described by

$$v_m(t) = v_{mi} + (v_{mf} - v_{mi})[1 - e^{-t/\tau}] \qquad (2\text{-}1)$$

where τ = time constant in seconds. Equation (2-1) shows that the measurement system output cannot track an instantaneous change of the measured variable. Rather, there is a lag in the output, which slowly decreases until the correct output is finally reached. The value of the time constant, τ, determines the speed by which the output "catches up" with the input. Small values of τ mean *fast* response, and large values of τ mean *slow* response. The time constant is also called the *63% time* since, in a time equal to one time constant after the step change, the output will have changed by about 63% of the required amount. A step change represents a *worst-case* situation, since the measured variable will typically not change so fast.

EXAMPLE 2-1   A measurement system has a time constant of 3.5 seconds (s). Under worst-case conditions, how long will it take for the measured indication to be 95% accurate in representing the true input?

Solution: This means that the value of $v_m(t)$ must be such that 95% of the total *change*, $v_{mf} - v_{mi}$, has occurred. From Eq. (2-1),

$$\frac{v_m(t) - v_{mi}}{v_{mf} - v_{mi}} = 1 - e^{-t/\tau}$$

Thus

$$0.95 = 1 - e^{-t/3.5}$$
$$e^{-t/3.5} = 0.05$$

Taking natural logarithms (base e) of both sides gives

$$\frac{-t}{3.5} = \ln(0.05) = -3$$
$$t = 10.5 \text{ s}$$

First-order time response is very common in measurement systems, and the design of an appropriate control strategy must take into account the effect of this lag on overall performance.

Second-Order Time Response.   The second-order time response, or second-order lag, is characterized by an output of the measurement system that *oscillates* even though the input signal has simply executed a step change! From the graph

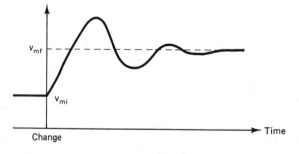

FIG. 2-3 In second-order time response, an oscillation occurs even though the actual variable changed as in Fig. 2-2a.

of Fig. 2-3, you can see that the measured indication gives highly erroneous information about variations of the measured variable, until the inherent oscillations finally decay away. It is of extreme importance when using a system with this response to wait until the transient oscillation is decayed away before trusting the measurement indication. If the control system, whether analog or computer controlled, is allowed to respond to this phantom oscillation, an instability in control could occur. Often, filters are used to block frequencies at which inherent measurement oscillations occur.

2-1.3   Linearity

One of the greatest problems in the measurement operation has to do with the fact that the *output* of a transducer often varies *nonlinearly* with the *input* of the transducer. This nonlinearity can prevent a control system from functioning. In analog

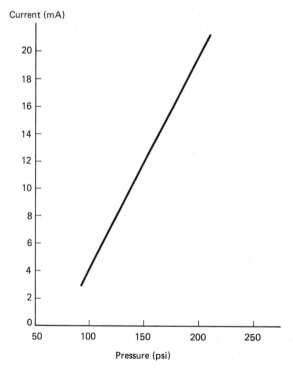

FIG. 2-4 This graph shows a linear transduction of pressure to current.

control it is very difficult to compensate for the problem, although special circuits are constructed to "linearize" transducer response. As you will see in Ch. 4, in computer control systems such linearization can be accomplished much easier using software after the data have been inputted. It is important for you to realize why linearity is so important to process control.

Controller operation, analog or computer, is based on calculations using a common range of input signal. In analog processing, input data are often reduced to the range from 4 to 20mA, where the lower current is the minimum value of the controlled variable and the higher current is the maximum value. In computer control (assuming 8 bits) the range (in hexadecimal) is 00H to FFH, where 00H represents the minimum value of the controlled variable and FFH, the maximum. The control system is designed assuming that variation within these ranges represents the controlled variable, linearly.

Figure 2-4 shows a pressure measurement system that produces a 4- to 20-mA signal linearly from a 100- to 200-psi pressure. Suppose that the pressure increases from a set point at 150 to 175 psi. The current will increase from the 12-mA set point to 16 mA. The controller sends a correction back to the process based on the 4-mA change in current representing a 25-psi change in pressure. The controller would send the same correction back, but with opposite sign, if the pressure changed from 150 to 125 psi.

Figure 2-5 shows the same situation with a nonlinear transducer. For convenience the same end points and set point are used, but notice the nonlinearity. You can

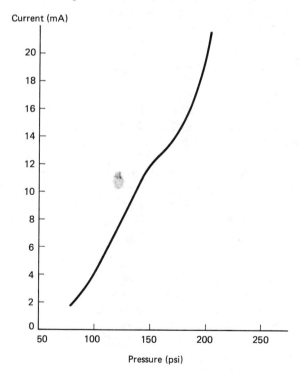

FIG. 2-5 This graph shows the same range as Fig. 2-4, but with nonlinear response.

see that equivalent changes of pressure in different parts of the range do not produce equivalent changes in current. A change of 150 to 175 psi produces a change of 2.4 mA from 12 to 14.4 mA. On the other hand, a change of 150 to 125 psi produces a 3.6-mA current change from 12 to 8.4 mA. Yet the control system *must assume* that all current variations represent the same pressure variations. The only way to assure this is if the transducer is linear, or its output can be linearized.

The same situation occurs with computer control systems where the 4 to 20 mA used in Figs. 2-4 and 2-5 become 00H to FFH digital signals. The nonlinearity is still present in the digital signal, because a change of 1 bit does not represent the same amount of physical variable change over the range of the physical variable.

2-2   TRANSDUCERS

The first stage of measurement is a device, the transducer, that converts the variable to be measured into a form suitable for process control. In most cases this means conversion into an electrical variable such as resistance, capacitance, or inductance. Some transducers convert the measured variable directly into voltage. In this section a brief summary will be given of the types of transducers that are used for measurement of common physical process variables.

2-2.1   Temperature Transducers

The measurement and control of temperature is a very important part of many manufacturing and processing industries. Many transducers have been developed to perform the primary measurement function. In this section, three very common types will be presented.

Units.   The proper unit of temperature is defined by the International System of Units (SI) to be the kelvin (K). This unit is called *absolute* since an object with no thermal energy would have a temperature of zero kelvin. Then each kelvin unit of temperature represents a certain amount of energy per molecule added to a system. The unit is defined by calibration points wherein a specific, reproducible state of matter is defined to have a certain temperature in kelvins. For example, when a quantity of pure water is held in equilibrium with a quantity of pure ice, the kelvin temperature of the mixture is 273.15 K. Another unit, in more common daily use, is the *Celsius* (formerly the centigrade) temperature. The temperature in Celsius is measured in degrees Celsius (°C). The relationship between kelvin and Celsius is given by the equation

$$T(°C) = T(K) - 273.15 \tag{2-2}$$

where $T(°C)$ = temperature in degrees Celsius

$T(K)$ = temperature in kelvins.

Another unit of temperature in common use in the United States, although its use is being deprecated, is the *Fahrenheit* temperature scale. In this case the temperature is measured in degrees Fahrenheit (°F). The relation between this temperature unit and Celsius is given by

$$T(°F) = \tfrac{9}{5}T(°C) + 32 \tag{2-3}$$

where $T(°F)$ = temperature in degrees Fahrenheit.

EXAMPLE 2-2   Given the temperature of 325 K, find the equivalent temperature in degrees Celsius and degrees Fahrenheit.

Solution: This is just an application of Eqs. (2-2) and (2-3).

$$T(°C) = 325 - 273.15 = 51.85°C$$

and

$$T(°F) = \tfrac{9}{5}(51.85°C) + 32 = 125.3°F$$

The following sections will present a brief description of the characteristics of several types of transducers. Since the ultimate goal is a voltage or current representing the temperature, only those transducers with an electrical property will be considered. It is good to remember, however, that there are many other types of temperature transducers that will not be discussed in this text. If you are ever asked to set up a temperature measurement system, you should learn about the other types also.

Resistance Temperature Detector (RTD).   This transducer is based on the increase of metal wire resistance with temperature. In its most common form, it consists of a small coil of platinum or nickel wire protected by a sheath of stainless steel. This is immersed in the environment whose temperature is to be measured, and the resistance of the coil is then a measure of the temperature. The range of these transducers extends from below 0°C to well over 600°C (1112°F).

For very accurate measurements, tables of resistance versus temperature are provided by the manufacturer of the RTD. Although the graph of resistance versus temperature is not linear, there is sufficient linearity over short spans to make a good approximation of resistance versus temperature as the equation of a straight line. It is important to remember that such an equation is only accurate over a limited range of temperature. The equation is defined in the form

$$R(T) = R(T_0)[1 + \alpha_0(T - T_0)] \tag{2-4}$$

where T = temperature at which the resistance is desired

T_0 = midpoint of valid temperature range

$R(T)$ = resistance at T predicted

$R(T_0)$ = resistance at T_0 from tables

α_0 = fractional change in temperature per unit of temperature at T_0.

The value of α_0 is determined from the table of resistance versus temperature of the RTD, using

$$\alpha_0 = \frac{1}{R(T_0)} \frac{R(T_2) - R(T_1)}{T_2 - T_1} \tag{2-5}$$

where T_2 = upper limit of temperature range

T_1 = lower limit of temperature range

T_0 = midpoint of range

$R(T_2)$ = resistance at T_2 from tables

$R(T_1)$ = resistance at T_1 from tables.

When using Eqs. (2-4) and (2-5), it is very important to be consistent with units. If the tables are in degrees Celsius, the units of α_0 will be the fractional change of resistance per degree Celsius.

It turns out that all metals have values of α that do not differ appreciably from each other. Furthermore, for any given metal, α does not vary by a great deal over the usable range of RTD temperatures. The value will be on the order of 0.004/°C. This means that there will be a change of only 0.4% of the RTD resistance for every change of 1°C. Thus for accurate measurements the changes in resistance that must be detected are very small. An RTD with a resistance of 100 ohms (Ω) at 20°C would change to 100.4 Ω at 21°C. This lack of sensitivity is a problem with the application of RTDs. The resistance is usually measured with bridge circuits, as discussed later in this chapter.

Another problem with RTDs is how the RTD affects the temperature of the environment whose temperature it is being used to measure. Usually, a current is passed through the RTD to make a measurement of resistance. But this means there will be some heating of the RTD due to i^2R power dissipated in the RTD. This heating will cause the RTD to indicate a higher temperature than actually exists (i.e., it "heats up" the environment whose temperature is being measured). This *self-heating* is defined by the *dissipation constant*, P_D, of the transducer. P_D has units of watts per degree Celsius (W/°C) and represents the number of watts of dissipation that will heat the RTD by 1°C in either still air or an oil bath (whichever is specified by the manufacturer). Self-heating must be considered in any accurate measurement.

EXAMPLE 2-3   An RTD has $\alpha_0 = 0.0037$/°C at $T_0 = 50$°C. The resistance at 50°C is given by $R(T_0) = 350$ Ω. Find the resistance at 75°C.

Solution: Equation (2-4) is used directly:

$$R(75°C) = 350[1 + 0.0037(75 - 50)]$$
$$= 350(1 + 0.0925)$$
$$= 382.4 \ \Omega$$

EXAMPLE 2-4   Suppose the resistance at 75°C is measured by passing a current of 20 mA through the RTD. If the RTD has $P_D = 30$ mW/°C, find the temperature that will be *indicated* by the RTD and its resistance.

Solution: Self-heating by the RTD will cause it to heat up and indicate a higher temperature for the environment. In this case, using the resistance at 75°C of 382.4 Ω and 20-mA current, the power dissipated by the RTD is

$$P = i^2R = (0.02)^2(382.4) = 153 \ \text{mW}$$

The temperature rise due to self-heating is now found from the dissipation constant:

$$\Delta T = \frac{153 \ \text{mW}}{30 \ \text{mW/°C}} = 5.1°C$$

Thus the indicated temperature is

$$T_i = 75 + 5.1 = 80.1°C$$

The resistance at this temperature is now found with Eq. (2-4):

$$R(80.1°C) = 350[1 + 0.0037(80.1 - 50)]$$
$$= 389 \ \Omega$$

You can see that self-heating contributes considerable error to the measurement.

Self-heating errors are reduced by making resistance measurements at as low a current as possible.

The time constant of RTDs depends on the size and construction. Typical values range from a low of about 1 s to as much as 20 s for large units.

Thermistor.   Another resistance-versus-temperature type of transducer is based upon the change in semiconductor resistance with temperature. This type of transducer, called a thermistor, usually has the characteristic that the resistance decreases with temperature in a highly nonlinear fashion. This nonlinearity, along with the rather limited typical range of perhaps $-80°$ to $200°C$, restricts the thermistor's use in industrial process control installations. The basic advantage is the high sensitivity, which can be as great as $-10\%/°C$ compared to $0.4\%/°C$ for the RTD. Because of the nonlinearity, the slope will change with temperature. Certain special types of thermistors have a nearly linear response over small ranges of temperatures.

Generally, the manufacturer provides tables of resistance versus temperature that can be used to deduce the temperature from a resistance measurement. Figure 2-6 shows the resistance-versus-temperature curve for a typical industrial-grade ther-

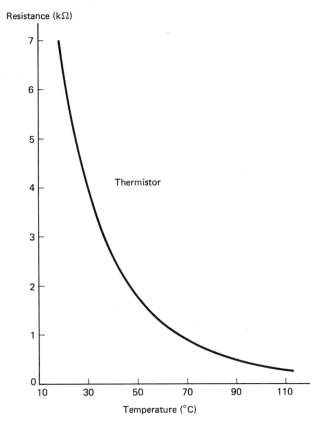

FIG. 2-6 A thermistor exhibits a nonlinear variation of resistance with temperature.

mistor. Note the negative slope and the nonlinearity. For computer control installations, this nonlinearity is not as much a problem as in analog control, since software linearization routines can be used. This will be discussed in Ch. 4. As with the RTD, the thermistor has a dissipation constant, P_D, that specifies the self-heating due to current passed through the transducer.

EXAMPLE 2-5 Find the change in resistance and percent of change in resistance with temperature for the thermistor around 30°C and again around 100°C.

Solution: The change is just the slope of the curve, which can be found by taking differences of temperature and resistance about the given values.

$$\text{slope}_{30} = \frac{3.6 - 4.3}{32 - 28}$$

$$= -0.175 \text{ k}\Omega/°C$$

or, dividing by the resistance of 4 kΩ at 30°C, -4 %/°C. For the other case,

$$\text{slope}_{100} = \frac{0.325 - 0.375}{102 - 98}$$

$$= -0.0125 \text{ k}\Omega/°C$$

or, dividing by the resistance of 0.35 kΩ at 100°C, -3.5 %/°C. So the percent of change is nearly constant, but the resistance change per degree Celsius is very different.

The dissipation constants for thermistors are generally much smaller than for RTDs, perhaps as little as 5 mW/°C. Thus great care must be taken to keep measurement current very low to avoid self-heating errors.

The time constants for thermistors range from $\frac{1}{2}$ s to 20 s, depending on size and construction.

Thermocouple. The thermocouple (TC) is a temperature transducer that produces a voltage, directly, as a function of temperature. The range of measurement varies from type to type but spans $-150°C$ to well over 1500°C for all types. The time constant depends upon the size of the wires used to construct the transducer. For small-wire thermocouples the time constant in good thermal contact can be as small as 20 ms. An important disadvantage is that the voltage produced is small, being less than 10 mV/°C, which means that amplifiers must be used to boost this voltage to usable levels. Another disadvantage is that the instrument is inherently susceptible to electrical noise. Special shielding and compensation circuits must be used to protect the measurement circuit from the high electrical noise environments encountered in industry.

The basic idea of the thermocouple is illustrated in Fig. 2-7. Two dissimilar metal wires, A and B, are joined together, forming the measurement junction, and to a third wire, forming what are called the reference junctions. A voltage is produced between wires C, which depends on the difference between the measurement junction temperature, T_m, and the reference junction temperature, T_{ref}. Both reference junctions must have the same temperature. The voltage for a given temperature difference also depends on the type of metals used for wires A and B. Various standard combina-

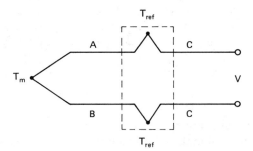

FIG. 2-7 This diagram illustrates the basic structure of a thermocouple.

tions of wire types have been developed, each having special characteristics with respect to range, sensitivity, or ruggedness. In Appendix A is a table (Table A-1) of output voltage versus measurement junction temperature for a type J thermocouple, which is made with *iron* for one wire and with an alloy, *constantan*, for the other wire. The reference junction is assumed to be 0°C.

EXAMPLE 2-6   Find the temperature if a type J TC with a 0°C reference measures 34.58 mV.

Solution: Table A-1 is arranged in rows and columns for temperature, with the corresponding voltages in the body of the table. The value of 34.58 mV is found in the 600°C row and the 25°C column. Thus the temperature is 625°C.

EXAMPLE 2-7   What voltage would be produced by a type J TC with a 0°C reference if the junction temperature were 270°C?

Solution: The voltage is found at the intersection of the row of 250°C and the column of 20°C. The value is 14.67 mV.

Interpolation.   Often the desired value of temperature or voltage is not in the table directly. For example, 314°C is not in the table because the temperature changes in 5°C increments. Also, it would be surprising if a measured voltage were exactly the same as some table entry. Instead of just guessing between two values, a *linear interpolation formula* can be used to calculate values between table entries. This same formula can be used in a computer to provide interpolation between table values entered into computer memory. A linear interpolation formula can be written

$$T(v) = T_1 + \frac{T_2 - T_1}{v_2 - v_1} (v - v_1) \qquad (2\text{-}6)$$

where $T(v)$ = interpolated temperature at voltage v
   v_1 = table voltage just less than v
   v_2 = table voltage just greater than v
   T_1 = table temperature corresponding to v_1
   T_2 = table temperature corresponding to v_2.

EXAMPLE 2-8   A type J TC with a 0°C reference measures 31.21 mV. What is the temperature?

Solution: Table A-1 shows that this voltage lies between two values; $v_1 = 31.08$ mV is just less and $v_2 = 31.37$ mV is just greater. The corresponding temperatures are 565°C and 570°C. Using the interpolation formula of Eq. (2-6) gives

$$I(31.21) = \frac{570 - 565}{31.37 - 31.08} (31.21 - 31.08)$$

$$= 567.2°C$$

This same interpolation can be used in reverse (i.e., to find the voltage for some temperature not in the table). When doing this, just interchange all the *T*'s and *v*'s in Eq. (2-6).

It would be a great hindrance to the use of a thermocouple if the reference junctions had to be maintained at a specific temperature, such as 0°C for the type J TC of Table A-1. Yet the values of measurement junction temperature and voltage depend on the value of reference temperature. There is no way around the fact that the reference junction temperature must be *known* to use a thermocouple for temperature measurement. However, it is possible to let the reference junction temperature be other than the value for which the table was constructed and still use the table. This is done by using a *correction factor* to alter the voltages of the table. Suppose the reference junctions are at some temperature, t_{ref}, that is not the same as the tables. Then the voltage of that reference temperature, as found from the tables, is used as a correction factor as follows.

1. *Finding temperature from a voltage measurement.*   Suppose a thermocouple with a reference temperature, T_{ref}, gives a voltage v_m for some temperature. Then the voltage of the reference temperature, $v(T_{ref})$, found from the tables, is added to that measured to give a corrected voltage:

$$v_{mc} = v_m + v(T_{ref}) \qquad (2\text{-}7)$$

   The temperature of this corrected voltage, as found in the tables, is that measured.

2. *Finding voltage for a temperature.*   Suppose a thermocouple with a reference temperature, T_{ref}, will be used to measure a temperature, *T*. Then the voltage of the reference, $v(T_{ref})$, found from the tables is subtracted from the voltage for the temperature, also found from the tables.

$$v_m = v(T) - v(T_{ref}) \qquad (2\text{-}8)$$

   This is the voltage that will be measured.

EXAMPLE 2-9   A type J TC has a 20°C reference. A voltage of 18.90 mV is measured. What is the temperature? Suppose this thermocouple is to be used to measure 180°C; what voltage will be measured?

Solution: For the first part of the problem it will be necessary to correct the voltage measured as indicated by Eq. (2-7) before the Table A-1 can be used. From the table the voltage of 20°C is found to be $v(20°C) = 1.02$ mV. Using this value in Eq. (2-7) gives

$$v_{mc} = 18.90 + 1.02 = 19.92 \text{ mV}$$

This voltage is now looked up in the table to find the temperature. The value is found in the 350°C row and the 15°C column, so the temperature is 365°C. For the second part of the problem it will be necessary to use Eq. (2-8) to find the voltage to be measured. The voltage of 180°C is found from the table to be $v(180°C) = 9.67$ mV. Then the voltage is

$$v = 9.67 - 1.02 = 8.65 \text{ mV}$$

This is the voltage that will be measured.

Integrated Temperature Transducers.   Many other types of temperature transducers are employed in industry and other commercial applications. Of particular interest are a class that are constructed with customized integrated-circuit assemblies that perform linearization and level adjustment. Such a transducer is little large than standard units and yet will output a voltage that is linearly dependent on temperature over some specified range. In some cases the assemblies even output a digitized signal directly, making interface to computers very easy. The problem with most of these units is that the temperature range is quite limited and seldom over 150°C maximum.

2-2.2 Displacement Transducers

There are many instances in the process industries when the physical displacement of an object must be measured. In some cases there is direct interest in this displacement, such as the positioning of a work piece for drilling or machining. In other cases the displacement is an intermediate indication of some other variable to be measured. For example, the displacement of a float may actually measure the level of liquid in a tank. In both types of applications, direct and intermediate, the same types of displacement transducers are used. In this section, several of the most common types of displacement transducers will be discussed.

Potentiometric.   The potentiometric transducer operates by a displacement causing the wiper of a variable resistor to move in proportion to the displacement. Thus the displacement is converted into a change in resistance. Figure 2-8 schematically illustrates the principle of operation. A great variety of designs are used for the physical manner by which the wiper is moved and for the structure of the resistance element. The transducer has the advantage of simplicity of design and ease of signal conditioning, since a changing resistance is easily converted into a changing voltage. The resistance change is also linear with respect to displacement. The disadvantages are in the wear-out, since there is a physical rubbing of wiper against wires, and the

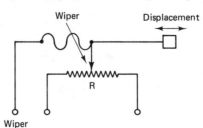

FIG. 2-8 A potentiometric displacement transducer converts displacement to resistance change.

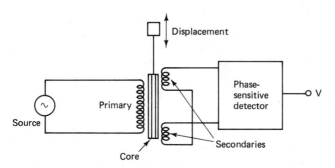

FIG. 2-9 The LVDT measures displacement via a transformer action. The transduction is very linear.

electrical noise that results from such a physical motion. The inherent range of the device is limited to the displacement that takes the wiper from one extreme of the resistance element to the other extreme. This range can be extended by the use of gears or levers, which either amplify or attenuate the range of measurable motion.

Linear Variable Differential Transformer (LVDT). One of the most common devices used in industry for converting displacement into an electrical signal is the LVDT. This transducer produces a dc voltage that is linearly proportional to displacement. There is virtually no friction to the displacement, since no physical rubbing is required, and hence no wear-out. The schematic of Fig. 2-9 can be used to understand the principle of operation. The central coil, or primary, is excited by an oscillator, which often operates at 1 kilohertz (kHz) or greater. The secondary coils are wired, as shown, in series opposition so that the two ac voltages produced are subtracted from each other to produce the output. The core of the transformer is free to move in and out of the coil assembly and is connected to the displacement system. If the core is centrally located, the secondary voltages will be identical and the output will be zero. As the core moves in either direction, the voltage induced in one secondary will exceed that in the other, and a net voltage will appear at the output. The phase-sensitive demodulator provides a dc output voltage from this ac voltage with a polarity indicating in which direction the core has moved.

LVDTs are available with total ranges of motion from ± 0.05 in. to ± 10 in. The oscillator and demodulator are often built into the unit so that the output is a dc voltage directly proportional to displacement. The output voltage is highly linear with displacement, often deviating from linearity by no more than 0.25% over the range of motion. The LVDT is used in many measurement systems as an intermediate stage, such as pressure transducers, flow transducers, and weighing stations.

Strain Gauge. The strain gauge is a transducer that measures very small displacements, such as the stretching of a metal bar under load. The basic principle is that, if a fine wire is stretched or compressed, its electric resistance will change. By measuring this change in resistance, the amount of stretching or compression can be determined. Figure 2-10 shows a strain gauge mounted on a metal bar. The gauge is

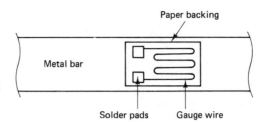

FIG. 2-10 The strain gauge converts stretching or compression into a change of resistance.

securely fastened to the bar, so if the bar stretches or compresses, the gauge will be likewise affected. Notice that the gauge is constructed by a back-and-forth arrangement of the wires to keep the dimensions small and yet provide a large total wire length.

The relationship between resistance change and length change is given by a manufacturer's constant for the gauge, called the *gauge factor*:

$$\text{GF} = \frac{\Delta R/R}{\Delta L/L} \tag{2-9}$$

where GF = gauge factor

$\Delta R/R$ = fractional change in resistance

$\Delta L/L$ = fractional change in length.

The fractional change in length, $\Delta L/L$, is also called the *strain*, which is why the transducer is called a strain gauge. For strain gauges constructed from metal wire or foil, the gauge factor is always approximately 2, GF $\approx$ 2, and is a constant. Some strain gauges are made from semiconductor material. For these gauges the gauge factor is much larger, perhaps as large as 150, but it is negative and varies nonlinearly with the strain. This makes their use somewhat limited.

EXAMPLE 2-10   Suppose a 5-m rod is placed under a heavy stress and stretches by 2 mm. If a strain gauge of 120-Ω nominal resistance and with a GF = 2.03 is mounted on the rod, find the change in resistance.

Solution: The change in resistance can be found from Eq. (2-9) by solving for ΔR:

$$\Delta R = (GF)(R)\frac{\Delta L}{L}$$

$$= (2.03)(120)\frac{0.002}{5} = 0.097\ \Omega$$

Example 2-10 illustrates a very important point about strain gauges; the change in resistance is very small. In this case the change of 0.097 Ω out of 120 is only 0.08%! This is much smaller than the changes due to temperature as noted for the RTD, which amounts to about 0.4%/°C. For this reason, very special care must be taken to protect gauge measurements against electrical noise and the overpowering effects of temperature variation. This is accomplished by using the gauge in combination with a

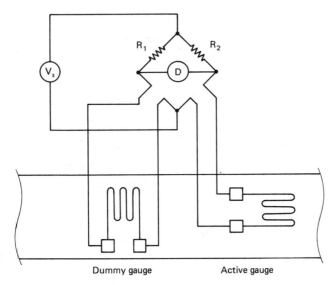

FIG. 2-11 Since the strain gauge is very temperature sensitive, a dummy gauge is used to compensate.

Dummy gauge   Active gauge

"dummy" gauge and a bridge circuit. Figure 2-11 shows the mounting of a strain measurement gauge and a dummy gauge on a bar. Notice that the dummy gauge will not respond to stretching or compression, but it will react to temperature changes. This is called *temperature compensation*. Later in this chapter you will see how the bridge circuit provides this compensation.

Strain gauges by themselves are used to monitor and measure the stretching and compression of bridges, buildings, and many other constructions. They are also used extensively as intermediate measurement devices in pressure gauges, flow meters, level transducers, and a host of other measurement instrumentation.

2-2.3 Optical Transducers

There is a growing application of optical methods of making measurements in the process industries. This is because an optical measurement does not require direct physical contact and consequential disturbance of the system being measured. As examples, to measure level, one can use light reflected from the surface; for distance, one can use the time of flight of a pulse of light to reflect from an object. Of course the use of light beams to detect the presence of objects in a continuous manufacturing process is well known. Many types of transducers are used to detect the light, either directly from a source or reflected. The properties of the photoconductive cell will be summarized as a representative example.

Photoconductive Cell. A very common type of optical detector is composed of a semiconductor material whose resistance is a function of the *intensity* of light striking the cell. In this device the resistance *decreases* with *increasing* light intensity in a highly nonlinear fashion. Figure 2-12 shows a typical curve of resistance versus light intensity. The device will only function for light that falls within a certain

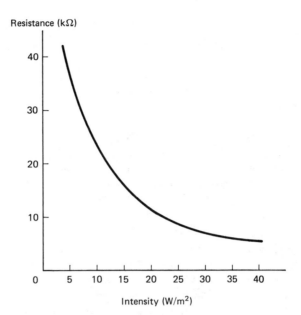

FIG. 2-12 The photoconductive cell converts light variations into resistance changes. Is it linear?

band of the spectrum. For the most common photoconductive cell, made from cadmium sulfide (CdS), the band is from 0.47 to 0.71 micrometer (μ_m) of light wavelength. This straddles the visible band. The time constant for these transducers is typically about 20 ms, which is quite slow for optical detectors.

2-2.4 Physical Transducers

A great number of other transducers are used to measure the many physical variables in the process industries. Each will have special characteristics making it suitable for particular applications. When using a transducer, care must be taken to evaluate the transducer with respect to the following points:

1. Determine the transfer function of the transducer. If the output is nonlinearly dependent on the measured variable, determine what the nonlinearity is and how it can be corrected for by software or hardware.
2. Determine the time constant of the transducer and assure that this time is fast enough that interference or errors will not result from use of this transducer in the measurement and control process.
3. Study the nature of the electrical output signal of the transducer and determine what kind of signal conditioning, as will be discussed in the next section, will be required. Pay particular attention to the sensitivity of the device to electrical noise, which could cause erroneous measurements.

The following paragraphs summarize some of the typical variables of the process industries and the transducers that are used to measure these variables.

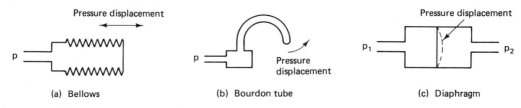

FIG. 2-13 These three pressure transducers all convert pressure information into a displacement.

Pressure. Devices to measure pressure occur in many forms in industry, but in all cases the measurement is the force per unit area that is exerted by a medium on the walls of its container. If the medium is a gas, the pressue is uniform over all the walls enclosing the gas. If it is a liquid, the pressure varies with the depth of the liquid and any gas pressure that may exist above the liquid surface. The pressure may be measured in a static environment, such as in a tank, or in a dynamic environment, such as when the medium is flowing in a pipe. Typical units are pounds per square inch (lb/in.^{2} or psi), inches of water (≈ 0.036 psi), inches of mercury (≈ 0.48 psi), and in the metric system the *pascal* [newton per square meter (N/m^2) ≈ 0.00015 psi].

Pressure is commonly measured using devices that execute a displacement with increasing pressure. This displacement is then measured with a displacement transducer, such as those discussed earlier. Figure 2-13 shows some common types of pressure displacement elements.

Flow Transducers. The measurement of the rate at which a substance moves is of great importance to many industries. The flow could be composed of solid material, such as grain or other dry products, or of liquid material, such as chemicals or even gaseous substances such as natural gas. A flow measurement may indicate the volume of material moving (gal/min, m^3/h, etc.), the speed of movement (ft/min, m/h, etc.), the mass moving (kg/h), or the weight moving (lb/h). The units in parentheses show typical units that may be involved, although there are certainly many others. The flow may be on conveyors, in open channels, or in pipes. A great variety of transducers exists to measure this physical variable. In most cases the flow is converted to an intermediate form, such as pressure or displacement, which is then measured by one of the previous techniques.

Level Transducers. Measurement of level refers to the depth of solid or liquid material in a container. The units will then be a distance measurement such as feet or meters. Many transducers perform such measurements, but most depend upon conversion of the level into a displacement, which is then measured by one of the techniques already discussed.

2-3 SIGNAL CONDITIONING

The ultimate goal of the measurement function in computer-based process control is a digital signal that is a function of the controlled variable. The first step in such a measurement is the conversion of that variable into an electrical variable via the transducers discussed in the previous section. The final stage of the measurement will be conversion of the analog electrical signal into a digital format. The intermediate step, to be discussed in this section, is to transform the transducer output into a form suitable for the analog-to-digital conversion process. This may or may not also involve the transmission of this signal, in analog form, from the measurement site to the location of the computer. The objective of this section is to present the standard types of analog signal conditioning that may be required.

2-3.1 Passive Signal Conditioning

The first type of signal conditioning to be considered does not involve the use of any amplifiers, oscillators, or other special circuit devices. These types of circuits are called *passive* since they usually involve the use of only resistors, capacitors, inductors, and voltage sources, but no devices like transistors or op amps. There are three basic types of circuits used in process control for passive applications: voltage dividers, bridge circuits, and passive filters.

Voltage Divider.   The most basic signal conditioning is the simple voltage divider. This circuit is used to convert a changing resistance to a changing voltage. The voltage divider is most useful in situations where interest is only in an alarm level or where a resistance changes over a considerable range and linearly with the variable measured. It would be very difficult to use the divider to convert RTD or strain gauge resistance change to voltage, since these devices exhibit a very small change in resistance with input variable. Example 2-11 illustrates how such a circuit might be used.

EXAMPLE 2-11   A photoconductive cell with a characteristic such as that shown in Fig. 2-12 is to be used for an alarm in light level. When the light reaches an intensity of 10 W/m^2, the alarm is to be triggered by a voltage of 5 V. The voltage should increase with light intensity.

Solution: This problem can be solved with a voltage divider such as that shown in Fig. 2-14. Note that the photocell has been chosen as the upper resistor, since this will make the voltage, v_T, increase as the light intensity increases (and the resistance of the cell decreases). The value of R_2 is found from the 5-V trigger requirement:

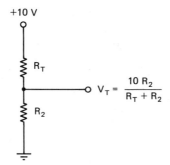

$$+10\ V$$

$$V_T = \frac{10\ R_2}{R_T + R_2}$$

FIG. 2-14 A simple voltage divider converts resistance variation into voltage variation.

$$v_T = 5 = \frac{10}{R_T + R_2} R_2$$

From Fig. 2-12 the cell resistance at 10 W/m^2 is found to be 23 kΩ. Then the preceding equation can be solved for the divider resistance:

$$R_2 = 23 \text{ k}\Omega$$

Bridge Circuit. The bridge circuit is used extensively for instrumentation signal conditioning since it can resolve very small changes in resistance or impedance. You have seen that the RTD and strain gauge both involve small changes in resistance, so the bridge is used as the first level of signal conditioning for both of these devices. The most basic bridge circuit, from which all the rest derive, is called the Wheatstone bridge, and is shown in Fig. 2-15. Notice that there are four resistors and one source. The *detector* placed between points *a* and *b* of the bridge circuit is used to perform measurements of bridge arm resistance. There are two conditions of interest relating to the detector and the values of the resistances:

1. *Null condition.* When the values of the resistors have a certain specified set, the detector will read zero voltage between points *a* and *b*. This is called a null condition. In this case the resistors *must* satisfy the condition

$$R_1R_4 = R_2R_3 \tag{2-10}$$

   Notice that this condition is independent of the voltage source used to drive the bridge. From this relation, if three of the resistors are known, the value of the fourth can be found.

2. *Off-null condition.* When the bridge is not at null, the open-circuit voltage from *a* to *b* can be used to express a relation between the resistors and the exciting voltage source:

$$\Delta v = v_a - v_b = v_s \frac{R_2R_3 - R_1R_4}{(R_1 + R_3)(R_2 + R_4)} \tag{2-11}$$

This relationship provides a conversion of resistance to voltage. However, this voltage will vary nonlinearly with the resistances since all resistors appear in both the numerator and denominator of Eq. (2-11). Approximately linear variation can be obtained by proper selection of the resistors.

Example 2-12 illustrates use of the bridge circuit.

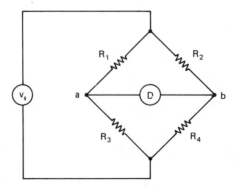

FIG. 2-15 The Wheatstone bridge is the basic circuit for measuring small fractional changes of resistance.

EXAMPLE 2-12   An RTD is used for R_4 in a bridge circuit. The RTD has $R(25°C) = $
350 Ω and $\alpha_0 = 0.0037/°C$. The bridge has $R_1 = 4.7$ kΩ, $R_2 = 1$ kΩ, and R_3 is a 2-kΩ
variable resistance. The bridge source is $v_s = 10$ V. (a) If the bridge nulls with $R_3 = 1400$
Ω, find the temperature. (b) If the detector can resolve a change in voltage of 4 mV, find
the smallest temperature change that can be resolved.

Solution: For part (a) it is merely necessary to use the bridge null equation, Eq. (2-10), to
find the value of R_4, and then to find the temperature from Eq. (2-4). For the value
of R_4,

$$R_4 = \frac{R_2 R_3}{R_1}$$

$$= \frac{(1 \text{ k}\Omega)(1.4 \text{ k}\Omega)}{4.7 \text{ k}\Omega} = 297.9 \ \Omega$$

Now Eq. (2-4) is used to find the temperature:

$$297.9 = 350[1 + 0.0037(T - 25)]$$

Solving for T,

$$T = \frac{297.9 - 350}{1.295} + 25$$

$$= -15.2°C$$

For part (b) it will be necessary to find the change in temperature that *causes* a bridge
offset voltage of 4 mV. Working backward, let's find the resistance change that causes 4
mV and then the temperature change from that. So, from Eq. (2-11),

$$\Delta v = 0.004 = 10 \frac{(4.7 \text{ k}\Omega)(R_4) - (1 \text{ k}\Omega)(1.4 \text{ k}\Omega)}{(4.7 \text{ k}\Omega + 1.4 \text{ k}\Omega)(1 \text{ k}\Omega + R_4)}$$

This equation is to be solved for R_4:

$$0.00244(1 + R_4) = 4.7R_4 - 1.4$$

$$R_4 = 298.5 \ \Omega$$

Now the temperature corresponding to this resistance is found from Eq. (2-4), as before:

$$298.5 = 350[1 + 0.0037(T - 25)]$$

$$T = -14.8°C$$

The difference between this temperature and that found before is the temperature
change that will cause an offset voltage of 4 mV and therefore be resolvable: $\Delta T = $
$-15.2 - (-14.8) = -0.4°C$.

AC Bridge.   When the arms of the bridge are replaced by impedances composed of resistors, capacitors, and inductors, the Wheatstone bridge becomes an ac
bridge. The excitation voltage must now be an oscillating source (i.e., a signal genera-
tor). A null condition can still be found and an off-null voltage. The null condition is
now, for the impedance,

$$Z_1 Z_4 = Z_2 Z_3 \qquad (2\text{-}12)$$

and the offset voltage will be derived from an equation like Eq. (2-11), but with the
resistances replaced by impedances as in Eq. (2-12). The ac bridge circuit is often used
in signal conditioning for transducers that result in capacity changes.

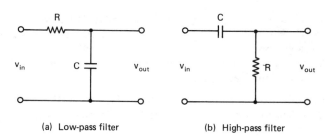

FIG. 2-16   Simple low-pass and high-pass filters can be constructed from a single resistor and capacitor.

Passive Filters.   Computer process control often has problems with electrical noise due to switching spikes from gates, flip-flops, and other digital circuitry. It is often necessary to use filters to reduce these high-frequency effects from the analog circuits. Furthermore, you will learn later that filters often must be used to reduce errors due to the rate at which a digital system samples analog data. In addition to these computer- or digital-related effects, there is often the need to reduce low-frequency noise from the ac line. In many cases, passive filters can be used to provide these protections.

Low Pass.   A low-pass filter can be constructed from a capacitor and resistor connected as shown in Fig. 2-16a. Such a circuit will attenuate signals with frequency near and above a critical value given by

$$f_c = \frac{1}{2\pi RC} \tag{2-13}$$

The relationship between the magnitude of v_{out} and the magnitude of v_{in} is given by

$$\left| \frac{v_{out}}{v_{in}} \right| = \frac{1}{[(2\pi fRC)^2 + 1]^{1/2}} \tag{2-14}$$

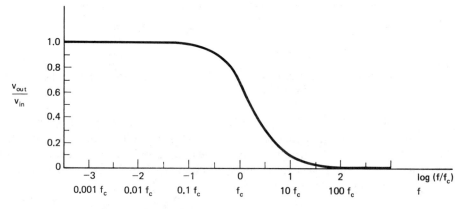

FIG. 2-17   This graph illustrates the pass characteristics of the simple low-pass filter with frequency.

Figure 2-17 shows a plot of the ratio of v_{out} to v_{in} versus frequency for such a circuit. The frequency has been plotted as the log (f) to show a larger range. Notice that the attenuation is gradual but centered about the critical value given by Eq. (2-13). These filters can be cascaded together to obtain more attenuation, but if this is done the impedance of each succeeding stage must be larger than the preceding stage.

EXAMPLE 2-13   A low-pass filter is needed to eliminate switching spikes at 1 megahertz (MHz). The fastest signal frequency is $f_s = 10$ kHz. Design a filter that reduces the signal frequency by no more than 5% but attenuates the 1-MHz noise.

Solution: The point here is that one must be careful where the critical frequency is selected so that the noise is reduced greatly but the signal is affected very little. If we choose the f_c to be, say, 20 kHz, the 1 MHz would be eliminated, *but* the signal frequency at 10 KHz would be reduced also. Let's use the 5% maximum reduction in Eq. (2-14):

$$0.95 = \frac{1}{[(2\pi f_s RC)^2 + 1]^{1/2}}$$

gives

$$2\pi f_s RC = 0.3287$$

or, for the signal frequency given,

$$RC = 5.23 \times 10^{-6}$$

Any combination of resistor and capacitor that gives this product will work. Often impedance requirements on preceding or following circuits help select the values. In this case, let's just use $R = 10$ kΩ, and then $C = 523$ picofarads (pF). The attenuation at 1 MHz can now be calculated to be

$$\left|\frac{v_{out}}{v_{in}}\right|_{1\,MHz} = \frac{1}{\{[2\pi 10^6 (5.23 \times 10^{-6})]^2 + 1\}^{1/2}}$$
$$= 0.03$$

So the 1-MHz signal is attenuated to 3% while the signal frequency is attenuated to 95%.

Many other types of passive low-pass filters can be designed with sharper cutoff bands (i.e, ranges of frequency over which the attenuation drops from unity to a small value).

High Pass.   A filter can also be constructed from a capacitor and resistor that attenuates *below* some critical frequency. This is called a high-pass filter. The circuit for this filter is shown in Fig. 2-16b. Note that the only difference is the position of the capacitor and resistor in the circuit. The critical frequency is the same as that defined in Eq. (2-13). The attenuation equation is changed now to be

$$\left|\frac{v_{out}}{v_{in}}\right| = \frac{2\pi fRC}{[(2\pi fRC)^2 + 1]^{1/2}} \qquad (2\text{-}15)$$

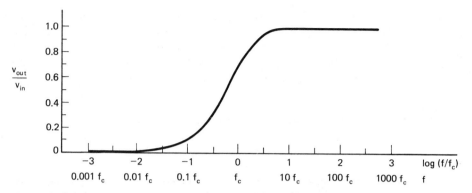

FIG. 2-18   This graph shows how the high-pass filter output is attenuated at low frequencies.

Figure 2-18 shows a plot of the voltage ratio of Eq. (2-15) versus log (f) for the high-pass filter. Note that lower frequencies are attenuated while higher frequencies are affected only very little by the circuit.

EXAMPLE 2-14   Construct a high-pass filter to attenuate the 60-Hz line noise to a factor of 0.01 (1%). Calculate the effect on a signal frequency at 10 kHz.

Solution: In this case the voltage ratio of Eq. (2-15) is to be set at 0.01 and RC found for a frequency of 60 Hz. This allows selection of R and C. These values are then used to calculate the attenuation, again using Eq. (2-15), for a signal at 10 kHz.

$$0.01 = \frac{2\pi(60)RC}{\{[2\pi(60)RC]^2 + 1\}^{1/2}}$$

This gives

$$377RC = 10^{-2}$$

or

$$RC = 2.65 \times 10^{-5}\text{s}$$

Let's select $R = 1\ k\Omega$ and then $C = 0.0265\ \mu F$. Using these values, the attenuation at 10 kHz can be found from Eq. (2-15); since $2\pi fRC = 2\pi(10^4)(2.65 \times 10^{-5}) = 1.665$, then

$$\left|\frac{v_{out}}{v_{in}}\right| = \frac{1.665}{[(1.665)^2 + 1]^{1/2}}$$
$$= 0.857$$

So the filter attenuates the 60-Hz line signal to 0.01 of its input value while leaving about 85.7% of the signal at a frequency of 10 kHz.

Many other types of high-pass filters can be constructed with improved characteristics over this simple RC type using inductors. This filter can be cascaded for improved performance, but care must be taken to keep loading effects from changing the effective characteristics.

2-3.2 Active Signal Conditioning

Active signal conditioning refers to those cases where special electronic devices or systems must be used on a signal, apart from resistors, capacitors, and inductors. There are a great many different types of active systems for signal conditioning. For the purposes of this text, it will be sufficient to consider a summary of the application of *operational amplifiers (op amps)* to the construction of required active circuits.

Op amps represent a general workhorse of analog electronics, which has replaced the transistor for the construction of specific electronic circuits. The use of op amps is quite simple, involving only the connection of specific external components, and of course a power source, to achieve the desired response. Op amp-based signal conditioning is used extensively in process control, both analog and computer controlled, to prepare signals for analog-to-digital conversion, and to adjust the levels of analog signals output by the computer. In this section a number of useful standard circuits will be given along with their electrical characteristics.

The circuits in this section will not show the power supply connections required by these op amps. In general, op amps require both plus and minus power supplies, typically of about 15V. Other connections are sometimes required for protection against oscillation. The specifications of individual units will tell you what connections are required. In this section, only the functional parts of the circuits are shown.

Inverting Amplifier.   The op-amp circuit of Fig. 2-19 uses only two resistors to construct a circuit that can amplify or attenuate an input signal. Notice that the sign of the output signal is the opposite of the input, as noted by the negative gain. The electrical characteristics are

$$v_{out} = -\frac{R_2}{R_1}v_{in} \qquad (2\text{-}16)$$

$$Z_{in} = R_1 \qquad (2\text{-}17)$$

$$Z_{out} < 50\ \Omega \qquad (2\text{-}18)$$

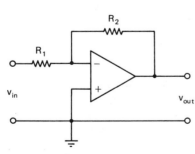

FIG. 2-19   A simple inverting amplifier can be constructed from an op amp and two resistors.

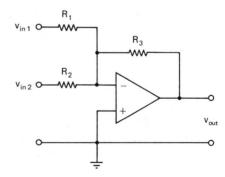

FIG. 2-20   This is a summing amplifier.

The output impedance value, z_{out}, depends on the gain chosen and the op amp used. The gain can be made less than 1 (attenuation) by making R_2 less than R_1. Two such inverting amplifiers in series can amplify without changing the sign of the input. The frequency response depends on the op amp, but it is generally flat for gains of less than 100 out to about 20 kHz.

Summing Amplifier.   A simple extension of the circuit of Fig. 2-19 makes an op-amp circuit that can sum two or more input voltages. The circuit is shown in Fig. 2-20 for the case of two input voltages. Note that the input circuit is simply split into two parts, each with an input resistor. The output is given by

$$v_{out} = -\left(\frac{R_3}{R_1}v_{in1} + \frac{R_3}{R_2}v_{in2}\right) \tag{2-19}$$

Notice that, if the resistors are all equal, $v_{out} = -(v_{in1} + v_{in2})$. In other cases the ratio of the resistors can be varied to construct a variety of circuit responses.

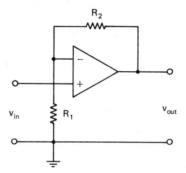

FIG. 2-21   The noninverting amplifier cannot have a gain less than unity.

Noninverting Amplifier.   The op-amp circuit of Fig. 2-21 uses two resistors also, but with different connections to produce an amplifier that does not invert the sign of the input signal. This amplifier can never have a gain of less than 1 (i.e., it cannot be an attenuator). The characteristics are

$$v_{out} = \left(1 + \frac{R_2}{R_1}\right)v_{in} \tag{2-20}$$

$$Z_{in} > 100 \text{ M}\Omega \tag{2-21}$$

$$Z_{out} < 50 \text{ }\Omega \tag{2-22}$$

The actual value of input impedance depends on the gain of the op amp and the op amp used. By eliminating R_1 and making $R_2 = 0$ (a short), a *voltage follower* results, which has a gain of unity. The advantage of this circuit is a very large input impedance, so it does not load down the preceding circuit.

Instrumentation Amplifier.   The circuit of Fig. 2-22 is called an instrumentation amplifier. It is extensively used in instrumentation, particularly where amplification of a differential voltage is required, as the bridge offset voltage. The two

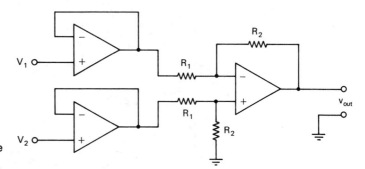

FIG. 2-22 The instrumentation amplifier is often used with bridge circuits.

amplifiers on the front are voltage followers for isolation, and the third op amp is used in a differential gain configuration. The characteristics of this circuit are

$$v_{out} = \frac{R_2}{R_1}(v_2 - v_1) \qquad (2\text{-}23)$$

$$Z_{in} > 100 \text{ M}\Omega \quad (\text{each side}) \qquad (2\text{-}24)$$

$$Z_{out} < 50 \ \Omega \qquad (2\text{-}25)$$

The two pairs of resistors must be very closely matched for these equations to be valid. Notice that the output depends only on the difference of the input voltages. If the resistor pairs are not matched well, some output will result from the individual input voltages as well as the difference. This is called poor common-mode rejection. Note that this amplifier can amplify or attenuate the input difference.

EXAMPLE 2-15 Signal conditioning is required to provide an output of 0 to 5 V as the input varies from 0.5 to 1.3 V. Use op amps to provide this function.

Solution: To provide this signal conditioning, let's first write an equation that describes the relationship between input and output. In general, this will be a straight line (linear) relation,

$$v_{out} = mv_{in} + b$$

where m and b are the slope and intercept. These can be found by using the given data in the equation:

$$0 = 0.5m + b$$
$$5 = 1.3m + b$$

The first equation gives $b = -0.5m$. If this is substituted into the second, the result is

$$5 = 1.3m - 0.5m = 0.8m$$

or $m = 6.25$. Then $b = -3.125$, and the equation is

$$v_{out} = 6.25v_{in} - 3.125$$

which can be written

$$v_{out} = 6.25(v_{in} - 0.5)$$

This equation can be constructed by a summing amplifier with v_{in} on one input and -0.5 V on the other input, followed by an inverting amplifier with a gain of 6.25. This

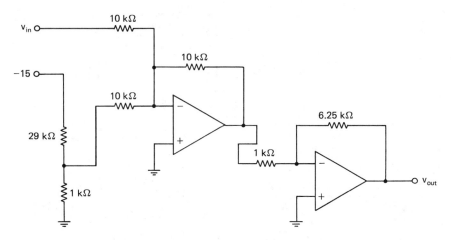

FIG. 2-23   This is a possible solution to Ex. 2-15.

circuit is shown in Fig. 2-23. The -0.5 V could be obtained from a divider off of the negative supply to the op amp, as shown.

2-3.3 Transmitters

As was pointed out earlier, it is often necessary to get measurement information from the site of measurement to a control facility located some distance away. This is accomplished by means of a transmitter. This word is not used in the traditional sense of a device that sends out electromagnetic signals, but rather as a device that can propagate signals, usually through wires, with little loss in the data information.

Pneumatic.   Historically, process control was accomplished to a large extent by pneumatic systems. In such cases the transmitter was a device that converted measurement information into an air pressure signal, usually between 3 and 15 psi, which was carried by pipes to the control room. These systems are still very much in use today.

Electronic—Analog.   When electronic processing is employed, the most common form of transmitter converts the data information into a range of current, usually from 4 to 20 mA. The idea here is that the range of physical-variable measurement is operated on by the transmitter until that range produces a current from 4 mA for the minimum to 20 mA for the maximum.

A current signal is used because this will be independent of load resistance, as long as the load is lower than some maximum. If a voltage was used, for example, the voltage drop in the wires from the measurement site to the control room would introduce an error in the measurement. With current, this does not occur, since if 10 mA (for example) is injected into the wires at one end, then 10 mA will come out the other, unless there is a shunt path between the wires.

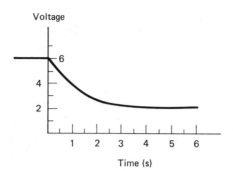

Voltage

6

4

2

1 2 3 4 5 6

Time (s)

FIG. 2-24   Graph for Prob. 2-3.

PROBLEMS

2-1   A pressure transducer has a time constant of 3.5 s. The output transfer function is 0.05 V/psi. At $t = 0$ the pressure suddenly changes from 75 to 149 psi. Find the transducer output at 0.5, 2, 3.0, and 5 s.

2-2   For Prob. 2-1, find the time after the $t = 0$ change at which the transducer output indicates the pressure to be 100 psi.

2-3   Figure 2-24 shows the measured response of a transducer to a sudden change of input. What is the transducer time response, τ? [*Hint*: Use Eq. (2-1) with all values taken from the graph, leaving only τ unknown.]

2-4   A temperature transducer has a transfer function for voltage output with temperature in degrees Celsius given by

$$V = 0.02(T - 20) + 0.0004(T - 20)^2$$

Plot this voltage versus temperature from 0° to 100°C. Is the relationship linear or nonlinear? Compare the change in voltage for a 5°C temperature change if the initial temperature is 30°C, and if it is 90°C.

2-5   Convert the following temperature to degrees Celsius and degrees Fahrenheit: 50 K, 320 K, 757 K.

2-6   Convert the following temperatures to degrees Celsius and kelvins: $-77°F$, $0°F$, $437°F$.

2-7   An RTD has $\alpha = 0.0042/°C$ and $R = 100\ \Omega$ at 25°C. Find the resistance at 0°C and 87°C.

2-8   For the RTD of Prob. 2-7, find the temperature if the resistance is found to be 279 Ω.

2-9   Suppose the RTD of Prob. 2-7 has a dissipation constant of $P_D = 20$ mW/°C. If it is placed in a bath at 25°C, find the maximum current that can be used for measurement if the error due to self-heating is to be less than 0.25°C. (*Hint*: Find the maximum power for that temperature rise and from this the current, assuming the resistance at 25°C.)

2-10   The thermistor of Fig. 2-6 is used in the divider shown in Fig. 2-25. Plot the voltage output versus temperature from 30° to 90°C. Is the result linear? How does it compare to the resistance versus temperature?

2-11   Suppose a regulated voltage of 8.0 V is placed across the thermistor of Fig. 2-6 and that its dissipation constant is 6 mW/°C. Compare the temperature error due to self-heating if the bath temperature is 20°C, 50°C, and 100°C.

2-12   Find the voltage of a type J thermocouple with a 0°C reference if the measurement temperature is $-45°C$, 115°C, 327°C, and 563°C.

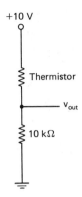

+10 V

Thermistor

V_{out}

10 kΩ

FIG. 2-25   Circuit for Prob. 2-10.

2-13 A type J TC with a 0°C reference measures 37.71 mV. What is the temperature? What is the temperature for a measurement of 22.44 mV?

2-14 Repeat Prob. 2-12 if the reference is 20°C.

2-15 Repeat Prob. 2-13 if the reference is 25°C.

2-16 A strain gauge has a GF = 2.14 and R = 120 Ω. Find the resistance if the strain is 0.0004 (tension).

2-17 Suppose the gauge wire of Prob. 2-16 has a temperature coefficient of α = 0.0037/°C at 20°C. Find the temperature rise that would produce a thermal resistance change equal to that of the strain.

2-18 The RTD of Prob. 2-7 is used for R_4 in the bridge circuit given in Fig. 2-15. Given V_s = 10 V, R_1 = 5 kΩ, and R_2 = 200 Ω, find the R_3 to null the bridge at a temperature of 25°C.

2-19 Using the same values as in Prob. 2-18 but with R_3 = 2500 Ω, plot the offset voltage versus temperature from 0° to 100°C. Is the result linear?

2-20 What bridge null detector voltage resolution is necessary for the circuit of Prob. 2-18 to just resolve a temperature change of 0.1°C?

2-21 A signal has high-frequency noise spikes at 2.5 MHz. Design an RC low-pass filter to attenuate this noise by 98%. What effect does this have on the data that are at 500 Hz?

2-22 Plot the ratio of V_{out} to V_{in} versus frequency for the two-stage RC high-pass filter of Fig. 2-26. Assume the input of the second stage is the output of the first stage. Compare the curve with that of a single stage by finding the frequency difference between ratios of 0.1 and 0.9.

2-23 Design a single-stage RC high-pass filter with a 1-kHz critical frequency. Compare the attenuation of 120 Hz with a signal at 12 kHz.

2-24 The inverting amplifier of Fig. 2-19 has the thermistor of Fig. 2-6 in the feedback (R_2). Use a constant input voltage of V_{in} = −2.0 V and R_1 = 20 KΩ. Plot the output voltage versus temperature. Is it linear?

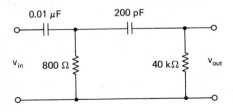

0.01 μF   200 pF

V_{in} 800 Ω   40 kΩ V_{out}

FIG. 2-26   Two-stage high-pass filter for Prob. 2-22.

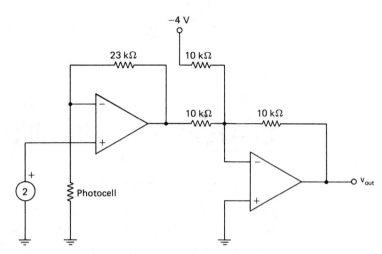

FIG. 2-27 Circuit for Prob. 2-25.

2-25 The photocell of Fig. 2-12 is used in the circuit given in Fig. 2-27. Plot the output voltage versus light intensity.

2-26 A transducer outputs a voltage, V_T, with a range of 4 to 12 V. Design an op-amp circuit that converts this to an output, V_{out}, with a range of 0 to 5 V. (*Hint*: First develop an equation for V_{out} as a function of V_T. From this the required op-amp circuits can be deduced.)

2-27 Show the circuit and values for an instrumentation amplifier with a gain of 480.

2-28 A type J TC with a 0°C reference is used for temperature measurement between 100° and 500°C. Signal conditioning must convert this to 0 to 10 V. Assuming the TC must be connected first to an instrumentation amplifier with a gain of 100, design the rest of the op-amp circuit to provide this conditioning.

2-29 Develop signal conditioning that will provide a voltage signal from 0 to 5 V as the light intensity, measured by the photocell of Fig. 2-12, varies from 4 to 10 W/m².

CHAPTER 3

DATA INPUT AND OUTPUT

OBJECTIVES

The objectives of this chapter are all concerned with the hardware by which data are input to the computer and output from the computer. Obviously, if the computer is to be used for control, then data about the controlled variables must be input and controlling signals must be output. After studying this chapter and doing the problems at the end of the chapter, you will be able to:

1. Describe the elements of data-acquisition systems (DAS) and data-output systems (DOS) for computer control.
2. Define the required hardware to interface data to a microprocessor-based computer.
3. Describe the timing requirements for data interface to a microprocessor-based computer.
4. Explain the operation and typical application specifications of digital-to-analog converters (DACs) and analog-to-digital converters (ADCs).
5. Given an application specification, design a DAS and DOS using ADCs and DACs and other support hardware, assuming a microprocessor-based computer.
6. Given an application specification, design a DAS and DOS using modularized input and output devices, assuming a microprocessor-based computer.

3-1 INTRODUCTION

There are some basic problems to be faced when a digital computer is considered for applications in control. Many of these problems must be dealt with when the variables related to the control are input to the computer or output from the computer, that is, at the *interface* between the "real world" and the "computer" world.

One problem is that the real world is fundamentally *analog*, but the digital computer is fundamentally *digital*. This has a number of consequences. First, a method of converting analog data to digital data for input must be developed. Second, a method of converting digital data back to analog data for output must be developed. Third, accounting must be made for the *loss* of information when analog data are converted to digital form. This means, for example, if temperature from 0° to 100°C is represented by a digital signal of 8 bits, then there can only be 256 values of temperature represented. So there will be ignorance of temperature variation of less than $\frac{100}{256}$ = 0.39°C. Fourth, accounting must be made for the limited ability of the digital output to be converted into analog data. Obviously, if 8 bits are converted into a voltage, there can only be 256 voltage values. Thus the output is not really analog. These are not all the issues, but they give an idea of some of the concerns related to the analog-to-digital difference.

Another problem has to do with the inherent *time* difference between the real world and the computer world. Industrial and commercial control applications may involve variable variation with time scales from nanoseconds to years. Typically, however, the time scales will be seconds to minutes for physical variables such as flow, pressure, and temperature. The computer, on the other hand, has a time scale fixed in the range of microseconds. Thus, if the value of a physical variable is to be input to a computer, there will be a time "window" of less than one to at most a couple of microseconds when these data must be presented.

A third problem is related to the system by which numerical information is represented. In the real world, numerical information is represented in the base 10 counting system, and all processing is defined and carried out in this system. In the computer, all representation and processing is performed in the binary or base 2 system. When a computer is used for control, the translation of data and processing between the base 10 system and the base 2 system must be performed for both input and output.

In this chapter and the next, these problems and others will be considered and solutions will be defined.

3-2 ELEMENTS OF DATA INPUT AND OUTPUT

In this section the general elements and requirements of data input and output in computer control systems will be defined. The general term *interface* is used to describe the overall process of inputting and outputting data. Interface *hardware* consists of the actual parts that are required to support the data input and output. Interface *software* consists of the computer instructions that are necessary to produce

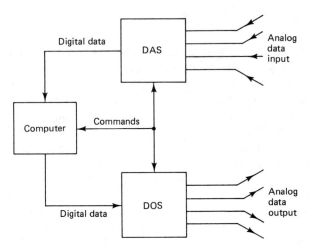

FIG. 3-1 The basic goal of digital data acquisition is to get analog data into digital form and into the computer.

the required input and output. The purpose of this section, and this chapter, is to define the hardware. Chapter 4 will discuss the software requirements.

Figure 3-1 is a diagram that defines the global system to be studied. The data-acquisition system (DAS) is used for input of analog data. The data are presented to this unit in analog form from one of many possible analog inputs or *channels*. Under command from the computer itself, the data are converted into digital form and presented to the computer as digital data. On the output side, the data-output system (DOS), the reverse process occurs. Again under command of the computer, digital data are presented to the DOS, converted to analog form, and output into one of several possible analog output channels.

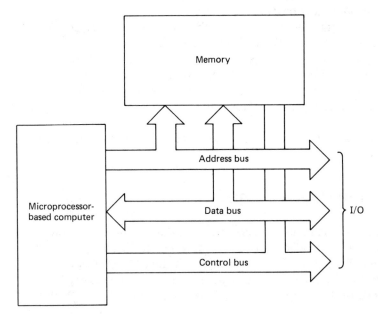

FIG. 3-2 All input and output is carried out using the address bus, data bus, and control bus.

3-2.1 The Computer Model

To define the nature of interface hardware, it is necessary to have a model of the computer to which the interface will occur. Fortunately, there are many common features of microprocessor-based computers so that a description can be constructed that can be used to define the input-output process for many different types of microprocessors. Examples will be related to specific microprocessor types.

All communication with a microprocessor is carried out by three sets of parallel wires or lines called *buses*. Any interface must use these buses for commands and to move the data between the DAS or DOS and the computer. Therefore, a model of a microprocessor for interface can be defined as in Fig. 3-2, with a "box" for the microprocessor itself and the buses as the communication links.

Data Bus.   The data bus represents the lines connected to the microprocessor by which information is input and output. When the DAS performs a conversion of some analog data to digital form, it will be input to the computer by depositing the digital signal on the data bus lines. The number of lines is determined by the size of the data word of the microprocessor. There are many 8-bit microprocessors, such as the 8080, 6800, 6502, and Z80. There are also 16-bit microprocessors, such as the 9900, 68000, and 8086, and a number of 32-bit devices are under development.

The data bus lines are *bidirectional*. This means that the same lines are used to carry digital signals into the microprocessor and to carry digital signals out. This feature of the bus creates some special requirements when external equipment is to use the bus for input and output. As illustrated in Fig. 3-2, the data lines are used for reading and writing memory, as well as for input and output.

Address Bus.   The address bus consists of the lines used by the computer to address memory locations, and it is also used for interface, as will be seen later. The number of address lines determines the maximum addressable memory of the microprocessor. For example, most 8-bit data word computers have a 16-bit address word. Thus these computers can address memory from 0000H to FFFFH. The total number of addressable memory locations is given by $2^{16} = 65,536$, or 65K, where one K is understood to mean 1024. Some microprocessors, particularly the 16-bit data word types, have more address lines for even greater addressing capability. A 20-bit address word would thus address $2^{20} = 1,048,576$ words of memory.

The address bus is typically unidirectional. The bus is used to carry address information from the microprocessor to external equipment, such as memory. The microprocessor may place an address on the bus for the purpose of reading from a memory, for example.

Control Bus.   The control bus is a set of parallel lines from the microprocessor by which commands can be issued to and from the microprocessor. The exact nature of these lines varies from microprocessor to microprocessor, but the following summary indicates the typical operations provided.

1. *Read or write.* The microprocessor will have one or two lines used to communicate with external equipment that a read or write operation is to occur. Thus, if the computer wishes to write to a memory location, the address bus would be loaded with the address and the appropriate write command would be issued on the control bus.

2. *Address bus status.* The control bus will have a line to indicate the status of information on the address bus. This line may indicate when the information on the address bus is valid or whether the address bus word is for memory operations or input–output operations.

3. *Interrupt.* There will be one or more lines connected to the microprocessor by which the interrupt feature of the computer can be exercised. When one of these lines is activated by external equipment, the normal sequence of instruction execution by the computer is interrupted. The computer is directed or *vectored* to a new set of instructions stored in memory. Execution of these instructions is carried out now to service the interrupt, which may be to input data for example. When finished, instruction execution is returned to that in effect when the interrupt occurred.

There are other lines in the control bus that will be introduced as needed, and particular microprocessors will have special lines as part of their design. However, the basic set listed will be sufficient for the initial purposes of our model computer.

3-2.2   Data Bus Usage

There are special restrictions on the use of the data bus by external equipment because of its bidirectional nature. The address bus and the lines of the control bus do not suffer the same restrictions since they are typically used for either microprocessor input or output exclusively. As you can see from Fig. 3-2, the data bus is used to transfer data back and forth from memory and the microprocessor. But this same data bus will be used to transfer information about variables in the control system back and forth from the microprocessor. There is a special way this must be done.

Data Bus Loading.   Perhaps the best way to see the problem is to show how transfers on the data bus *cannot* be done. Suppose it is desired to input to the microprocessor the settings of four switches. These could be high–low switches in a pressure system, for example. One might imagine just connecting these switches to four lines of the data bus, as shown in Fig. 3-3. We have assumed the computer model has only 4 bits in the data word. The switches have been set up for the bit pattern 1010_2 and have been simply connected to the data bus. By doing this the computer has been *locked up*! Suppose the microprocessor tries to execute an instruction to read memory. Then the address is placed on the address bus and memory is activated by a READ command on the control bus. But when the memory places the contents of the addressed location on the data bus, it will be impossible to change from the 1010_2 set

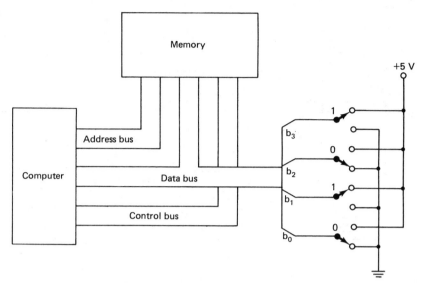

FIG. 3-3   In this example the data bus has been "loaded" with 1010 and cannot be used for data transfer with memory.

by the switches. The data bus cannot be used by memory or the microprocessor because the switches have fixed the lines to 1010_2. Obviously, this cannot be tolerated. The bus must be left available except at the precise moment when the switch settings are to be read by the computer.

Tristate Buffers.   This goal is accomplished by using a special circuit element called a tristate buffer. Although a solid-state device, this element functions like a switch that can be turned on and off by the computer. Figure 3-4a shows that the input of the tristate buffer is isolated from the output until the "switch" is closed by a signal on the ENABLE line. The figure also shows the proper schematic symbol of the device. Note that it can be enabled by either an active low, as in Fig. 3-4b, or an

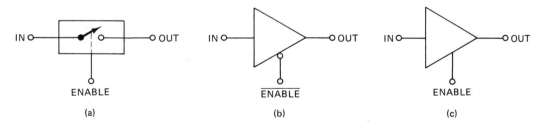

FIG. 3-4   The tristate buffer is much like a switch in that it has an "open circuit" or high impedance state.

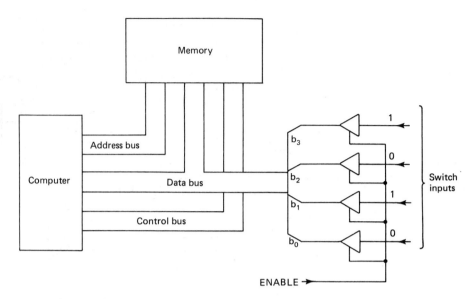

FIG. 3-5 This shows how the problem of Fig. 3-3 can be solved with tristate buffers.

active high, as shown in Fig. 3-4c. The word "tristate" is used to denote that the output can be one of three states, *high*, *low*, or *open*, which is called the *high-impedance* state.

The problem of reading the switch settings can now be solved as shown in Fig. 3-5 by using a tristate buffer between the switches and the data bus. Note that a new requirement has been added, because the computer must now initiate a *command* to enable the buffers and place the switch settings on the data bus. In one form or another, all equipment connected to the data bus must provide isolation so that the bus is free to be used by the microprocessor and other equipment.

Data Output.   When the computer is to output a signal to the DOS, the output will be carried on the data bus. In this case the computer executes an instruction that loads the required output bit pattern onto the data bus, and then the DOS "reads" this information for output, such as conversion to some analog signal. This is the same thing that occurs when the computer "writes" to memory. The problem is that the required output information is only on the data bus for a short length of time, perhaps only $\frac{1}{2}$ to 1 microsecond (μs). Thus the equipment that is to receive this information must *capture* the information during this time interval. This is made possible by the use of a *latch* connected to the data bus. As shown in Fig. 3-6, the latch is nothing more than a set of flip-flops (F/Fs) equal to the number of bits in the data bus. Since there is little loading on the input of the F/Fs, it is often not necessary to use isolation buffers between the latch and the data bus.

It will be necessary for the computer to generate a command to latch the data on the data bus during the interval when the desired output information is on the data bus. This is done by the LATCH (also called LOAD) input to the device. This input

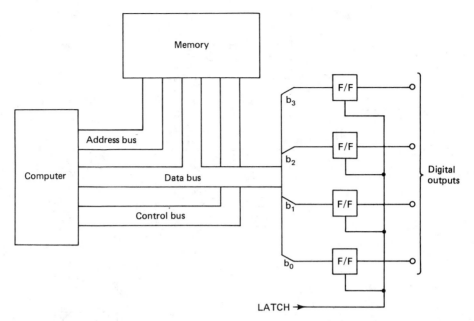

FIG. 3-6   For data output, F/Fs are used to capture data from the data bus lines using a LATCH or CLOCK input.

may be active low or active high depending on the particular unit used. Once the latch has captured the required data, it will be available to the DOS until the latch contents are changed. Such changes can be caused when the computer loads new data into the latch or if the latch is cleared by external equipment.

So you can see that in both input and output operations it is necessary for the microprocessor to generate commands to *cause* the operation. The next section considers how this command is generated.

3-2.3   Input–Output Device Selection

The manner by which the computer actually produces the commands for input and output depends upon the particular design of the microprocessor. There are two common methods for accomplishing this: *isolated I/O ports* and *memory mapping*. In either case, however, the required operations are the same. A general diagram of the hardware for input–output device selection is shown in Fig. 3-7. Note that the address bus and the control lines are decoded to provide the required ENABLE or LATCH commands for the I/O device. This decoding consists of a logic combination circuit that interprets the address and control lines from the microprocessor to produce the required I/O device signals.

Isolated I/O Ports.   This method of input–output operation results from specific instructions within the instruction set of the microprocessor. In the case of the 8080, for example, the instructions are denoted by the mnemonics

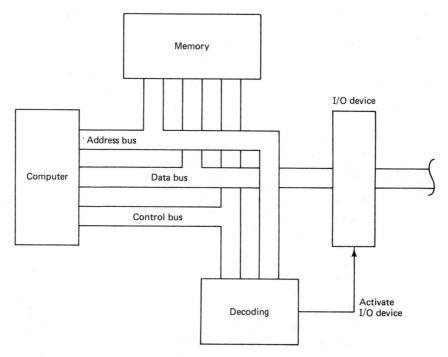

FIG. 3-7 Commands to buffers and latches are obtained by decoding the address bus lines and control bus lines.

> IN $\times\times$ inputs data from port $\times\times$ (in hex)
> OUT $\times\times$ outputs data to port $\times\times$ (in hex)

When these instructions are executed, the data bus is used along with the accumulator for data transfer between the external equipment and the microprocessor.

The port *address*, $\times\times$, is an 8-bit binary number that is loaded into the lower 8 bits of the address bus when the instruction is executed. To derive the command necessary to activate the I/O equipment, the port address is *decoded* to produce the required ENABLE (input) or LATCH (output) signal.

EXAMPLE 3-1 Develop the decoding required to input data from a tristate buffer with an instruction IN 2AH. Assume an 8080 system for which the control bus signal required is the I/OR low. The tristate buffer is enabled by a high.

Solution: As noted, the port address, 2AH, will be copied into the lower byte of the address bus. Also, $\overline{\text{I/OR}}$ is part of the control bus. Decoding will be accomplished by combining the three stated facts to obtain a high enable. The resulting system is shown in Fig. 3-8 as implemented by AND gates and inverters. This solution uses address lines A0 to A7 and the $\overline{\text{I/OR}}$ line.

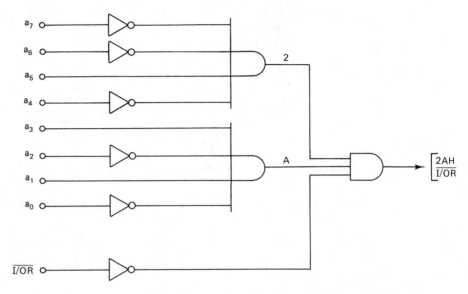

FIG. 3-8   In this example the decoding is a read from port 2AH.

Since 8 bits are used to determine the I/O port address, there are 256 possible ports that can be used, 00H to FFH. It is important to note that, when isolated I/O port techniques are used, all input and output operations occur through the accumulator of the microprocessor.

Memory-Mapped I/O.   Another common type of input–output processing used in microprocessors does not employ any special instructions or port addresses. In these systems the decoder of Fig. 3-7 actually causes the microprocessor to function as though it were reading or writing to memory. Thus the "port" becomes effectively like a memory address. This means that there cannot be any *real* memory using that address. In essence, then, in memory-mapped I/O, a block of memory addresses is set aside to function as input and output channels. When the microprocessor executes an instruction that reads one of these locations, what actually happens is that the input device is activated to place its data on the data bus, which is then read into the microprocessor. As far as microprocessor operation is concerned, a memory location has just been read. The same is true for writing to a memory location for outputting data. All microprocessors can support memory-mapped I/O, including those with input and output port structure. Some microprocessors, such as the 6800, can only support memory-mapped I/O.

EXAMPLE 3-2   Data output is to occur using a 6800 microprocessor. Such output is to occur to any address with 5H as the most significant digit (i.e., any 5×××H address reference, where ××× can be any hex digits). A memory write instruction loads the address bus with the address, takes the control bus VMA line high, and takes the $R/\overline{W}$ line low. Develop the decode circuit to activate a latch needing an active low.

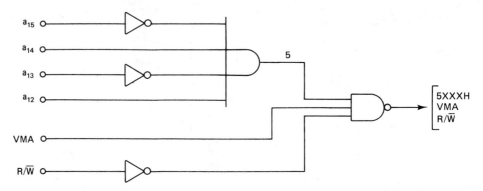

FIG. 3-9   This decoding is for a 6800, memory-mapped selection of address 5XXXH VMA and a write.

Solution: The decoding circuit must provide a low output when the high-order nibble of the 16-bit address bus contains a 5 and VMA is high and R/$\overline{\text{W}}$ is low. The system of Fig. 3-9 will provide this requirement.

Note that *any* instruction in the 6800 set that writes to a memory location 5×××H will cause the latch to capture the data placed on the data bus. An example would be STAA 5000H, which stores accumulator A in memory location 5000H.

One disadvantage of memory-mapped I/O is that it uses up memory addresses that can therefore not be used for actual memory. In the preceding example, all memory locations from 5000H to 5FFFH are now unavailable for real memory. Of course, one could have decoded all 16 address bits and made the address 53A2H or anything else. But then the decoding circuits become very large. One advantage of this type of intput–output is that there are many instructions that can be used to input and output data, and they do not necessarily involve the accumulator.

Universal I/O Ports.   Some integrated circuits have been designed to act as either 8-bit tristate input ports or latched output ports. These devices are designed to interface easily with microprocessor-based computers. Figure 3-10 shows a diagram of one such universal port, the 8212 (Intel Corporation). Note that this device contains eight D-type F/Fs and eight tristate buffers. Device selection can occur with either an active low (DS1) or active high (DS2). The mode (MD) and strobe (STB) lines are used to set up the device for input or output, or the *transparent* mode of operation. Transparent means that any data placed on the input lines also appear on the output lines. An interrupt line is also available with its F/F, which allows using the interrupt feature of the microprocessor to initiate an input cycle. This port will be used in numerous applications in this text.

EXAMPLE 3-3   Show how two 8212s can be used to input and output data to an 8080-based system using port address ×7H, where × means "don't care."

Solution: This is a matter of decoding the lower 4 address bits to a 7 and using this with $\overline{\text{I/OR}}$ and $\overline{\text{I/OW}}$ for the input enable and output latch. For the input mode, we take MD low,

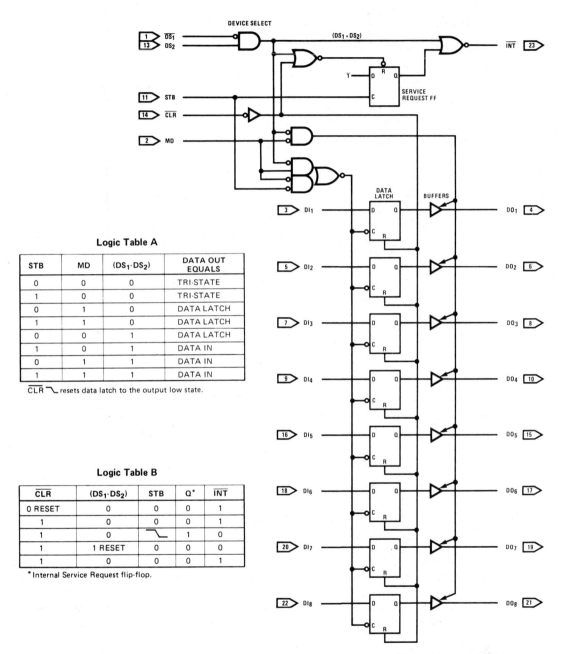

Logic Table A

STB	MD	$(DS_1 \cdot DS_2)$	DATA OUT EQUALS
0	0	0	TRI-STATE
1	0	0	TRI-STATE
0	1	0	DATA LATCH
1	1	0	DATA LATCH
0	0	1	DATA LATCH
1	0	1	DATA IN
0	1	1	DATA IN
1	1	1	DATA IN

$\overline{CLR}$ ⌐ resets data latch to the output low state.

Logic Table B

$\overline{CLR}$	$(DS_1 \cdot DS_2)$	STB	Q*	$\overline{INT}$
0 RESET	0	0	0	1
1	0	0	0	1
1	0	⌐	1	0
1	1 RESET	0	0	0
1	0	0	0	1

* Internal Service Request flip-flop.

FIG. 3-10 The 8212 is an example of a universal I/O port with both tristate buffers and latches. (Courtesy of INTEL Corporation)

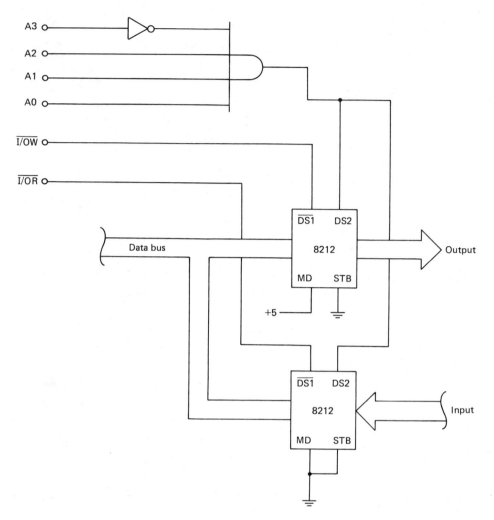

FIG. 3-11 The solution of Ex. 3-3.

tie DS2 to decoded 7, and $\overline{DS1}$ to $\overline{I/OR}$. This turns the buffers on when IN 07H is executed so that the data are loaded onto the data bus. External equipment signals latch data into the F/Fs using STB. For output, DS2 is connected to decoded 7 again, but I/OW is connected to DS1. If MD is tied high, the OUT 07H instruction will capture data from the data bus. MD high will leave the buffers on, making the latch outputs available at the device outputs. The diagram of this system is shown in Fig. 3-11.

3-2.4 Timing

The problem of timing has to do with the fact that the data that the computer will input or output will typically have a window of less than 1 μs in which to be processed. Thus, if a signal is to be input to a computer, it must be presented to the data

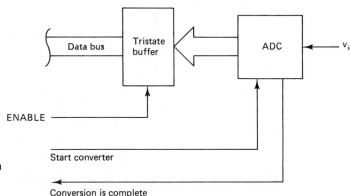

FIG. 3-12 A two-way communication is usually required to acquire analog data.

bus during a particular instant of time, which may very well be only 500 to 1000 nanoseconds (ns). In a similar way, output has a rigid timing constraint. If a digital signal is to be output, it will be placed upon the data bus by the microprocessor for a time of about 1 μs, and it must be captured during that period. These types of problems are solved by a two-step process.

1. As shown previously, we let the microprocessor issue the commands about when to ENABLE a tristate for input or when to LATCH data from the data bus. Thus the computer itself selects the particular instant when the data are to be input or output. For output this is enough, since the latch will hold the data until the DOS can read and convert them to an analog form. For input, however, there is still a problem, because the computer will not know exactly when the data are ready to be input.
2. For input the computer issues the commands that will start the data-collection process and then is programmed to wait until the data are ready before attempting a read. Thus, as shown in Fig. 3-12, there is a *two-way* communication process occurring between the DAS and the computer. The computer issues a command saying "get me some data" and then waits until the DAS loads the data into the tristate and informs it that the data are ready before performing an input.

3-3 OUTPUT OPERATIONS

As a first step toward understanding the process by which the computer inputs and outputs data for control, let us consider the output function. In the previous section the necessary latches and controls were presented by which the microprocessor can output a digital word to a latch. The latch captures the data as they are placed on the data bus. Now we have a binary signal on the output lines of the latch. The next question is what is done with this signal in terms of output to the real world. In this section the various techniques of using the output digital data are considered.

3-3.1 Digital Control Outputs

In some cases the digital signal appearing on the output of the latch is sufficient in itself for the control function. This is particularly true when on–off types of control functions are involved. In these cases, no digital-to-analog conversion is required. The output from the data latch can be used directly to drive compatible solid-state or electromagnetic relays. In other cases it may be necessary to use the latch output to drive a transistor or buffer amplifier in order to boost the available power for some later stage.

In Ch. 5, specific examples of control operations using the direct digital outputs will be considered. Insofar as the output operation itself is concerned, the description given previously of loading the latch from the data bus is sufficient.

3-3.2 Digital-to-Analog Conversion

The more interesting problem in the use of computers for control is when the output is required to be an analog signal. In this case it is necessary to perform a conversion of the digital signal on the output of the latch to a proportional analog signal. In this section the most common technique for performing this conversion will be considered.

Principles.   The basic principle of digital-to-analog conversion (DAC) is that the digital data word is considered to define *percentage* or *fraction* of some *reference* signal. The fractional amount is determined from the original input signal by the DAC. The actual output signal may be a current or voltage, but it is usually a voltage. In Fig. 3-13, the operation of the DAC is shown symbolically as producing an output voltage from the reference input based upon the value of the digital input. In equation form this would be written

$$V_{\text{out}} = \alpha V_{\text{ref}}$$

where V_{out} = DAC output voltage
  V_{ref} = DAC reference voltage
  α = a fraction (<1) determined by the digital input signal.
The relationship between the fraction α and the digital signal is defined by considering the binary number of the digital data to be a *fractional* number. Thus, if an 8-bit digital output from the computer is 10110101_2, this is considered to be 0.10110101_2,

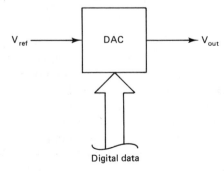

$V_{\text{ref}} \longrightarrow$ | DAC | $\longrightarrow V_{\text{out}}$

Digital data

FIG. 3-13 The digital-to-analog converter (DAC) produces an output voltage that is some fraction of a reference voltage.

with the decimal point to the left of the most significant bit (MSB). In this case, α is defined by

$$\alpha = b_1 2^{-1} + b_2 2^{-2} + b_3 2^{-3} + \cdots + b_n 2^{-n} \qquad (3\text{-}2)$$

where $b_1 b_2 \cdots b_n$ = the binary number with b_1 the MSB. Of course, Eq. (3-2) can be generalized to any number of bits in the data bus of the computer. Basically, the DAC simply calculates the value of α using Eq. (3-2) and multiplies this times a reference voltage. This then forms the output voltage.

Output Step Size.   If the input digital data are composed of 8 bits, you know there are 256 possible states or values of this number, from 00H to FFH. Thus there will be 256 steps in the output voltage as determined by Eqs. (3-1) and (3-2). The *size* of each step is simply the reference divided into 256 values. This is also called the *resolution* of the output voltage:

$$\Delta V_{\text{out}} = \frac{V_{\text{ref}}}{256} \qquad (3\text{-}3)$$

For the general case of a digital signal of n bits, the resolution equation can be generalized to

$$\Delta V_{\text{out}} = V_{\text{ref}} 2^{-n} \qquad (3\text{-}4)$$

where ΔV_{out} = step size of output voltage. The step size is very important because it indicates the *fineness* by which the output voltage can be varied. If very delicate and smooth control is desired, the step size must be very small.

EXAMPLE 3-4   Compare the step size of converters with a 10-V reference and 4, 8, and 16 bits.

Solution: Using Eq. (3-4), the step sizes are found as

$$\begin{aligned}
\text{4-bit:} \quad & \Delta V_{\text{out}} = (10)(2^{-4}) = 0.625 \text{ V/step} \\
\text{8-bit:} \quad & \Delta V_{\text{out}} = (10)(2^{-8}) = 0.039 \text{ V/step} \\
\text{16-bit:} \quad & \Delta V_{\text{out}} = (10)(2^{-16}) = 0.00015 \text{ V/step}
\end{aligned}$$

Maximum Output.   Another important point to remember regarding the use of DACs is that the maximum output voltage is *not* equal to the reference. The reason for this is that α will always be less than 1, even with the maximum digital input of all 1's.

EXAMPLE 3-5   Find the maximum output voltage of DACs with 4, 8, and 12 bits and with 5-V references.

Solution: The maximum output voltage occurs when all input bits are 1. Thus Eq. (3-2) can be used to find the output voltages:

$$\begin{aligned}
\text{4-bit:} \quad V_{\text{max}} &= 5(\tfrac{1}{2} + \tfrac{1}{4} + \tfrac{1}{8} + \tfrac{1}{16}) \\
&= 4.6875 \text{ V} \\[6pt]
\text{8-bit:} \quad V_{\text{max}} &= 5(\tfrac{1}{2} + \tfrac{1}{4} + \tfrac{1}{8} + \tfrac{1}{16} + \tfrac{1}{32} + \tfrac{1}{64} + \tfrac{1}{128} + \tfrac{1}{256}) \\
&= 4.9805 \text{ V}
\end{aligned}$$

16-bit: $V_{max} = 5(\frac{1}{2} + \frac{1}{4} + \frac{1}{8} + \frac{1}{16} + \frac{1}{32} + \frac{1}{64} + \frac{1}{128} + \frac{1}{256} + \frac{1}{512} + \frac{1}{1024} + \frac{1}{2048} + \frac{1}{4096})$

$$= 4.9988 \text{ V}$$

In those cases when a *particular* maximum value of output is desired, the reference is adjusted to give the required value of output when all bits are set.

EXAMPLE 3-6   Find the reference required so that the maximum output of a 6-bit DAC is 12 V.

Solution: This can be done by using Eq. (3-2) to solve for the reference:

$$12 = V_{ref}(\frac{1}{2} + \frac{1}{4} + \frac{1}{8} + \frac{1}{16} + \frac{1}{32} + \frac{1}{64})$$

$$= 0.984375 \ V_{ref}$$

Solving for the reference voltage gives

$$V_{ref} = 12.1905 \text{ V}$$

Input–Output Relations.   It is quite easy to calculate the analog output from Eq. (3-2) when the digital input is known. The reverse problem, of finding the digital input that produces a specific output, is somewhat more complicated. Part of the problem is that, since the output jumps in increments of the step size, it is only possible to find the digital input that gives an output closest to that desired. This is done by finding the fraction α and then converting this to the closest binary number with the specified number of bits. One method of finding the binary number is by successive multiplication by 2.

Decimal to Binary Fraction Conversion.   From Eqs. (3-1) and (3-2), you can see that the fraction is given by

$$\alpha = b_1 2^{-1} + b_2 2^{-2} + b_3 2^{-3} + \cdots + b_n 2^{-n}$$

Now suppose this expression is multiplied by 2:

$$2\alpha = b_1 + b_2 2^{-1} + b_3 2^{-2} + \cdots + b_n 2^{n-1}$$

The first term on the right will be a 1 if b_1 is a 1 and a 0 if b_1 is a 0. The rest of the expression is a fraction (i.e., less than 1). This means that 2α will be less than 1 if b_1 is zero and greater than 1 if b_1 is 1. So we have determined the value of b_1. Now, by multiplying the remaining fractional term by 2, we determine b_2. The fraction left over from that operation is multiplied by 2 to determine b_3, and so on, until all n bits have been determined. Example 3-7 illustrates this process.

EXAMPLE 3-7   An 8-bit DAC has an 8-V reference. Determine the analog output voltage for inputs of 0EH and A3H. Find the digital input that would give an output closest to 6.35 V.

Solution: The analog output voltages can be found from Eq. (3-2). For the first case, 0EH $= 00001110_2$, so the output voltage is:

For 0EH: $V_{out} = 8(\frac{1}{32} + \frac{1}{64} + \frac{1}{128}) = 0.4375 \text{ V}$

In the second number, A3H $= 10100011_2$, so the output voltage is given by:

For A3H: $V_{out} = 8(\frac{1}{2} + \frac{1}{8} + \frac{1}{128} + \frac{1}{256}) = 5.09375$ V

To determine the digital input giving the closest value to 6.35 V out, we first find α:

$$\alpha = \frac{V_{out}}{V_{ref}} = \frac{6.35}{8} = 0.79375$$

Now successive multiplication by 2 is started:

$$2(0.79375) = 1.5875 > 1 \quad \text{therefore } b_1 = 1$$
$$2(0.5875) = 1.175 > 1 \quad \text{therefore } b_2 = 1$$
$$2(0.175) = 0.35 < 1 \quad \text{therefore } b_3 = 0$$
$$2(0.35) = 0.7 < 1 \quad \text{therefore } b_4 = 0$$
$$2(0.7) = 1.4 > 1 \quad \text{therefore } b_5 = 1$$
$$2(0.4) = 0.8 < 1 \quad \text{therefore } b_6 = 0$$
$$2(0.8) = 1.6 > 1 \quad \text{therefore } b_7 = 1$$
$$2(0.6) = 1.2 > 1 \quad \text{therefore } b_8 = 1$$

Notice that the process did not come out exactly, since after 8 bits there is still a remainder of 0.2. The input signal predicted is 11001011_2 or CBH. From Eq. (3-2) you can see that the output voltage actually produced by this is

CBH: $V_{out} = 8(\frac{1}{2} + \frac{1}{4} + \frac{1}{32} + \frac{1}{128} + \frac{1}{256})$

$$= 6.34375 \text{ V}$$

This is a difference of -0.00625. The most the difference could ever be is one step size or, in this case, $\frac{8}{256} = 0.03125$ V.

The difference in the actual output versus the desired output in this example is not an "error" in the true sense of the word, which might be corrected by building a better DAC. It is a result of the discrete possible output values of the DAC based upon the number of bits. The only possible outputs that bracket the desired value of 6.35 V are 6.34375 for CBH and 6.375 produced by CCH (one LSB higher). To improve on this would require using a DAC with more bits.

Bipolar Operation.   Often DACs can be configured to interpret the incoming digital data in such a way that a bipolar output is produced. For example, the output may swing between -5 and $+5$ V instead of 0 to 10 V. The specifications of the DAC will explain the relationship between the digital signal and the resulting output voltage magnitude and polarity. One of the most common relationships is called *offset binary* or *modified 2's complement*. In this mode, if a negative voltage is desired, the 2's complement of a binary number is taken, and then the MSB is complemented. The equation for the output voltage is given by

$$V_{out} = \alpha V_{ref} - \frac{V_{ref}}{2}$$

or

$$V_{out} = V_{ref}(b_1 2^{-1} + b_2 2^{-2} + \cdots + b_n 2^{-n}) - \frac{V_{ref}}{2} \qquad (3-5)$$

To see how this equation works, let's consider an 8-bit converter. You can see that, if the binary input is 10000000_2 or 80H, the output will be

$$V_{\text{out}} = V_{\text{ref}}(\tfrac{1}{2}) - \frac{V_{\text{ref}}}{2} = 0 \text{ V}$$

Now, a binary 1 would be 00000001_2 or 01H, but in modified 2's complement operations we must complement the MSB so that the required input is 10000001_2 or 81H. According to Eq. (3-5), this will give an output of

$$V_{\text{out}} = V_{\text{ref}}(\tfrac{1}{2} + \tfrac{1}{256}) - V_{\text{ref}} = \frac{+ V_{\text{ref}}}{256}$$

but this is just the minimum step voltage, as would be expected from a single bit. Now suppose the input is to be a binary -1, -00000001_2 or -01H. In 2's complement this would be 11111111_2 or FFH. But since the DAC used modified 2's complement, the MSB must be complemented, giving 01111111_2 or 7FH. Let's use this in Eq. (3-5):

$$V_{\text{out}} = V_{\text{ref}}(\tfrac{1}{4} + \tfrac{1}{8} + \tfrac{1}{16} + \tfrac{1}{32} + \tfrac{1}{64} + \tfrac{1}{128} + \tfrac{1}{256}) - \frac{V_{\text{ref}}}{2}$$

$$= \frac{- V_{\text{ref}}}{256}$$

So you can see that a -1 does indeed give a negative output voltage equal to one step

TABLE 3-1

Digital Input	Analog Output		
11111111	$\dfrac{+ V_{\text{ref}}}{2}$		
11111110	$\dfrac{+ V_{\text{ref}}}{2} - \dfrac{V_{\text{ref}}}{256}$		
11111101	$\dfrac{+ V_{\text{ref}}}{2} - \dfrac{2 V_{\text{ref}}}{256}$		
.	.		
.	.		
.	.		
10000001	$\dfrac{+ V_{\text{ref}}}{2} - \dfrac{127 V_{\text{ref}}}{256}$	$= \dfrac{V_{\text{ref}}}{256}$	
10000000	$\dfrac{+ V_{\text{ref}}}{2} - \dfrac{128 V_{\text{ref}}}{256}$	$= 0$	
01111111	$\dfrac{+ V_{\text{ref}}}{2} - \dfrac{129 V_{\text{ref}}}{256}$	$= \dfrac{- V_{\text{ref}}}{256}$	
.	.		
.	.		
.	.		
00000010	$\dfrac{+ V_{\text{ref}}}{2} - \dfrac{254 V_{\text{ref}}}{256}$		
00000001	$\dfrac{+ V_{\text{ref}}}{2} - \dfrac{255 V_{\text{ref}}}{256}$		
00000000	$\dfrac{+ V_{\text{ref}}}{2} - \dfrac{256 V_{\text{ref}}}{256}$	$= \dfrac{- V_{\text{ref}}}{2}$	

size. Table 3-1 summarizes the relationship between the modified 2's complement digital input and the output voltage for 8 bits.

EXAMPLE 3-8   Given an 8-bit DAC operating in the bipolar mode with a 10-V reference, find the output voltage for digital inputs of A6H and 5DH. What digital input would be required for output voltages of $+4.5$ and -3.7 V.

Solution: As with the unipolar operation, the first problem, finding the output for a given digital input, is simple, in this case using Eq. (3-5). First let's take the case of A6H = 10100110_2. You can see that this will give a positive voltage since the MSB is set. The value is found from Eq. (3-5):

$$\text{A6H:} \quad V_{\text{out}} = 10(\tfrac{1}{2} + \tfrac{1}{8} + \tfrac{1}{64} + \tfrac{1}{128}) - \tfrac{10}{2}$$

$$= 1.484375 \text{ V} \quad \text{(exact)}$$

In a similar way, 5DH = 01011101_2 will give a negative value since the MSB is a 0. From Eq. (3-5) we write

$$\text{5DH:} \quad V_{\text{out}} = 10(\tfrac{1}{4} + \tfrac{1}{16} + \tfrac{1}{32} + \tfrac{1}{64} + \tfrac{1}{256}) - \tfrac{10}{2}$$

$$= 1.3671875 \text{ V} \quad \text{(exact)}$$

Now, to find the input to produce a specific output, one can simply find α as before and perform successive multiplication. For the first case,

$$\alpha = \frac{V_{\text{out}} + (V_{\text{ref}}/2)}{V_{\text{ref}}}$$

$$= \frac{4.5 + 5}{10} = \frac{9.5}{2} = 0.95$$

Performing the successive multiplication by 2 gives the result of 11110011_2 = F3H. Note that the MSB is a 1 as required. For the other case we get

$$\alpha = \frac{-3.7 + 5}{10} = \frac{1.3}{10} = 0.13$$

Performing the successive multiplication by 2 gives the result as 00100001_2 = 21H. Here the LSB is a zero as specified for a negative output voltage. The actual output voltages can be found from Eq. (3-5) to be

$$\text{F3H:} \quad V_{\text{out}} = 10(\tfrac{1}{2} + \tfrac{1}{4} + \tfrac{1}{8} + \tfrac{1}{16} + \tfrac{1}{128} + \tfrac{1}{256}) - \tfrac{10}{2}$$

$$= 4.492 \text{ V}$$

$$\text{21H:} \quad V_{\text{out}} = 10(\tfrac{1}{8} + \tfrac{1}{256}) - \tfrac{10}{2} = -3.711 \text{ V}$$

Microprocessor-Compatible DACs.   In general, a DAC will output the analog voltage of whatever digital signal is placed on its input lines. As seen in the previous section, a latch is used to capture the digital word from the data bus of the computer, and this value is held until changed by appropriate commands from the computer. Therefore, the DAC output will be held at whatever voltage corresponds to this latched digital word.

Because of the extensive use of microprocessors, a number of DACs are available that have built-in latches. These units are designed to be compatible with microprocessors and can often be connected directly to the data bus and control bus lines.

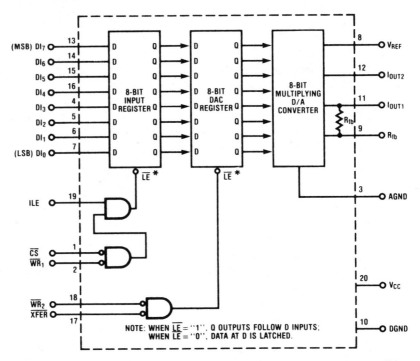

FIG. 3-14 The DAC0830 is an example of a DAC designed to be compatible with microprocessors. (Courtesy of National Semiconductor Corporation)

Figure 3-14 shows a diagram of a typical microprocessor-compatible DAC called the DAC0830 (National Semiconductor). A decoder generates the chip-select signal ($\overline{CS}$) as a port address or memory address (if memory mapped) by use of the combination logic on address lines and control lines. The other inputs are used to capture data and transfer data. This particular device actually outputs a current instead of a voltage directly. An op amp is used to convert the current to a voltage. This unit, as with most types, can be connected in such a way as to give either a unipolar or bipolar output.

3-4 INPUT HARDWARE

In this section the hardware used to input control system variable data into the computer will be studied. In some cases, data may be in digital form already, and therefore input directly, while in other cases the data will be analog and must be converted into a digital form before input can occur.

3-4.1 Digital Data Input

Some types of control equipment produce digital information directly in response to variation of a process variable. In such cases the input process is entirely digital. The procedure used to input these data depends on many factors, such as the number of bits, serial or parallel format, and timing of the data. For the purposes of this text, only the general process of such data input will be considered, since such subjects are more properly treated in specialized texts on digital communication.

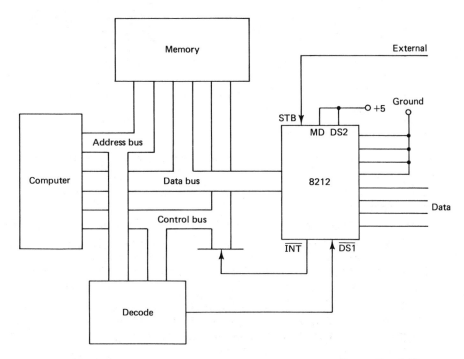

FIG. 3-15 Digital data can be input through a tristate buffer and latch like the 8212.

Parallel Data. In many cases the digital data to be input will already be in parallel form. Then it will merely be necessary to load these data into a latch and allow the computer to read the data in on the data bus by enabling a tristate buffer under program control. Generally, the external equipment will load the data into a latch and notify the computer that data are available. This process is important since the same procedure will be followed when parallel digital data resulting from analog-to-digital conversion are input to the computer. The hardware required to implement parallel input is simplified by the use of integrated latch–tristate buffer circuits. One such device was presented in Fig. 3-10. This device consists of eight individual F/F cells, which can be loaded to hold data, and the tristate buffers required to interface data to a bus.

In Fig. 3-15 it has been assumed that the external equipment provides a signal to the buffer–latch to capture and hold the data, while at the same time setting the internal F/F, which will be input to the computer by an interrupt to show that data are ready to be input. When the input is required, the computer will provide the proper address and control line information for the decoder. The decoder will output a signal to the buffer–latch to enable the tristate buffers and place the data on the data bus.

In the example shown in Fig. 3-15, only 4 bits of actual digital data are to be input. The rest of the bits of the data word are simply tied low (in this case) or high.

Serial Data. In some cases, such as communication of digital data over long distances, a parallel presentation of the data is inconvenient or even impossible. Under these circumstances the data may be propagated to the computer in a serial for-

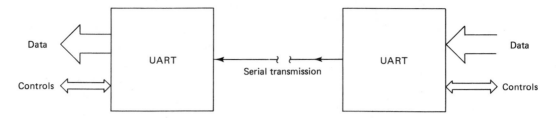

FIG. 3-16   A UART is used to transmit digital data serially.

mat. In most cases these data must be converted back to a parallel format for input to the computer on the data bus. A specialized circuit module called a *universal asynchronous receiver–transmitter* (UART) is often used for this purpose. In this case the digital data are converted to a serial bit stream at the measurement site by a UART and propagated, on a single wire, to the computer. At the computer site another UART is used to convert the serial bit stream back to individual parallel bits. These are then input to the computer, either directly or through a buffer–latch as described in the previous section. Figure 3-16 shows a block diagram of how such a measurement process may be visualized. Of course, there must be communication with the computer by the UART to indicate that data have been received.

3-4.2   Two-Level Analog Data

There are many instances in the process and control fields when data regarding a variable can be represented by two-level information. Common examples of ON/OFF control systems are those used for home and auto air-conditioning temperature control. There are a host of other examples from business, industry, and the consumer world. For these types of control systems, a transducer may convert the controlled variable into an analog electrical signal, but all that is needed for control is the relation between the variable value and some limit. That is, is the value greater or lesser than the limit? Thus the information is binary in nature and a natural for the computer. A special integrated circuit is used to convert such analog comparison into the proper one-digit digital signal.

Comparator.   The comparator, with the symbol shown in Fig. 3-17, compares two analog voltages. The output of the comparator, b, will be a digital *one* if V_1 exceeds V_2 and a digital *zero* if not. This can be represented as

$$b = \begin{cases} 1, & V_1 > V_2 \\ 0, & V_1 < V_2 \end{cases} \qquad (3\text{-}6)$$

The comparator is also used to provide alarm information to a computer, using the interrupt lines, when a critical process variable exceeds a limit.

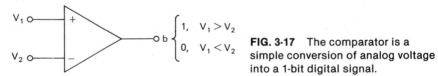

FIG. 3-17   The comparator is a simple conversion of analog voltage into a 1-bit digital signal.

EXAMPLE 3-9   A process has three critical variables, pressure, level, and temperature. These are not under control but must be monitored to be under specific alarm levels. Temperature is available at 10 mV/°C, pressure at 50 mV/psi, and level at −1.5 V/ft. The alarm levels are 100°C, 30 psi, and 3 ft, respectively. Devise a system to input this information to an 8080-based computer using an 8212 tristate buffer where the data are input on port 07H. Level voltage is 9 V at zero ft.

Solution: It is clear that each alarm level can be converted to an equivalent voltage, and this can be used with a comparator to provide a digital high when an alarm condition occurs. A decoder must be devised to enable the tristate when an input to port 07 occurs. For the 8080, this must be accompanied by the I/OR low. The alarm voltages can be provided by simple voltage dividers. The values are given by:

$$\text{Temperature:} \quad (10 \text{ mV/°C})(100°\text{C}) = 1 \text{ V}$$
$$\text{Pressure:} \quad (50 \text{ mV/psi})(30 \text{ psi}) = 1.5 \text{ V}$$
$$\text{Level:} \quad (-1.5 \text{ V/ft})(3 \text{ ft}) + 9 = 4.5 \text{ V}$$

Level voltage has negative slope so it will be necessary to reverse the connections to the comparator that evaluates this comparison. Figure 3-18 shows the resulting system.

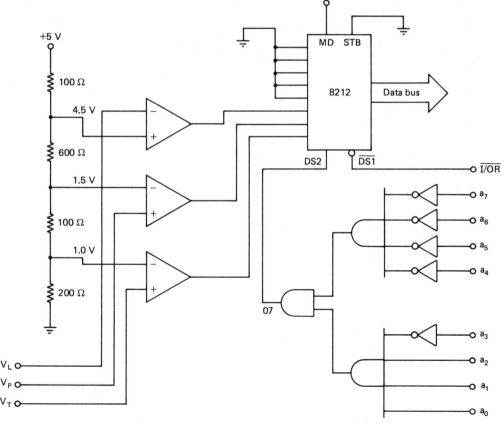

FIG. 3-18   This circuit is one solution to Ex. 3-9.

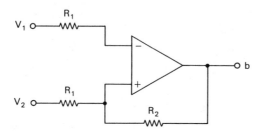

FIG. 3-19 A hysteresis comparator can be constructed by adding three resistors.

Note that voltage dividers have been used to develop the required alarm-level voltages.

Hysteresis Comparator. One problem with the use of comparators for alarm-level detection is the effect of noise on the analog voltage lines input to the device. If noise is present on the signal, the comparator can be set, reset, set, and so on, when the signal plus noise level is close to the alarm level. Many techniques are used to combat this "jitter" of the comparator output. One method is to use the first setting of the comparator to set a F/F. The F/F will then ignore subsequent transitions of the comparator output until reset by external circuitry. Another method is the use of filters to cut down on noise on the signal lines. A very common technique, however, is to use a system that inserts an *offset* or *hysteresis* between the voltage level that will cause the comparator output to go high and that which will cause the output to return low.

A typical circuit for this is shown in Fig. 3-19. Note that the polarity of input signals has been reversed from Fig. 3-17. The system works by feeding back some of the output level (typically TTL $+5$ V) to the positive comparator input. The response of this comparator for variations of voltages V_1 and V_2 is shown in Fig. 3-20. In this figure, V_1 is assumed to be the varying signal and V_2 the alarm-level setting. Note that if $V_1 << V_2$ the comparator output will be high, and that V_1 must rise to V_2 and beyond by a factor of $(R_1/R_2)V_0$ before the output changes state.

$$V_1 \geq V_2 + (R_1/R_2)V_0$$

Once having changed state, the signal must drop all the way back to V_2 before the output once again goes high.

$$V_1 \geq V_2$$

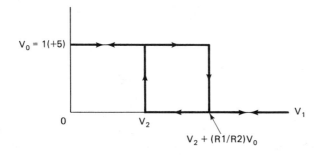

FIG. 3-20 The response of the hysteresis comparator is like two-position control.

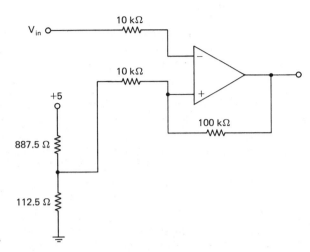

FIG. 3-21   One solution of Ex. 3-10.

This "window" provides the protection that the comparator output will not jitter due to noise, as long as the window is greater than the noise.

EXAMPLE 3-10   Suppose rpm information is available as a voltage scaled at 225 mV/1000 rpm but with 40 mV of noise. If an alarm level is to be 2500 rpm, devise a comparator that will provide 50-mV immunity from this noise. What rpm error does this noise immunity window represent? Assume the comparator output will be at TTL levels.

Solution: To provide the 50-mV noise immunity, the hysteresis comparator will need

$$\frac{R_1}{R_2}(5) = 50 \text{ mV}$$

or

$$R_2 = 100R_1$$

If R_1 is chosen to be 1000 Ω, then $R_2 = 100$ kΩ. The alarm level is (225 mV/1000 rpm)(2500 rpm) = 0.5625 V. The circuit of Fig. 3-21 will then provide the specification of this problem. The rpm error introduced by this window is

$$\text{error} = \frac{50 \text{ mV}}{225 \text{ mV}/1000 \text{ rpm}} = 222.2 \text{ rpm}$$

Of course, if the computer requires a high-going signal for the alarm condition, then the output of a hysteresis comparator will be put through an inverter before being input by the computer.

3-4.3   Analog-to-Digital Conversion

When a computer control system involves continuous variation of an analog variable over a range, the value of this variable must be converted into a proportional digital signal for input to the computer. This is the reverse of the problem of digital-to-analog conversion considered previously. It turns out that there are more difficulties associated with the analog-to-digital conversion, however, which makes their use in control systems a little more complicated.

General Principles.   The basic idea is to consider the analog data to be a "number" and to convert this into the equivalent binary number. The difficulty is at once obvious; the binary number can only have a finite number of bits, such as the common 8-bit microprocessor-based computers, and therefore can only represent a limited range of numbers. In fact, for 8 bits one can only represent 256 counting states (including zero). So you can see immediately that there will be a *loss* in knowledge of the variable value in going from continuous analog information to finite bits of digital information. We must be very careful to account for this new ignorance in subsequent treatments of the data. Anyway, as in the DAC, it turns out to be easiest to treat the analog data as a fraction of some reference. If voltage is taken to be the analog medium, input voltage will be considered some fraction of a reference voltage, V_{ref}. This means that the input voltage will have to be *less* than this reference.

What most ADCs do is to find a fractional number, given by the binary output, that is the closest *smaller* fraction of the analog input voltage. In equation form,

$$V_{in} > \alpha V_{ref} \tag{3-7}$$

where V_{in} = analog input voltage

V_{ref} = analog reference voltage

$$\alpha = b_1 2^{-1} + b_2 2^{-2} + b_3 2^{-3} + \cdots + b_n 2^{-n}. \tag{3-8}$$

Equation (3-8) assumes an n-bit word results from the conversion. The inequality of Eq. (3-7) means that the voltage on the right side of the equation will always be less than the input voltage, but never by more than the step-size voltage represented by one LSB of the digital signal. Thus the uncertainty in this ideal case is never greater than

$$\Delta V = V_{ref} 2^{-n} \tag{3-9}$$

Input–Output Relations.   The actual relationship between the input and output can be deduced by procedures like that used for the DAC. If the digital output is known, and the reference, then limits can be placed upon the possible values of the analog input voltage. The limit is just that represented by the step-size voltage given by Eq. (3-9). When the input analog voltage is known, and the reference, and the binary output is desired, a calculation is performed like that for the DAC. The fractional ratio of input voltage to reference is first calculated. Then this is converted to a binary by the process of successive multiplication by 2, as described earlier.

EXAMPLE 3-11   Given an 8-bit ADC with a 10-V reference, (a) if the output is 5EH, find the range of input voltage. (b) What output will be produced by an input of 7.6 V?

Solution: For (a), Eq. (3-6) can be used to find the fraction represented by the binary number 5EH $= 01011110_2$, as

$$\alpha = \tfrac{1}{4} + \tfrac{1}{16} + \tfrac{1}{32} + \tfrac{1}{64} + \tfrac{1}{128} = 0.3671875 \quad \text{(exact)}$$

When this is multiplied by the reference, we get a voltage of 3.671875 V. This means that the input voltage is between this value and this value plus the step size of $\tfrac{10}{256} = 0.0390625$ V. The input range is 3.671875 to 3.7109375 V. Of course this answer is probably not physical, since most real-world problems cannot deal with this many significant figures.

For (b), let us first find the fraction represented by the specified input voltage, $\alpha = 7.6/10 = 0.76$. Now the process of successive multiplication is used:

$$
\begin{array}{ll}
2(0.76) = 1.52 > 1 & \text{therefore } b_1 = 1 \\
2(0.52) = 1.04 > 1 & \text{therefore } b_2 = 1 \\
2(0.04) = 0.08 < 1 & \text{therefore } b_3 = 0 \\
2(0.08) = 0.16 < 1 & \text{therefore } b_4 = 0 \\
2(0.16) = 0.32 < 1 & \text{therefore } b_5 = 0 \\
2(0.32) = 0.64 < 1 & \text{therefore } b_6 = 0 \\
2(0.64) = 1.28 > 1 & \text{therefore } b_7 = 1 \\
2(0.28) = 0.56 < 1 & \text{therefore } b_8 = 0
\end{array}
$$

So the binary output will be 11000010_2 or C2H. This actually represents a fraction that is less than 0.76 but not by more than the step size of one LSB, $\tfrac{1}{256} = 0.00390625$. In fact, you can show that the fraction represented by C2H is 0.7578125, which is less than the input by 0.0021875. *Note*: Instead of successive multiplication, it is often easier to find the fraction of 256 and to convert this to an integer and then a hex number. Thus $(0.76)(256) = 194.56$, and the integer part, 194, converts to C2H.

In this example the results have been shown to the full significant figures of the problem. In practice, it will be necessary to consider the numbers in light of the least significant figures of variables used in the problem. For example, if the reference voltage is known to three significant figures, the fractions used to deduce the outputs cannot be specified to any more than three significant figures.

Conversion Time.   One of the most important characteristics of ADCs is that a finite amount of time is required for the device to produce a digital output from the input analog voltage. The length of time required for the ADC to calculate the binary output of an analog input varies over a large range, depending upon the type of conversion process employed. One of the most common processes is called the *successive approximation* ADC. This device will typically convert 8 bits in 30 to 50 μs. Another type, commonly used for digital voltmeters, is called the *dual-slope* ADC and may take up to 1000 μs for a conversion. The *flash* converters are among the fastest, since an 8-bit conversion may be completed in only a few nanoseconds, but this ADC suffers from other disadvantages that limit its usefulness.

The finite conversion time of ADCs has several important consequences when the ADC is used in data-acquisition systems. The following paragraphs describe factors in the application of ADCs that result from the finite conversion time.

1. *Start convert command.* Since the ADC takes a finite length of time to determine the binary output of an analog input, the binary output does not represent the input at every instant of time. In fact, most ADCs do not even calculate the binary output until receiving a command, in the form of a digital signal input, to start the conversion process. Thus the computer or external equipment must generate a command to the ADC to start the conversion process when the computer needs to input the data. This is often called the START CONVERT (SC) command.

2. *Conversion complete signal.* The length of time required to perform a conversion is not constant, even for a given ADC. The time is dependent on the frequency of an internal ADC clock. For this reason the ADC generates a digital output signal that notifies the computer or other external equipment when the conversion process is complete. This is a signal that the computer can input the binary output of the ADC. This is often called the END OF CONVERT (EOC) or CONVERSION COMPLETE (CC) signal.

3. *Analog voltage.* Since a finite length of time is required for the ADC to compute the binary output, it stands to reason that the input voltage must remain *constant* during this interval. The ADC refers to the value of the input voltage during the conversion process. Therefore, if this voltage were changing, the conversion process would become confused and the output would be in error. Thus either the change in input voltage must be very slow compared to the conversion time or a system must be used to "hold" the voltage value at the moment a conversion is started by a *convert start* signal.

The most important consequence of the conversion time is its impact on the process of analog data input to a computer. In general, a four-step sequence must occur:

1. The computer issues a command to the ADC to start conversion (SC).
2. The computer goes into a wait mode while the conversion process is taking place. (Or the interrupt feature may be used, as will be discussed in Ch. 4.)
3. The ADC sends a conversion complete (CC) signal to the computer when the binary output has been determined and placed on the ADC binary output lines.
4. The computer reads the ADC binary output into the data bus.

Bipolar Input.   As in the case of the DAC, it is possible for the ADC to be configured to convert bipolar input signals into a binary output. It is most important in this case to study the specifications of the ADC to determine the way in which the positive and negative voltages will be represented in binary. The most common representation is modified 2's complement or offset binary, as discussed in the section on DACs. As noted, this system has the zero represented by a binary MSB of one and the rest zero, as 10000000_2 for 8 bits. For computers using 2's complement representation of signed numbers, the MSB would have to be complemented as soon as the input had been made. The equation relating input voltage and binary output is simply shifted by one-half the reference:

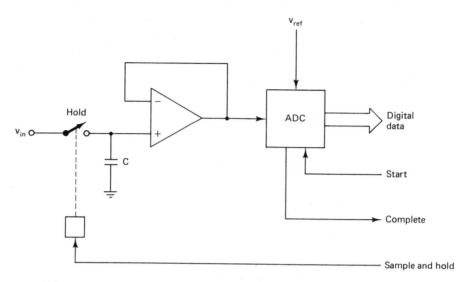

FIG. 3-22   Often a data input system will have a sample and hold as well as analog-to-digital converter (ADC). Note the convert start signal and conversion complete signal.

$$V_{in} > \alpha V_{ref} - \frac{V_{ref}}{2} \tag{3-18}$$

Sample and Hold.   In those cases when the input voltage changes at a rate *not* slow compared to the conversion time, it will be necessary to capture and "hold" an input value at the moment a sample of analog voltage is to be converted. This is accomplished by a *sample-and-hold* circuit constructed using op amps. The basic principle of such a circuit is shown in Fig. 3-22. The switch is a solid-state device, usually an FET, which is turned on by a digital input signal. In the on state the circuit is in the *sample* mode, and the changing input voltage will appear across the capacitor, C. The voltage-follower op amp is selected to have very high input impedance. When the digital input signal opens the switch, the circuit enters the *hold* mode. Whatever voltage was on the capacitor at the instant the switch was opened will now remain, regardless of subsequent changes of input voltage. The capacitor voltage will not change, even when "measured" by the ADC, since the high input impedance of the voltage follower prevents discharge of the stored voltage. Figure 3-23 illustrates the time sequence of successive sampling and holding of a changing analog voltage. Note that the actual binary signal input by the computer will be samples of the analog voltage at intervals determined by the time from one hold to the next hold. The fact that the computer has only periodic samples of process variables will be found to have important consequences on control.

The ability of the capacitor voltage to track fast changes in the input voltage in the sample mode is determined by the source resistance, R_s, of the circuit providing V_{in} to the sample-and-hold circuit. The time constant $R_s C$ must be as small as possi-

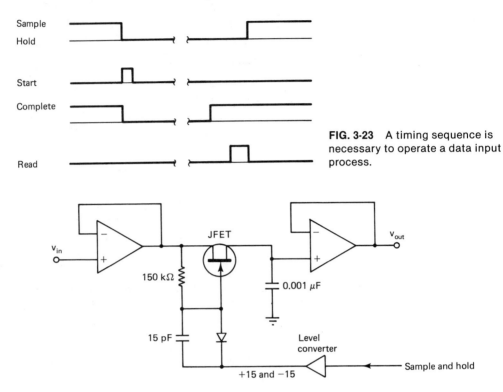

FIG. 3-23 A timing sequence is necessary to operate a data input process.

FIG. 3-24 An actual sample-and-hold circuit usually uses a JFET transistor because of its very high OFF resistance. It must be driven by high voltage, such as 15 V.

ble. This is often assured by using a voltage follower on the input before the switch. The low output resistance of the follower and low "on" resistance of the switch provide for fast tracking of input voltage changes. A typical sample-and-hold circuit is shown in Fig. 3-24.

Use of the sample-and-hold circuit introduces the need for another command in the data-acquisition process. Now the computer must issue a hold command in addition to the START CONVERT command.

Input-Level Adjustment.   The voltage generated by measurement of some process variable has a level and range dependent on the transducer and signal conditioning of the measurement process. The ADC will perform conversion on the basis of a voltage varying between 0 and V_{ref} (for unipolar operation). To obtain compatibility between the measurement and ADC, it is often necessary to use amplifiers, attenuators, and voltage bias circuits between the measurement system and the ADC.

These circuits typically use standard op-amp approaches. It is very important to maintain *traceability* throughout such conditioning between the signal levels and ranges and the process variable.

EXAMPLE 3-12   Temperature is measured with a transfer function of 0.15 V/°C. An 8-bit ADC with a 5-V reference will be used to convert temperature from 20° to 100°C to 00H to FFH. Input will be to port EH of an 8080. START CONVERT will be issued by simply writing to port E4, and CONVERSION COMPLETE will be examined as data bit 6 input from port E4. A high indicates the conversion is complete. Construct the interface circuit and specify the degrees of temperature per LSB.

Solution: A problem like this is best solved by drawing a block diagram of all the essential features of the system. This has been done in Fig. 3-25 by including the following requirements:

1. A measurement block inputting temperature and outputting voltage at 0.15V/°C. Therefore, the limit voltages are

$$20°C: \quad (0.15 \text{ V/°C})(20°C) \quad = 3.0 \text{ V}$$
$$100°C: \quad (0.15 \text{ V/°C})(100°C) = 15.0 \text{ V}$$

2. A signal conditioning block that must convert the 3- to 15-V signal to 0 to 5 V for the ADC. This can be done by subtracting 3 from the measurement voltage to get 0 V at 20°C. Then the range is 0 to 12 V. Now an attenuation of $\frac{5}{12} = 0.417$ is needed to convert the range to 0 to 5 V.

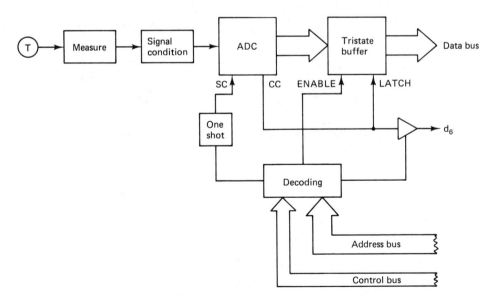

FIG. 3-25   This is the general hardware configuration for Ex. 3-12.

3. The next block is the ADC with the voltage input, 8-bit output to an 8-bit tristate buffer and the data bus, START CONVERT input, and CONVERSION COMPLETE output.

4. There must be a 1-bit tristate buffer to carry the CONVERSION COMPLETE signal to the computer data bus.

5. Then a decoding system is needed to provide the proper signals for port E4H and E5H usage. For the 8080, this means the port address, $\overline{I/OR}$ low for input and $\overline{I/OW}$ low for ouput.

6. A one-shot multivibrator is started by the START CONVERT command. The multivibrator may be necessary because ADC requires a certain pulse length to start conversion.

Now each block is considered in more detail, and the appropriate system is designed. The measurement block and ADC are self-contained. The signal conditioning block can be constructed from op amps. Figure 3-26 shows one circuit that will work. The decoding is accomplished by using combination logic to provide the required buffer enable signals and F/F signals. One method of providing this is shown in Fig. 3-27. The entire DAS is shown in Fig. 3-28. The resolution is simply $(100°C - 20°C)/256 = 0.3125°C$ per LSB.

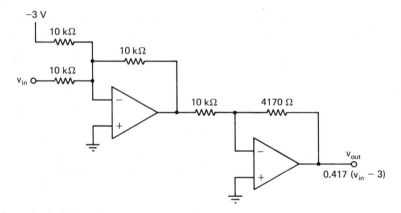

FIG. 3-26   The signal conditioning can be provided by this circuit.

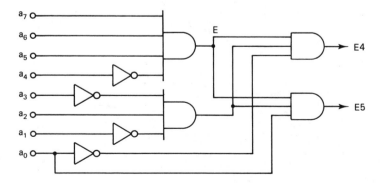

FIG. 3-27   Decoding for Ex. 3-12 can be provided by this circuit.

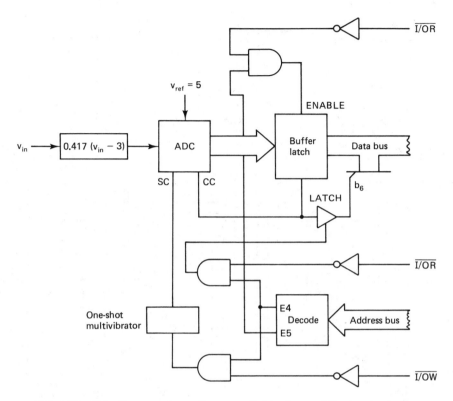

FIG. 3-28 This diagram shows the essential features of the hardware for Ex. 3-12.

Microprocessor-Compatible ADCs.   A number of ADCs have been developed that are specifically compatible with microprocessors. These devices have built-in tristate buffers so that the outputs can be directly connected to the data bus of the computer. In many cases the appropriate control lines necessary to sequence the ADC through a data-conversion process can be connected directly to the unit.

Figure 3-29 shows a block diagram of the functional elements of one such ADC, called the ADC0801 (National Semiconductor) which was designed for compatibility with the 8080, although it can be easily used with other microprocessor types. The functional characteristics of this device will be considered from the digital signal side and then from the analog side.

The $\overline{\text{I/OR}}$ and $\overline{\text{I/OW}}$ lines from the control bus and the computer data bus lines are connected directly to the ADC. The device has a built-in tristate output latch. The $\overline{\text{CS}}$ line is provided by decoding the required port or memory address as desired from the address bus. The converter is started by providing the $\overline{\text{CS}}$ signal and the $\overline{\text{I/OW}}$. When the conversion is completed, the $\overline{\text{INTR}}$ line is taken low. This can be used as an interrupt or be read by the computer to determine that data are ready. The data are loaded on the data bus by providing $\overline{\text{CS}}$ along with $\overline{\text{I/OR}}$ to the unit.

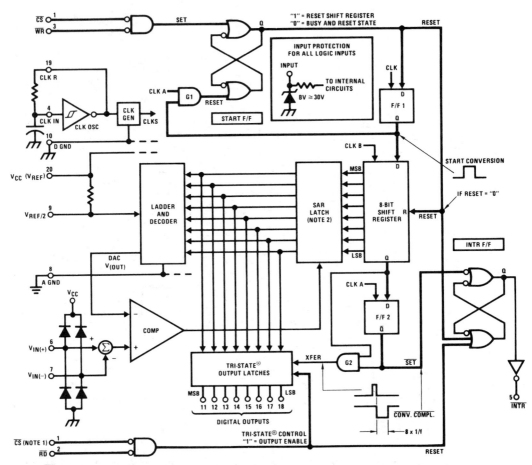

Note 1: $\overline{CS}$ shown twice for clarity.

Note 2: SAR = Successive Approximation Register.

FIG. 3-29 The ADC0801 is an example of a ADC designed to be compatible with microprocessors. (Courtesy of National Semiconductor Corporation)

The analog characteristics of this ADC are interesting in the variety of options available. The unit can be used with a reference of 5 or 2.5 V or an adjusted reference. It is possible to use an input offset directly into the ADC so that conversion is obtained between two limits instead of 0 to the V_{ref}. The actual conversion is made from $V_+ - V_- = 0$ to $V_+ - V_- = V_{ref}$.

3-5   MODULARIZED DATA INPUT AND OUTPUT

A majority of the applications of microprocessor-based computers to control systems involves the input and output of more than one quantity. An application that requires the input and output of many variables could be implemented by using as many

ADCs and DACs as there were inputs and outputs. This would be costly and not very efficient since the unused ADCs and DACs would be idle whenever that particular variable was not being input or output. This problem has been addressed and solved by the development of modularized data-acquisition (input) systems and data-output systems.

Data-Acquisition System (DAS).   A modularized data-acquisition system is designed to be compatible with particular computers or microprocessors and can handle many different analog inputs. The analog inputs are referred to as *channels*. Figure 3-30 shows a block diagram of the essential features of such a system, which is designed to handle 16 single-ended analog channels or 8 differential input channels

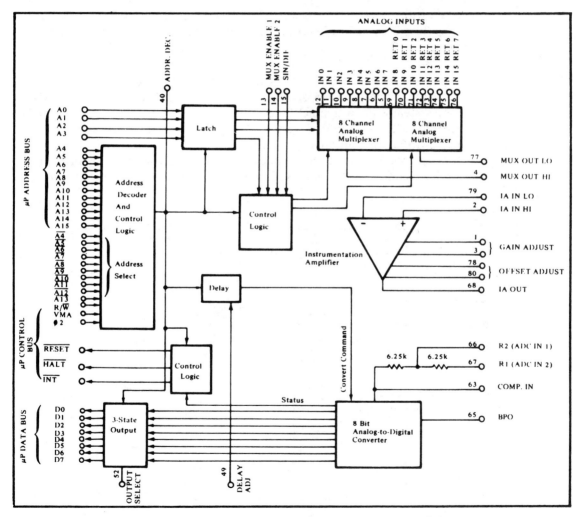

FIG. 3-30   A complete, multichannel data-acquisition system makes interface to a microprocessor quite easy. (Courtesy of Burr-Brown Corporation)

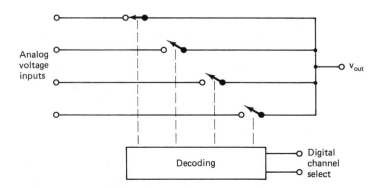

Analog voltage inputs

Decoding

Digital channel select

v_{out}

FIG. 3-31 An analog multiplexer can select one of several analog data channels for input. The switches are usually a JFET transistor.

for interface with a 6800 microprocessor. The device is called the MP21 and is manufactured by Burr-Brown. The following description explains the nature and function of each block.

1. *Analog multiplexer.* This device is essentially a switch that can be digitally addressed to channel the analog data from one input to the amplifier and ADC. For a system with 16 channels, there will be four digital lines to address the 16 possible switch positions. Figure 3-31 illustrates schematically the nature of such a switch for four analog channels.
2. *Address decoder.* The DAS is connected directly to the address bus and control bus of the computer. The address decoder is *programmed* by hardwired jumpers

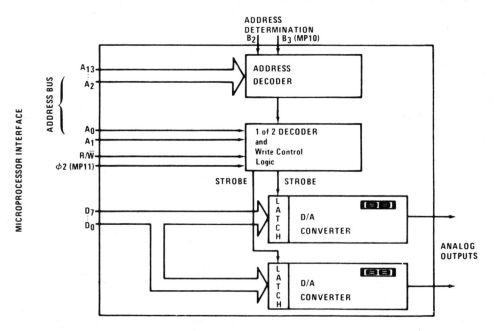

FIG. 3-32 The modularized output system makes output design much easier for microprocessor-based systems. (Courtesy of Burr-Brown Corporation)

to respond to a particular set of addresses and control signals appearing on the buses. In the unit of Fig. 3-30 the lower-order 4 bits are used to address the 16 input channels while the higher-order 12 bits are used in conjunction with control lines for device selection and read and write operations. Note that the VMA, R/W, and ϕ_2 are directly connected to the decoder.

3. *Amplifier and ADC.* The unit has a built-in signal-conditioning amplifier and ADC that operates on the data passed through the multiplexer. Thus any channel can be addressed and passed through to the amplifier and ADC. The gain of the amplifier can be externally adjusted.

4. *Tristate output latch.* Since the output of the ADC is connected to the tristate latch, the DAS output lines can be connected directly to the data bus of the computer. When a read operation occurs, the DAS will enable the tristate buffers and load the data onto the data bus.

So you can see that this one unit can be used to provide input capabilities for up to 16 data channels with full analog-to-digital conversion. Such systems have capabilities beyond this basic description, such as bipolar operation, differential input modes, and programmable gain. In particular applications it will be necessary to study the specifications very carefully to make use of as many capabilities as possible.

Data-Output System (DOS).   Figure 3-32 shows a block diagram of a typical data-output system. Much the same as the DAS, a DOS with an analog multiplexer can provide the capability of using one DAC to output to many different output channels. For the example shown, the system can output two channels. The address decoder serves the same function as that described fro the DAS. Note the latch that captures data from the data bus under control of the computer via the control lines and the decoded address bus lines.

PROBLEMS

3-1 Construct the decoding circuit for Ex. 3-1 using two-input NAND/NOR gate logic.

3-2 Repeat Ex. 3-1 if the port address is changed to E4H.

3-3 Construct the decoding circuit of Ex. 3-2 using two-input NAND/NOR gate logic.

3-4 A 6800 will input 8 bits through a tristate buffer that is enabled by a LOW, through address E000H. The 6800 read requires control lines VMA to be HIGH and the R/$\overline{\text{W}}$ line HIGH. Construct the enable circuit.

3-5 Suppose adress 5×××H is used for an input address in memory-mapped operation. How much real memory space is unavailable as a result?

3-6 An 8080-based computer will input from port A7 using an 8-bit tristate enabled by a LOW and output through port A7 using an 8-bit latch activated by a HIGH. The computer requires $\overline{\text{I/OR}}$ for a read and $\overline{\text{I/OW}}$ for a write (both active low). Develop the required decoding hardware.

3-7 Find the analog output voltages for an 8-bit DAC with a 5-V reference for the following inputs: **(a)** 00010101_2; **(b)** 35H; **(c)** 10010010_2; **(d)** A3H; **(e)** F7H.

3-8 A 5-bit DAC must output 8.00 V for a 11111_2 input. What reference voltage is required? What is the output step size?

3-9 A 12-bit DAC with a 10-V reference is supposed to output 7.450 V under some circumstance. What is the required binary output for the closest possible output voltage? What is the error?

3-10 A 10-bit bipolar DAC using offset binary has an 8-V reference. What is the step size? Find the output voltage for inputs of **(a)** 008H; **(b)** 052H; **(c)** 1F6H; **(d)** 25BH; **(e)** 308H; **(f)** 3F3H.

3-11 Suppose the converter of Prob. 3-10 must output as close as possible to $+2.2$ V and -3.15 V. Find the required digital inputs and the errors.

3-12 A positioner has 48 positions activated by 48 voltage levels from 0 at the first position in steps of 0.15 volts. A 6-bit DAC will be used to provide the required voltages. What reference will be required? What digital input will produce position 33?

3-13 A pressure transducer has a transfer function of 0.05 V/psi. Develop the circuit for two comparators providing digital HIGH alarms for pressures of 78 and 105 psi.

3-14 The pressure alarms of Prob. 3-13 are to be input to port 7×H ($\times$ = don't care) of an 8080-based computer. Show how a tristate buffer can be used for input, including the decoding.

3-15 Light level is converted to voltage as 0.015 V/lumen. A comparator will be used to detect a level of 595 lumens. Electrical noise is found to run 30 mV and light noise is 2 lumens. Construct a hysteresis comparator circuit to provide noise immunity with a 10-mV margin above normal signal noise. What are the resulting light levels for the comparator ON and OFF transitions?

3-16 A 6-bit unipolar ADC has an 8.0-V reference. Find the digital output results from inputs of: **(a)** 1.43V; **(b)** 3.39V; **(c)** 5.12 V; **(d)** 7.43 V.

3-17 Suppose the ADC of Prob. 3-16 must have the output changed from 111110_2 to 111111_2 at 8.00 V. What reference is required?

3-18 An 8-bit ADC has a 10.0-V reference. For each of the following outputs, specify the possible input voltage range: **(a)** 01010101_2; **(b)** 9CH; **(c)** F3H.

3-19 Supppose the ADC of Prob. 3-18 is modified to operate bipolar in modified 2's complement. Find the binary output for input voltages of: **(a)** 3.49 V; **(b)** -2.24 V.

3-20 The converter of Prob. 3-19 has an output of 10111010_2. What is the range of input voltages? Repeat for an output of 00111101_2.

3-21 Suppose the ADC output in Ex. 3-12 is B4H. Find the temperature. If the temperature is 73°C, find the digital output.

3-22 An 8-bit ADC with a 10-V reference will be used to input pressure from 50 psi (00H) to 200 psi (FFH) into a 6800-based computer. The transducer has a transfer function of 40 mV/psi. START CONVERT is a low signal that will be sent from the computer on bit zero of the data bus using memory-mapped address E000H. CONVERT COMPLETE will be read into the computer as a low on bit one again using address E000H. Data input will be taken by enabling an 8212 tristate latch using address F000H. Construct the interface circuit. The required control lines are VMA HIGH, R/$\overline{\text{W}}$ HIGH to read, and LOW to write.

CHAPTER 4

DATA INPUT AND PROCESSING SOFTWARE

OBJECTIVES

The overall objective of this chapter is a study of typical software required for the input and initial processing of data in microprocessor-based control systems. This primary objective can be broken down into a number of secondary objectives. After studying this chapter and doing the problems at the end of the chapter, you will be able to:

1. Explain the type of instructions to input using isolated I/O port or memory-mapped techniques.
2. Describe three methods of accounting for the time required for hardware input signal processing.
3. Compare the fixed-point and floating-point representation of data in the computer.
4. Explain the significance of variable traceability.
5. Describe the effects of aliasing and averaging on sampled data systems.
6. Compare the equation inversion and table methods of data linearization.
7. Explain and compare the full range and real variable modes of representing data in digital format.

4-1   INTRODUCTION

In Ch. 1 an overview of process control was presented and the role of the computer was explained. The next two chapters showed how process variable data are measured and transformed into digital format suitable for use by a computer. For the most part these operations have involved hardware (i.e., the actual equipment that performs measurement, conversion, and so forth). Now, following this logical progression, we find ourselves at the entrance of the computer. The data have been digitized and placed on the data bus, or at least in a tristate buffer ready to be enabled by the computer, which will then place the data on the data bus. From this point until a control signal is output by the computer, all operations will be in software, that is, will consist of appropriate sets of computer instructions operating on the data according to stored programs.

This chapter represents the initial software operations that must be performed on the raw digital data as captured from the DAS. We consider this initial processing in a number of distinct categories, and those make up the major sections of the chapter.

The first category will consider the software required to get data into the computer. The problems here are in part associated with the fact that there will be a delay, whose exact value is never known, between when the computer requests data and when the data are actually available for input.

Another important category is the form of the data relative to the physical variables that the data actually represent. When temperature is converted to voltage and this is converted into an 8-bit digital signal and input to the computer, what is the relation between that binary number and the temperature from which it all started? This is considered along with problems associated with how such data are "passed" into a higher-level language, such as FORTRAN, which may be used to program the control algorithms.

The last major category is concerned with the relation between *how* the data were taken and the *information* content of the data in binary form in the computer. Since the information is both sampled (not continuously known in time) and digitized (not continuously known in value), it is natural to expect that inherent errors exist between the binary data and the real data. This category also considers different ways of representing physical data in the computer.

Software Representation.   To study software, it is convenient to consider the topic in three parts:

1. *Algorithm.* The algorithm is the set of equations and/or sequence of operations that solve some problem. Since it is simply a statement of procedure, it is independent of the computer. In many cases the algorithms required to solve a control problem are presented as statements of what operations are required.
2. *Flowchart.* A flowchart is the first step to converting an algorithm into a computer program that allows the computer to solve the problem. The flowchart shows a step-by-step pictorial view of how the algorithm is accomplished. A

general flowchart describes the required steps in terms not specialized to any particular computer. A *detailed* flowchart specializes some of the operations to a particular computer in terms of registers used, flags tested, and so on. Both types of flowcharts are used in the software descriptions.

3. *Program*. A program results when the detailed flowchart is translated or *coded* into the actual instructions of the particular microprocessor employed. In the software examples presented, both 8080 and 6800 code are used. The common manner of representation of such programs uses the mnemonics and assembly language conventions of each microprocessor.

In the software studied in this chapter and this text, some of all three of the above parts are presented. In terms of applications, however, it is most important that the algorithm and the associated general flowchart be understood, since these can then be adpated to particular microprocessors.

4-2   INTERFACE SOFTWARE

Chapter 3 presented the hardware necessary to input analog data into a micro-processor-based computer. It was also shown that the computer plays an important, active role in this process in initiating commands both to start the measurement–conversion process and to cause the data to be deposited on the system data bus. The commands that are initiated occur as a result of instructions executed by the computer (i.e., software). This represents the first level of software required in control by computer. Two important topics are associated with this level of software. The first concerns the actual *instructional sequence* that produces the input. The second concerns the *time sequence* involved in the input.

4-2.1   Input Instruction Sequence

The underlying assumption about data input is that analog data are being converted to digital format and input to a microprocessor-based computer. Under this assumption a number of generalizations can be made about the events that must occur in hardware and software.

Operation Sequence.   A certain common sequence of operations must precede the input of data by a microcomputer. These operations can be summarized as follows:

1. Send a command to the DAS requesting a data sample. This operation has the basic objective of starting the analog-to-digital conversion process. It may also first select a data channel of a multichannel DAS and perhaps switch a sample-hold module to HOLD before starting the conversion process.
2. Interrogate the DAS to see if the data are ready. This operation is used by the computer to deduce if the data are ready by looking for a conversion complete

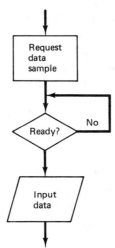

FIG. 4-1 Software actions for input are illustrated by this flowchart.

signal from the DAS. In some cases the computer must periodically perform the interrogation until the data are actually ready, while in other cases the DAS uses the computer interrupt procedure.

3. Send a command to the DAS to input the data. This operation is the objective of the whole process and results in the data value being placed on the data bus by the DAS and therefore input. This operation may also perform certain important reset operations in the DAS to ready it for the next sample conversion.

The actual form of the instructions required to perform these operations depends on the type of computer and type of input process being used. Figure 4-1 shows the general flowchart for this procedure.

Isolated I/O Port.   Many microprocessors support a type of input, as discussed in Ch. 3, by which special instructions produce input (and output). In the 8080, as an example, input is accomplished by execution of the instruction

$$\text{IN XYH}$$

where IN is the mnemonic of the instruction and XYH is a hex *port address*, which is from 00H to FFH. Thus there are 256_{10} possible input ports. The effect of the instruction is described as follows:

1. The port address, XYH, is copied into the lower-order byte (A_0 to A_7). The 16-bit bus would thus contain ZZXYH, where ZZ is undefined.
2. The 8080 system control line I/OR is taken low by the computer.
3. The contents of the data bus are copied into the A register (accumulator) of the microprocessor.

Although other microprocessors may vary in the type of control lines and other details, these basic operations will be required for any isolated I/O port input. Note that the input data end up in the accumulator. Generally, flags and condition codes are not affected.

The equivalent instruction for output is given by

OUT XYH

where OUT is the mnemonic and XY the address byte again. This instruction takes $\overline{I/OW}$ low and then places the data in the A register on the data bus. There are 00H to FFH output port addresses and thus 256_{10} possible ports.

The three steps of the input process would thus be accomplished by loading the accumulator with the desired output commands to the DAS and then executing an OUT XYH instruction. Input is accomplished by executing an IN XYH instruction to actually input the data when they are ready.

EXAMPLE 4-1   A DAS uses port address E4H for both the data request output command and to interrogate when the data are ready. Bit d_0 HIGH is used to request data from the DAS and bit d_7 is returned LOW, which is the sign bit LOW, when data are ready. Data are read by inputting from port E5H. Construct the detailed flowchart and give the required 8080 instructions to implement the basic operations of the input process.

Solution: For the first step, the data must be requested. This will require loading the accumulator with 01H and executing OUT E4H. Interrogation will involve the instruction IN E4H and then testing d_7 of the accumulator to see if it is LOW. This can be done by testing the sign-flag bit. The actual data input is accomplished by IN E5H. The detailed flowchart is shown in Fig. 4-2. When this flowchart is coded the resulting code is:

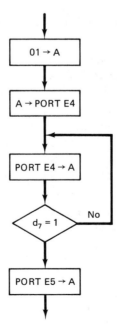

FIG. 4-2 This flowchart shows the operations necessary for Ex. 4-1 using isolated I/O ports.

```
                ·
                ·
        MVI A,01H              ;loads A with 01H

        OUT 0E4H               ;outputs data request

WAIT:   IN  0E4H              ;check if data is ready

        ORA A                 ;set flags

        JM WAIT               ;if D₇ high wait

INPUT:  IN  0E5H              ;data into accumulator

                ·
                ·
```

Another method of checking if the data are ready uses the interrupt features of the microprocessor, as discussed in Sec. 4-2.2.

Memory-Mapped I/O.   As pointed out in Ch. 3, the memory-mapped I/O procedure is characterized by using the DAS like a memory location. Thus any read instruction from the memory location decoded to activate the DAS will result in an input of the data. Virtually any microprocessor can support this type of I/O as long as the DAS system reacts to the instruction in the same fashion as memory. The microprocessor has no inherent way of knowing if memory or a DAS is being accessed. The 6800 is typical of some microprocessors that support *only* this type of I/O mechanism (i.e., it has no port instructions). This means that any memory reference instruction can be used for input. For example, an input from a DAS with an address of XYWZH could be accomplished by the followng ($ means a hex number in 6800 assembly language):

LDAA $XYWZ   (data into accumulator A)
LDAB $XYWZ   (data into accumulator B)
ADDA $XYWZ   (data plus A into A)

and there are others within the instruction set that could be used. Note that the data need not be brought into the A accumulator.

The basic three sequences involved in an input process would thus be accomplished by using *memory write* instructions to send signals or commands to the DAS and *memory read* instructions to interrogate or input data from the DAS.

EXAMPLE 4-2   If a HIGH on d_7 is sent to a DAS at address F100H, the ADC is started. When conversion is complete, a HIGH is returned in d_7 of the same address. The data are input by a read of address F101H. Show the 6800 detailed flowchart and sequence of instructions that will accomplish this.

Solution: The required operations can be accomplished by first loading the A accumulator with 80H and "writing" this to memory address F100H. Then the interrogate for conversion complete is accomplished by "reading" location F100H and looking for d_7 HIGH, which is equivalent to the sign bit. A read of memory address F101H will input the data.

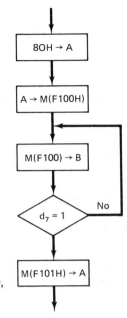

FIG. 4-3 For memory-mapped I/O, the same basic operations are necessary.

The flowchart is shown in Fig. 4-3. This flowchart is easily coded as follows (# means immediate operation):

```
        .
        .
        .
        LDAA   #$80      ;load A with D₇ HIGH
        STAA   $F100     ;start ADC
WAIT:   LDAB   $F100     ;get status of DAS
        BPL    WAIT      ;input data if D₇ HIGH
INPUT:  LDAA   $F101     ;load data into A
        .
        .
        .
```

4-2.2 Input Time Sequence

The ADC will take a certain length of time to perform the conversion of an analog input voltage to a binary number for input to the computer. The input time sequence refers to just what the computer does, in time, while waiting for the binary input to be ready after requesting an input. There are a number of possibilities. The choice depends on just how tight a schedule there is on the activities of the computer. Three common approaches will be presented.

Interrogated Wait Loops. When the schedule of the computer is light, it can simply wait until the DAS indicates that the data are ready. In this case the computer repeatedly interrogates the DAS until an indication is received that the data are ready. One way of doing this was illustrated by the flowcharts of Figs. 4-1 through 4-3. The

109

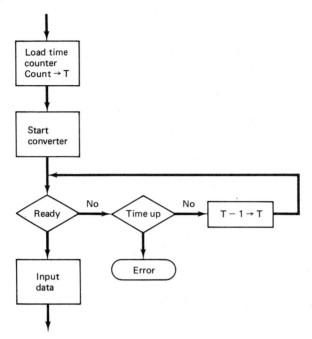

FIG. 4-4 Timers are often used to protect against failures of the DAS causing the computer to lock up waiting.

danger in this approach is that, if an error condition occurs in the DAS such that a conversion complete signal is never valid, the computer will be caught in an endless loop. Recovery would require a reset.

A better approach is shown in the flowchart of Fig. 4-4. Here a software counter or *timer* is used to provide a fixed amount of time for the DAS to respond to the data request. The time is provided by fixing the number of times that the interrogate loop can be performed. The initial load of COUNT is selected in conjunction with the total time consumed by one run through the loop to give plenty of time for the ADC to complete the conversion. If a data ready response is not received in this time, an error condition is indicated and some other action is taken.

EXAMPLE 4-3   An ADC specification indicates that 80 to 100 μs is required for an 8-bit conversion. The following 8080 routine is used for the wait loop. The number of computer states for each instruction is given, assuming about 0.5 μs per state.

```
            MVI  B,TIME      ;TIME = counts
            MVI  A,01H       ;D₀ = 1 to start ADC
            OUT  0E4H        ;start ADC
    WAIT:   IN   07H         ;interrogate  (10 states)
            ORA  A           ;set flags    (4 states)
            JP   INPUT       ;data ready   (10 states)
            DCR  B           ;B - 1 → B    (5 states)
            JNZ  WAIT        ;not zero     (10 states)
            JMP  ERROR       ;time up go to error
    INPUT:  IN   08H         ;input the data
```

Determine what value should be used for TIME if a time margin of 100% is to be allotted for conversion.

Solution: The converter takes a maximum of 100 μs and for a 100% margin it means the loop should wait 200 μs before jumping to the error routine. The total number of states in the loop is 39 so that the total time in one run through the loop is $(39)(0.5 \mu s) = 19.5$ μs. Then the number of times allowed through the loop is $200/19.5 = 10.3$, so let's use 11 times. Then TIME = 0BH.

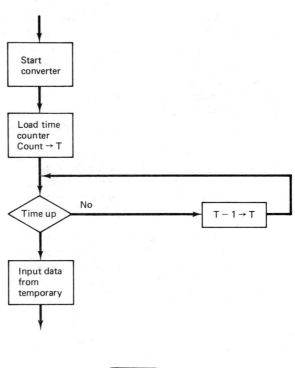

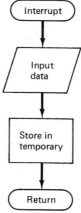

FIG. 4-5   An interrupt-driven timer and input process operate as shown in this flowchart.

Interrupts.   Another approach to computer activity during the wait time of the ADC involves using the interrupt feature of microprocessors. In this mode of operation the computer is free to perform other operations while waiting for the DAS to indicate that data are ready. When the conversion is complete, the DAS signals the microcomputer on one of the interrupt lines. This will cause the computer to transfer operation to an interrupt service routine, which will input the data. Such an interrupt can be used in many different ways.

Interrupt-Driven Wait Loop.   In this mode of operation a wait loop is entered after initiation of the data input request to the DAS. The difference is that the DAS is never interrogated to see if the data are ready. Rather, the DAS simply takes the microprocessor interrupt line active when the data are ready, and the service routine inputs the data and, perhaps, stores them in some memory location. The wait loop is then reentered and finished prior to further processing of the data. In such a case the interrupt routine simply inputs the data and stores them in a temporary location. The flowchart of Fig. 4-5 illustrates how such a system might appear. Of course, this is not any more time efficient than the previous process.

EXAMPLE 4-4   A 6800 system will input data according to the procedure of Ex. 4-2, except a conversion complete will generate an interrupt, $\overline{IRQ}$, which vectors the computer to an interrupt service routine to input the data. There will be a wait loop in the main program counting down from 1BH. Show the main program and the interrupt routine.

Solution: In the 6800 an $\overline{IRQ}$ vectors the computer to the routine whose starting address is in FFF8H and FFF9H. The program counter, index registers, accumulators A and B, and the flags are all pushed on the stack when transfer to the interrupt routine occurs and then popped back upon return. Thus any input in the interrupt service must be saved before returning to the main program. The program might have the form:

```
              LDAB    #$1B        ;use B as counter

              LDAA    #$80        ;load A with D_7 HIGH

              STAA    $F100       :start ADC

       WAIT:  DECB                ;B - 1 → B

              BNE     WAIT        ;still looping

              LDAA    $0300       ;get the data

                .

                .

                .

       ;Interrupt service routine - input data and store
       ;in location 0300H

              LDAA    $F101       ;get the data

              STAA    $0300       ;put in 0300 temporary

              RTS                 ;return
```

An obvious flaw in the routine presented in this example is that, if something went wrong and the ADC data were never presented, the program would go on until the wait loop was finished. The accumulator would be loaded with whatever data 0300H held when the loop was finished. It would be better to construct software routines to protect against this and also to terminate the loop when the data interrupt occurred.

Interrupt-Driven Processing.   When there are a number of jobs for the computer to do during the input process, the interrupt feature provides a mechanism to input new data while the processing of old data is still occurring. In this case a more efficient use of computer time results than a simple wait loop. One restriction is that the input process must not proceed at a rate exceeding the processing rate or data will get "backed up," which may cause a breakdown of the whole input and processing procedure.

Real-Time Processing.   When the control system must process data and initiate control commands on a time sequence basis, real-time processing is often used. In this system a real-time clock is tied to the interrupt process. Suppose data must be taken from some process at a regular clock interval. Then the real-time clock system is programmed such that whenever the data-collection time arrives an interrupt is generated that vectors or directs the computer to execute the necessary instructions to input the data. These data are stored in a common location accessible by another routine that will be executed in the normal events of the master program. In this way the data are always updated at the required time period. The input routine would be similar to those already considered involving wait loops following a request for data.

4-3   DATA REPRESENTATION

The results of the previous operations leave the data in an accumulator of the microprocessor and ready for the next stage of processing. The ultimate goal will be to process these data through an algorithm that produces an output to a controlling variable.

At this point it is important to understand the form of the data in the computer, how this relates to the physical data, and how the computer interprets this number.

4-3.1   Relation to the Physical Variable

The data started out as an analog measurement of some physical variable that is to be input to the computer as part of the control process. When the information about this variable finally appears in the computer, many factors must be considered about its relation to the actual variable. The most significant factor is that mathematical computations will be carried out on this variable, such as finding the error by subtracting the set point. These computations are defined on the basis of the actual value of the variable. Such computations must be translated into the equivalent binary form for coding in the computer instruction set.

To be able to derive and code operations in the computer, it will be necessary to maintain *traceability* between the binary number and the physical variable it represents. Such traceability is provided by carefully documenting each phase of the process from transducer measurement, signal conditioning, and analog-to-digital conversion to input to the computer. The resulting relation can be expressed by three quantities: offset, range, and functional dependence.

Offset or Bias.   The binary signal in the computer varies from all zeros to all ones as the entire range of counting states is considered. It is not uncommon for the represented physical variable to have a range for which zero is not included. For example, a system may measure pressure from 300 to 900 psi and convert this to an 8-bit binary number, 00H to FFH. The offset, v_0, is the value of the physical variable at the zero of the binary number. In this example, $v_0 = 300$ psi. If the measurement resulted in a standard 4- to 20-mA current transmission signal, and this is converted to binary, the 00H may correspond to 4 mA, which in turn must be related back to the value of the physical variable.

Range.   The range refers to the difference between the minimum and maximum values of the physical variable represented by the binary number. In the preceding example, the pressure range is $(900 - 300) = 600$ psi. If the measurement and digital conversion process are bipolar, the range may involve a negative to positive value. In general, the range is defined by the difference between the maximum represented value and the minimum represented value:

$$R = v_{max} - v_{min} \qquad (4\text{-}1)$$

where v_{max} = maximum value of the physical variable
v_{min} = minimum value of the physical variable.

Functional Dependence.   Unfortunately, many transducers produce an output that is nonlinear with respect to the measured quantity. In general, this means that the binary number will also vary in a nonlinear fashion with respect to the physical variable. Figure 4-6 illustrates two functional relations for a measurement that has the same range and offset.

In case A of Fig. 4-6, the functional relation is *linear* or simply proportional. Note that, except for the finite step size of the analog-to-digital conversion, the relationship between the physical variable and binary number is a straight line. Such relations are preferred since the control system computations will be much easier. An equation can be written that allows the value of the physical variable to be deduced from the binary number. To do this, the range and offset are used as follows. First, a constant is defined as the amount of change of the physical variable per bit of the binary number. This constant also expresses the *resolution* of the representation.

$$K = R2^{-n} \qquad (4\text{-}2)$$

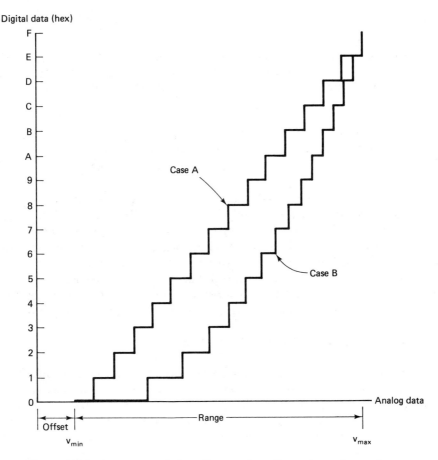

Digital data (hex)

Case A

Case B

Offset

Range

v_{min}

v_{max}

Analog data

FIG. 4-6 This chart contrasts how linear and nonlinear dependence shows up in the digital data. Notice that in case B each bit does not represent the same amount of analog data.

where R = range of the physical variable
n = number of bits in the binary number.
Now this is used to deduce the value of the physical variable from the binary number. The binary number is converted into its equivalent decimal value:

$$v = KN + v_0 \qquad (4\text{-}3)$$

where v = physical variable
K = slope defined by Eq. (4-2)
$N = b_n 2^n + b_{n-1} 2^{n-1} + \cdots + b_1 2^1 + b_0$
(decimal number equivalent to binary).

EXAMPLE 4-5 Temperature is converted linearly from 40° to 220°C into 00H to FFH. Specify the range and offset. Find the equation relating temperature and N. Suppose the binary number in the computer is 4AH. Find the temperature.

Solution: Since the problem states that 40°C converts to 00H, it is clear that the *offset* is v_0 = 40°C. The range is obviously given by R = (220 − 40) = 180°C. The equation is found from Eqs. (4-2) and (4-3). K = $(180)(2^{-8})$ = 0.703°C/LSB. The equation for temperature is

$$T = 0.703N + 40°C$$

The number 4AH = 01001010_2 so that the decimal number is $N = 2^6 + 2^3 + 2 = 74$. Substituting this into the temperature equation gives

$$T = 0.703(74) + 40 = 92°C$$

In case B of Fig. 4-6, the functional relation is *nonlinear.* As you can see, this means that the physical variable and binary number are not related by a straight line. Every LSB change of the binary number does *not* represent the same change in the physical variable. This is extremely important to the control process. In fact, the use of traditional process control procedures will require that a binary representation of the physical variable be developed that *is* linear with respect to the controlled variable. This is accomplished by a process called *linearization.* Linearization involves the coding of mathematical algorithms, as will be shown later in this chapter.

4-3.2   Relation to the Computer

The objective of getting the binary representation of the controlled variable into the computer is to perform the computations necessary to produce the controlling output. To do this, mathematical operations will be performed on and with the number. It is therefore very important that consideration be given to the relation of computer operations and the input number.

Unsigned Numbers.   In most cases the physical data will be input as coded (by the ADC) into an unsigned binary integer. For example, with an 8-bit system the data will come in as a binary number from 00H to FFH. Even though each bit may *represent* fractional data, the math operations that follow will treat the number as a simple unsigned binary integer. In fact, if the microprocessor uses 2's complement as the representation of negative numbers, then half the data (80H to FFH) could *seem* to be negative. It is at the option of the programmer to define how the numbers are considered, based on an understanding of the math operations in the instruction set. Example 4-6 illustrates how the apparent negative (2's complement) nature of input data does not present a problem.

EXAMPLE 4-6   The temperature of Ex. 4-5, which is converted into a unipolar 8-bit binary, has a set point of 150°C. Develop the coding in 8080 mnemonics to find the error, as TERR. Let TEMP be the binary temperature input contained in the accumulator. Calculate the error in binary and decimal for inputs of 120° and 180°C.

Solution: First find the set point in binary using the equation that resulted from Ex. 4-5. We simply solve for N:

$$N = \frac{T - 40}{0.703} = \frac{150 - 40}{0.703} = 157_{10} \quad \text{(rounded to an integer)}$$

The binary number can be easily found:
$$TSP = 10011100_2 = 9DH$$

Symbolically, the error is TERR = TEMP − TSP. This can be simply coded using the subtract immediate instruction:

$$SUI\ 9DH \qquad ;A - 9DH \rightarrow A$$

For an input of 120°C the binary is found to be 72H, and for 180°C it is C7H. The errors in decimal are (120 − 150) = −30°C and (180 − 150) = 30°C. In binary, using the preceding instruction, the results are found by performing a 2's complement add operation on the binary numbers. The 2's complement of 9DH is given by $01100100_2 = 64H$, and therefore the error is found by the computer as A + 63H → A. The results are

$$120°C: \quad 72H + 64H = D6H$$
$$180°C: \quad C7H + 64H = 2BH$$

Since each LSB is 0.703°C, it is easy to show that 2BH is 30°C (rounded). But what about D5H? Even though the input was not expressed as a bipolar number, that is, 9DH did *not* represent a negative number (MSB = 1), the result of the subtract instruction *is* automatically in 2's complement format. Note that D6H becomes 2AH when the 2's complement is taken, which shows that this actually represents −30°C (rounded).

The use of integer numbers for data representation and computation is called *fixed-point* representation. This means that the decimal point, which separates fractional and integer quantities, is assumed to be located at a fixed position in the number. If integers are assumed, the point is to the right of the LSB. If pure fractions are assumed, the point is to the left of the MSB. It is also possible to assume that the point is in the middle of the data word, say between the fifth and sixth bit. Then all math operations would be designed to remember that this assignment had been made. Generally, the integer assumption is made.

Signed Numbers.   In those cases when an ADC is set up to operate in a bipolar mode, adjustments will be necessary after the data have been input to the computer. Usually, the sign will be indicated by the MSB using offset binary. If the negative nature of the numbers is to be maintained, conversion to 2's complement will be necessary. This is simple to do since the only difference is the MSB. After input, the MSB is simply complemented.

Multiple Precision.   With the common 8-bit microprocessors, one data word can represent a range of data with a resolution of 256 states. For many applications this is sufficient. In applications where this resolution is not sufficient to achieve the desired degree of control, it may be necessary to use more than 8 bits to represent the data. In these cases the 8-bit microprocessor can still be used, but with *two* or more words to represent the data. For example, with 16 bits in the data word the resolution is expressed by the data-range spread over 65,536 states. This would mean that a 16-bit ADC would be required and that the input process would use two ports to input the data as two 8-bit words. Mathematical processing would then be programmed as 2-byte operations.

EXAMPLE 4-7   Motor speed is to be measured and controlled in the range of 1200 to 1600 rpm with the speed regulated to within 1.0 rpm of the set point. Find the minimum number of bits that must be used in the measurement.

Solution: The range is $R = (1600 - 1200) = 400$ rpm. If control is required to 1.0 rpm, the *minimum* resolution of the measurement would be 0.50 rpm. Why? Suppose the speed was 1400 rpm. If the resolution in measurement was 1.0 rpm, it would have to increase to 1401 rpm before the change could be detected and corrective action initiated. But it would have to *decrease* to 1399 rpm before a change could be detected also. This is a spread of 2 rpm in the control, not 1 as required. By making the resolution in measurement 0.5 rpm, the spread of measurement is 1.0 rpm. From a practical point of view, even better resolution would be required. Using 0.5 rpm and the range of 400 rpm gives the number of measurement *states* as

$$\text{states} = \frac{400}{0.5} = 800$$

Let's look at the states for different numbers of bits:

$$
\begin{aligned}
8 \text{ bits:} \quad & \text{states} = 2^8 = 256 \\
10 \text{ bits:} \quad & \text{states} = 2^{10} = 1024 \\
12 \text{ bits:} \quad & \text{states} = 2^{12} = 4096 \\
& \text{etc.}
\end{aligned}
$$

It is clear that a 10-bit ADC must be used for the measurement. If an 8-bit microprocessor is being used, 2 bytes must be used to represent the data.

4-3.3   Floating-Point Representation

In many cases the use of fixed-point representation of numbers is inconvenient or not possible. The most typical example is when the numbers used in calculations involve very small and very large values. It may be necessary to use numbers from, say, 123,000 to 0.00567 all in the same routines. When converted to binary, these would require many bytes for representation. Furthermore, it would become very difficult to keep track of the location of the decimal point if multiplication and division were involved. In these cases and others, floating-point representation is used.

Definition.   Floating point can be understood by comparison to the powers of 10 method of writing base 10 numbers. For example, the number 123,000 could be written as 1.23×10^5, which means $1.23 \times 100,000$. Likewise, $0.00567 = 5.67 \times 10^{-3}$ or 5.67×0.001. For computer operations the same representation is used, except, usually, the base of the power term is 2 instead of 10. The numerical part is called the *mantissa*. This would be 1.23 and 5.67 in the preceding examples. The power term is called the *exponent*. In the computer the decimal point is most often assumed to be to the left of the MSB of the mantissa. The representation of floating point in computers uses one or more bytes for the mantissa and another byte for the exponent. It is clear then that this representation of numbers requires the use of two or more bytes, as in multiple precision integer numbers.

Figure 4-7 illustrates the structure of a typical floating-point representation of numbers using a 2-byte mantissa and a 1-byte exponent. In this example the signs of

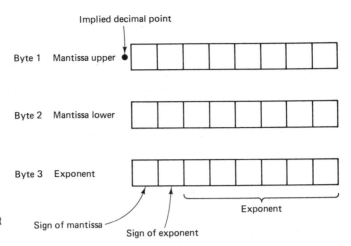

Byte 1   Mantissa upper

Byte 2   Mantissa lower

Byte 3   Exponent

Implied decimal point

Sign of mantissa

Sign of exponent

Exponent

FIG. 4-7 This illustrates one method of using a floating-point representation of numbers.

both the mantissa and the exponent are contained in the exponent byte. This means that the exponent has only 6 numeric bits. Thus it can vary from $+63$ to -63. The number has the form

$$\pm 0.XXXXXXXXXXXXXXXX \times 2^{\pm YYYYYY} \qquad (4\text{-}4)$$

where $XXXXXXXXXXXXXXXX = 16\text{-bit mantissa}$
$YYYYYY = 6\text{-bit exponent.}$

In this representation the sign of the exponent is usually indicated by a sign bit and the sign of the mantissa by a sign bit, such as the MSB of the exponent as shown in Fig. 4-7.

The maximum positive number that can be represented, according to Eq. (4-4), is $.1111111111111111_2 \times 2^{111111_2}$. Converting this to base 10, we get about $1. \times 2^{63}$ or about 10^{+19}. The minimum positive is about 10^{-19}. The resolution is the LSB of the mantissa, or $2^{-16} = 0.000015$. You can see that use of floating point allows much greater flexibility in the use of number ranges. This is contrasted with the increased complexity of programming and math operations with multiple-byte exponential representations.

Numbers. To illustrate the representation, consider the numbers given previously. First, 123,000 can be converted to 1E078H, which is 11110000001111000_2 as an integer. We move the decimal to the left of the MSB and count the number of left shifts. This will be the positive power, and it is seen to be 17_{10} or 11H. The floating point number in binary is then

$$0.1111000000111100 \times 2^{010001}$$

in terms of bytes, the mantissa bytes would be 11110000 for the most significant byte and 00111100 for the least significant byte. The exponent would be 00010001, which shows the mantissa to be positive (MSB = 0) and the exponent positive.

The second number was 0.00567. This can be converted to fractional binary by successive multiplication by two, as was done for the study of ADC operation. The result is the binary fraction 0.0000000101110011100010110, etc. We move the decimal to the right to the left of the first 1 and count the number of shifts. This is easily seen to be 7, so the binary number is 000111. The floating-point binary number is

$$0.1011100111001011 \times 2^{-000111}$$

where the mantissa has been truncated at 16 bits. In terms of the computer bytes, the exponential will be expressed with a sign bit; -000111 becomes 1000111. Thus the most significant byte is 10111001, the least is 11001011, and the exponent is 01000111. The MSB is 0, which shows the mantissa is positive.

Note that the microprocessor will not typically have instructions that deal with the addition, subtraction, and even formation of such floating-point representations. The programmer must construct codes that perform these functions.

Math Operations.   When a microcomputer is to be used with a floating-point representation of numbers, subroutines must be written that perform floating-point add, subtract, and perhaps multiply. These are then called on when the control algorithm is written. In general, these routines perform the math operations and then *normalize* the result so that it again has the decimal point to the left of the MSB of the mantissa. When input data are taken from an ADC, they too must be normalized to fit within the floating-point representation. Often a *floating-point accumulator* is used as the operation register set for all floating-point math operations. This is simply memory locations set aside to function as the accumulator.

Higher-Level Languages.   In some cases, higher-level languages are available with the control computer, such as BASIC or FORTRAN. In these cases the control algorithms are all written in these languages, which are much easier than machine language. When physical data are converted to binary and input to the computer, they must be *passed* to the higher-level language. This often means expressing the number in a compatible floating-point form. Most computers and languages with such capability also provide routines that will adjust input data and put them into the floating-point accumulator so they can be used in the language. In this text we are more concerned with small-scale dedicated microprocessor applications, so extensive treatment of floating-point procedures will not be given.

However, in some cases it may be necessary to construct floating-point representations of data even in small-scale applications, so it is important to understand the concepts of floating-point representations as presented here.

4-4   DATA PROCESSING

Prior to setting up the algorithm that will compute the controlling output, certain processing of the input data must often occur. Generally, such processing will require math operations on the input data. The first part of this section will consider the software tools by which common math operations are carried out in the microprocessor. The rest of this section studies two of the more common requirements of the data input and initial processing. The first concerns the effect of the periodic sampling of controlled variable data as opposed to continuous knowledge of this quantity. The second is concerned with nonlinearities between the input binary number and the actual value of the variable measured.

4-4.1 Microprocessor Math Operations

The instruction set of the microprocessor will contain single- and sometimes double-word math operations for addition and subtraction. In general, the instruction set will not include multiplication and division. Yet, of course, all but the very simple control requirements will require these math operations in the computations necessary to derive the control output. This is satisfied by the construction of subroutines to perform these operations. A number of algorithms exist for multiplication and division; selection of these is dependent on the time required, number of bits involved, and other factors. The principles and coding of these algorithms can be found in almost any software text on microprocessors. For specific routines in this text, the subroutines used are discussed in Appendix B and described briefly below.

Multiplication.   Software multiplication routines generally involve the elementary operations of shifting and adding performed just the same as when decimal numbers are multiplied by hand. In binary the process is somewhat more elementary because there are only two digits per state. In essence, a common algorithm then operates exactly like the following sequence for multiplying two binary numbers:

$$
\begin{array}{r}
1011 \\
\times \quad 1110 \\
\hline
0000 \\
1011 \\
1011 \\
1011 \\
\hline
10011010
\end{array}
$$

Notice that the multiplication of two 4-bit numbers ended up with an 8-bit result. It could have been less, of course, but in general the result *may* require twice as many bits as the numbers multiplied.

There are many different ways by which the operations required in the multiplication can be coded. Each has its special advantages. You can see, however, that the basic operations are shifting of the multiplicand and addition of it or zeros to the answer depending on the bit of the multiplier.

For the purposes of demonstration in this text, a subroutine is presented in Appendix B that multiplies two 8-bit numbers and gets a 16-bit number as a result. The code for this algorithm in 8080 mnemonics and a flowchart of the operations are presented in Appendix B. The subroutine is called MULT8. As written in 8080 instructions, the routine returns the answer in the HL 16-bit register pair.

Division.   Division, like multiplication, is often programmed to follow an algorithm much like the "division by hand" that a human would perform. There are many algorithms and many ways to code these algorithms. For the purposes of this text, the routine given in Appendix B will be used. This routine divides a 16-bit number by an 8-bit number and gives a 16-bit result. The flowchart and 8080 code for the algorithm are given in Appendix B. The subroutine is called DIV16.

Constant Multiplication and Division.   To multiply and/or divide a constant and some number, one can use MULT8 and DIV16. In many cases it is easier and faster to perform constant operations by specific routines for the specific constant. This is done using the fact that a right shift divides by 2 and a left shift multiplies by 2. Thus, if it necessary to multiply a number by 2.75:

$$\text{ANSWER} = 2.75 * (\text{NUMBER})$$

Whereas one could use MULT8 with proper adjustment for the fractional part, it would be easier to write

$$\text{ANSWER} = 2 * (\text{NUMBER}) + \frac{\text{NUMBER}}{2} + \frac{\text{NUMBER}}{4}$$

Then this multiplication would be programmed by the operations

ANSWER = (left shift of NUMBER) + (right shift of NUMBER) + (right shift NUMBER twice)

Of course, one would have to be careful that NUMBER did not contain a 1 in the MSB, which would be lost by the left shift.

Hardware Math.   When the multiply and divide operations carried out by software are too slow, it is possible to use special hardware that performs these operations on numbers passed by the micoprocessor. Actually, these units are simply dedicated computers that have been programmed for only the required functions, such as multiplication. Thus the routines are very efficient and much faster than software operations in the microprocessor.

4-4.2 Sampled Data Systems

We have seen that by using analog-to-digital conversion of the physical data, information is lost about the continuous variation of this variable. This discreteness of value knowledge has important consequences on the control system, as will be seen in Ch. 5. It was pointed out earlier that there is also a discreteness about knowledge of the variable in time, since the values are only available when "sampled" and input by the computer. This also can have important consequences on the control system.

The sampling of values of the controlled variable is a necessary part of a digital control system and not just an arbitrary choice of the design. One reason is the finite length of time taken by the DAS to acquire and convert a value of the analog data to digital. Another is the fact that, while computations are being made to determine a feedback for control, the computer can clearly not be inputting new data. Finally, in many cases even microprocessor-based computers will be performing other functions within the same time period, perhaps even controlling other variables in the system.

Sampling Interval.   The primary question to be asked and answered in setting up a microprocessor-based control system is the time interval, T_s, between samples of the controlled variable. This is sometimes expressed by the equivalent concept of *sampling frequency*, which is just 1 over the sampling period, $f_s = 1/T_s$. Con-

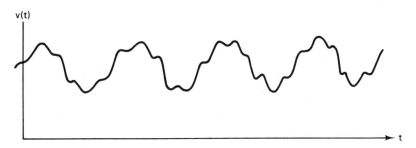

FIG. 4-8 This analog data signal shows the continuous variation of some variable in time.

straints will be placed on the *minimum* sampling interval (maximum frequency) owing to the data acquisition and conversion time and the time the computer must spend on other tasks. There are other constraints on the *maximum* sampling time (minimum frequency) based on the accuracy by which the samples reflect the time variation of the variable.

The general rule of thumb is to use the *shortest possible* sampling interval, which is the same as the highest possible sampling frequency.

Minimum Frequency Constraints.   Determination of the minimum frequency of sampling in a system involves complicated considerations of the Fourier transform of the sampled signal. Fortunately, it is possible to visualize the concepts by reference to some simple considerations. Simply put, the samples must be close enough together in time to faithfully reconstruct the variations of the signal. Consider the time-varying signal of Fig. 4-8 as the basis for illustrating sampling frequency effects. Remember that the only information the computer has about the time variation of the signal is provided by the samples. In essence, the computer must interpolate between samples to deduce variation between samples.

Figure 4-9 illustrates a case where samples are taken at a very high frequency. Each sample is joined by simple, straight line segments. Notice that the sampled version of the signal retains all the variation of the original signal.

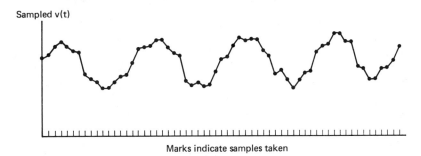

Marks indicate samples taken

FIG. 4-9 For a high sample rate, the computer would have nearly perfect information about signal variation.

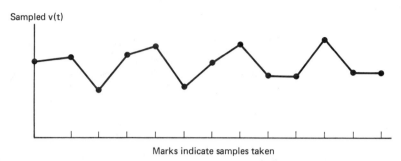

Marks indicate samples taken

FIG. 4-10   Notice that with the larger sample time the detailed information begins to disappear.

In Fig. 4-10 the sampling frequency has been decreased, and therefore the time between samples is correspondingly increased. Notice that certain variation of the signal is *lost* since it occurs between samples. Simply put, the samples are no longer a faithful reproduction of the original signal.

Figure 4-11 illustrates a particularly dangerous effect that may occur in some cases. Here you can see that not only has time variation information about the signal been lost, but another, lower-frequency variation of the signal is now falsely implied by the data. This is called *aliasing* and the false frequency is called the *alias frequency*. This can be dangerous because the control system will now go to work trying to feed back a signal to eliminate this oscillation, which does not really exist. In doing so, it may actually *create* oscillating instability in the system.

In general, then, you can see why selection of the highest practical sampling frequency is important.

Sampling Rate Determination.   Actual determination of the minimum frequency and thus the required sampling rate depends on knowledge of the time variation of the signal. If the Fourier transform is known, the maximum frequency content of the signal is also known. If not, as is usually the case, the maximum frequency must be estimated by examination of worst-case conditions. A sampling *theory* developed by Shannon and Nyquist tells us that the minimum sampling frequency

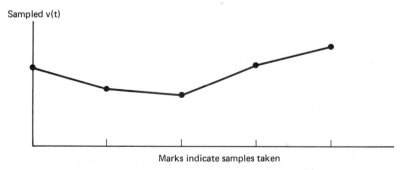

Marks indicate samples taken

FIG. 4-11   With a very low sample rate, the sampled data signal does not look anything like the actual data. Note the false variation.

for reconstruction of the signal from the samples is given by the *Nyquist rate*, which is simply twice the highest signal frequency:

$$f_{smin} = 2f_{max} \qquad (4\text{-}5)$$

where f_{smin} = minimum sampling frequency
$\quad\ f_{max}$ = maximum signal frequency.

Now the *practical* selection of sampling rate is quite a different matter. First, Eq. (4-5) was developed under the assumption of a continuous, periodic signal. The relation really says that if many, many samples are taken over many cycles of the signal, then reconstruction is possible at that rate. This is not the case in practical control problems, however. The signals are not present for long periods of time, and it is desirable that the control system have reliable information about signal variation with only a few samples. For these reasons, and remembering that Eq. (4-5) is a *minimum*, a general guide is that the sample frequency should be 10 times the maximum signal frequency:

$$f_s = 10f_{max} \qquad (4\text{-}6)$$

where f_s = practical estimated sample frequency. Using this sampling rate gives 10 samples within one period of the highest frequency variation of the signal and thereby some confidence that the signal can be reconstructed. It is important to remember that Eq. (4-6) is only a general guide, and that lower sampling rates could very well give adequate control in many circumstances.

Often the maximum signal frequency can be fixed by passing the signal through a low-pass filter with a cutoff frequency of f_{max}. In this case the cutoff frequency has been selected to be higher than any frequency for which the response of the control system would be important.

EXAMPLE 4-8   Given the typical pressure signal of Fig. 4-12, estimate the maximum signal frequency and the minimum sampling frequency.

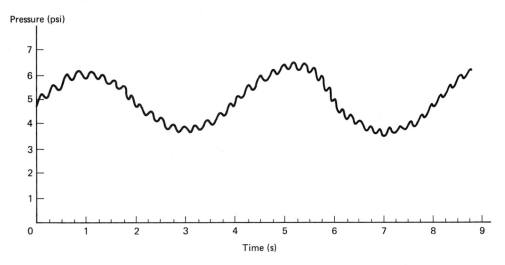

FIG. 4-12   Time variation for Ex. 4-8.

Solution: There is clearly a long period variation with a period of about 4 s. In addition, however, there are periodic oscillations with periods of about 0.2 s. Thus the maximum signal frequency is $f_{max} = 1/0.2 = 5$ Hz. Then, according to the Nyquist rate, the minimum sampling frequency is given by Eq. (4-5), $f_{smin} = 10$ Hz, or a sample every 0.1 s. This would give only two samples for every cycle of the higher-frequency variation. The practical guide of Eq. (4-6) suggests a sampling rate of $f_s = 50$ Hz or a sample every 0.02 s. So the computer must service the input routine every 20 ms, meaning that all computations must be completed in this time period. If we figure an average of $10\mu s$ per instruction, this is 2000 instructions, which is very likely plenty for a control system.

Maximum Frequency Constraints.   The maximum frequency of sampling is dependent mainly on the conversion rate and the rate at which the computer can service the input process. Obviously, the sampling period cannot be *faster* than the time required by the DAS to acquire and convert a signal. So that's one constraint. The other is an estimate of how much time the computer will spend on execution of instructions to provide for the control algorithm. This is a bit more difficult to answer. The best solution is to program the entire control system from input of the controlled variable to output of the controlling variable and see how much time is required. This time, plus the data-acquisition time, is the new shortest time between samples. Then there must be consideration of any other activities the computer must perform, such as servicing other loops.

One simply hopes that the required minimum frequency and the constrained maximum frequency do not disagree!

EXAMPLE 4-9   Temperature data will be sampled from five locations in a process. An 8080-based microcomputer will execute a control algorithm for each location to control temperature. The DAS requires a maximum of 100 μs to acquire and convert a temperature channel. Approximately 250 instructions are executed during the control algorithm for each channel. Estimate the maximum sampling frequency. From this, estimate the maximum frequency variation of the temperature signal that will be detectable.

Solution: To do this, let's assume a channel has just been sampled and determine how long it will be before the channel can be sampled again. This means the instructions will be $5(250) = 1250$ instructions. A common 8080 instruction requires 10 states at about 0.5 μs per state. Thus the instructions require a time of $(1250)(10)(0.5 \mu s) = 6250 \mu s$. There will be four other channels acquired for a time of $4(100) = 400 \mu s$. Thus the total time before the channel selection can occur again is 6650 μs. The inverse of this gives the maximum sampling frequency:

$$f_s = 160 \text{ Hz}$$

The maximum tolerable frequency variation of the temperature signal is given if this sample frequency is assumed to be 10 times the signal frequency as in Eq. (4-6). Then $f_{max} = 16$ Hz. Since time constants for temperature are generally in seconds, this probably presents no problems for reliable information about the temperature signals.

4-4.3   Linearization

It was pointed out in Ch. 1 that a linear relationship between the measured indication of a process variable and that variable itself is very important to providing a control

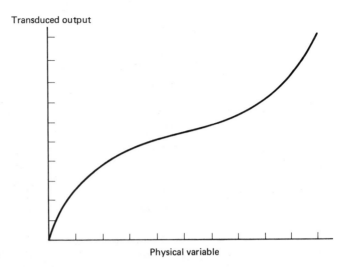

FIG. 4-13 This shows a very nonlinear transduction of a physical variable into an analog output signal.

system. It is unfortunate that many transducers used for measurement are *nonlinear* in their response. This means that the analog voltage presented to the DAS, although varying smoothly and continuously with the physical variable, varies in a nonlinear fashion. The output of the ADC will be linear with respect to the voltage and therefore will also be nonlinear with respect to the physical variable.

As an illustration of this, consider the relationship of Fig. 4-13. This shows a transducer transfer function whose output is nonlinear with respect to the variable input. You can see that this means that equal *changes* of voltage do *not* represent the equal changes of the variable. Now, after conversion to a binary number, a plot can be constructed of the binary number versus the physical variable. This is shown in Fig. 4-14. Notice that the nonlinearity is still present. This graph shows that changes of the binary by one LSB do *not* represent the same changes of the physical variable.

Why is this a problem? The control algorithm bases its feedback on the amount of change of the physical variable. The control may say, "If the variable changes by

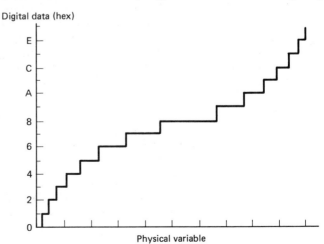

FIG. 4-14 When the analog signal is converted into digital, the digital signal shows the same nonlinearity with the physical variable.

1% of the range, then change the feedback by 2% of its range." Now, if the binary number is the only knowledge of the variable value, you can see that a change of 1% of the physical variable does not produce the same change in the binary number over the range. So the problem is how to determine what change in the binary *represents* a 1% change of the physical variable.

As a human this does not seem like much of a problem. You might say, "Given a change in the binary number, just look at the graph and figure out how much change in the physical variable has occurred." This is easy for a human but virtually impossible in an analog electronic control system. When the computer is used, a method analogous to "looking at the graph" can be used; it is called *linearization*. In essence, a mathematical process is used to convert the input binary to another binary number that *is* linear with respect to the physical variable. Two basic methods of providing linearization are discussed next.

Equation Inversion.   In some cases it is possible to perform the linearization by a mathematical process in the computer. These cases occur when the relation between the input and output of the transducer, although nonlinear, can be easily inverted. This method can be defined symbolically by the following construction. Suppose voltage input to a DAS is related to the physical variable by an equation of the form

$$V = f(v) \qquad\qquad (4\text{-}7)$$

In principle, this equation can always be inverted to find the value of the physical variable from the voltage:

$$v = g(V) \qquad\qquad (4\text{-}8)$$

where $g(V)$ = the inverse equation of $f(v)$. A common example of equations and inverses is the exponential and natural logarithm, where, for example, if $V = 5e^{2v}$, then $v = \text{In}\ (V/5)/2$.

This same process can be carried out in the computer using the digital signal that is input from the voltage. Since the binary number and voltage are linearly related, the same kind of inversion process can be used. The only problem is that coding transcendental equations like exponentials and logarithms is quite complicated and computer time costly. Given the constraints on time imposed by sampling, it is best to avoid long computational routines. Thus, except for simple cases, other methods of linearization are often more practical. Example 4-10 illustrates how equation inversion linearization can be used.

EXAMPLE 4-10   A transducer produces a nonlinear voltage as a function of pressure. After signal conditioning, the ADC input voltage varies from 0 to 5 V as the pressure varies from 0 to 100 psi, and is given by

$$V = 0.5\sqrt{P}$$

The ADC produces an output varying from 00H to FFH as the voltage varies from 0 to 5 V. Find the equation that will produce a 1-byte digital number that is linear with pressure and for which 00H corresponds to 0 psi and FFH corresponds to 100 psi.

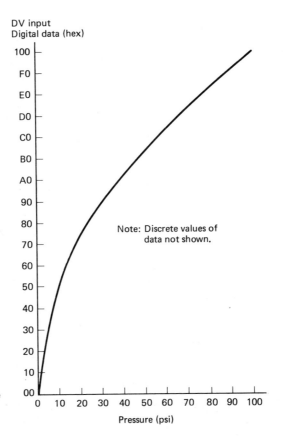

DV input
Digital data (hex)

Note: Discrete values of data not shown.

Pressure (psi)

FIG. 4-15 This graph shows the digital signal resulting from the transducer of Ex. 4-10.

Solution: This is simply a question of squaring the digital ADC output and then finding the appropriate scale factor. Let *DV* be the digitized voltage. This varies from 00H to FFH as the pressure varies from 0 to 100 psi, except that the variation is as the square root of the pressure, as shown roughly in Fig. 4-15. Let's simply square this number. Then $(DV)^2$ will be *linear* with respect to pressure, but the range is wrong. $(DV)^2$ will vary from 0 to $(FFH)^2$ = FE01H, not 0 to FFH as required. So a scale adjustment is necessary. In this case the scale adjustment is simply dividing by FFH. You can see this because when *DV* = FFH (100 psi) we want the output to be FFH, so if *DP* is the pressure digital signal,

$$DP = \frac{(DV)^2}{FFH}$$

and when *DV* = FFH, *DP* = (FFH)(FFH)/FFH = FFH as required. The solution is to program a routine that multiplies the input by itself, which produces a 16-bit number, and then divide this by FFH. The flowchart for doing this using the subroutines MULT8 and DIV16 is shown in Fig. 4-16. Note that of the 16-bit result returned by DIV16 only the lower 8 bits will have the answer since, as shown previously, *DP* can never exceed FFH. Thus moving E into A puts *DP* into A. Figure 4-17 shows a plot of *DP* versus pressure.

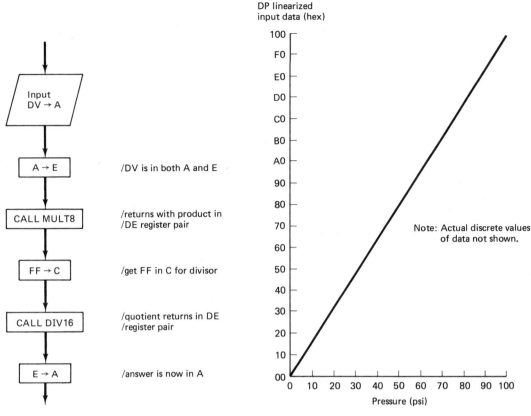

FIG. 4-16 Subroutines MULT8 and DIV16 can be used to linearize the measurement in Ex. 4-10.

FIG. 4-17 After linearization the digital data varies linearly with pressure.

Tables. A second method of linearization is more like the kind of linearization that a human uses when a graph of input versus output is available. In this case the graph is stored as a table of digital input versus physical variable. A program simply "looks up" the input binary number and thus finds the correct value of the physical variable, in binary form of course. In general, this method turns out to be faster and easier to code than equation inversion and is often used even when such an equation is available.

One of the first questions to be addressed when using this method is how many table entries to use. The longer the table is, the more memory required and the more time it takes to search the table for the correct values. Of course, the more values in the table, the more accurate the linearization will be. This conflict can be compromised by using a table without an excessive number of entries and then *interpolating* between the table values.

Interpolation. One common method of interpolation simply draws a straight line between two points on a graph and calculates a value in between as if the straight line were the actual curve. If the points (table values) are not too far apart, good accuracy can be achieved. The idea is illustrated by Fig. 4-18. The solid line represents

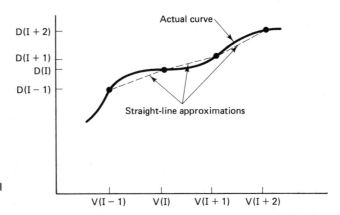

FIG. 4-18 The table in computer memory will contain pairs of digital data, $D(I)$, and variable $V(I)$.

the actual nonlinear variation of D with v, and the dots the values used for the table. Suppose the value of v is desired for some input, D, which lies between two table entries. Then using linear interpolation this value is found, assuming a straight line between the points, as shown. There is some error from the actual value, but this will be small if the table points are sufficiently close together. Even greater accuracy in interpolation can be obtained if curved lines are used as estimators between table values instead of straight lines. We will consider only linear interpolation in detail.

Linear Interpolation. Linear interpolation is performed by assuming a straight line joins two consecutive table points, as illustrated in Fig. 4-18. This line allows the calculation of an estimated value for inputs that lie between table entries.

To define the relationship, assume an input, DIN, varies in a nonlinear fashion with the physical variable being measured. Stored in memory is a table of values of DIN and the corresponding values of the physical variable. The values of DIN are denoted by $D(I)$, and the corresponding values of the physical variable by $V(I)$, where I identifies the location of the pair in the table, as shown in Fig. 4-19. Note that there

TABLE ENTRY NUMBER		DIGITAL INPUT DATA (HEX)		VARIABLE DATA (HEX)
1		D(1)		V(1)
.		.		.
.		.		.
.		.		.
I−1		D(I−1)		V(I−1)
I		D(I)		V(I)
I+1	DIN →	D(I+1)	VIN →	V(I+1)
.		.		.
.		.		.
N		D(N)		V(N)

FIG. 4-19 This shows how the table is structured. In this case a measurement, DIN, falls between $D(I)$ and $D(I + 1)$. Then the variable, VIN, will fall between $V(I)$ and $V(I + 1)$.

131

are N total entries in the table. The values making up the table may be taken from a graph, product specifications, or an equation. Suppose an input is taken and the value, DIN, is found to lie *between* $D(I)$ and $D(I + 1)$. This means that the value of the variable, VIN, lies between $V(I)$ and $V(I + 1)$. The following linear interpolation formula allows the value of VIN to be calculated:

$$\text{VIN} = V(I) + \frac{V(I + 1) - V(I)}{D(I + 1) - D(I)} [\text{DIN} - D(I)] \qquad (4\text{-}9)$$

The table of values can be set up so that the result, VIN, is scaled to vary over the range 00H to FFH as the variable changes over the control range, or to be the binary value of the variable itself.

Generally, a subroutine is written that takes the input value and outputs the linearized number back to the calling program. An example of this, with the flow-chart, is shown in Appendix B. This routine is called INTRP. The subroutine requires input consisting of the starting address of the table, the number of table entries, and the input data. Error conditions are returned if the input lies outside the range of the table. Of course, if the entire range of 00H to FFH is employed, such an error cannot occur.

EXAMPLE 4-11   Show how the problem of Ex. 4-10 would be solved using the table linearization method. Assume the table will use 17 entries, including 0. The pressure is to be linearly represented by 00H to FFH for the full range of 0 to 100 psi. So each bit of the linearized VIN will represent $100/256 = 0.391$ psi.

Solution: First, let's follow through the logic of the process to see just what the linearization is supposed to accomplish. Some pressure, p, is converted nonlinearly to a voltage according to $0.5\sqrt{p}$. This voltage varies from 0 to 5 V as the pressure varies from 0 to 100 psi. The voltage is converted into an 8-bit digital word, DIN, which varies from 00H to FFH linearly with respect to the voltage, but nonlinearly with respect to the pressure. We need a table and interpolation such that the input word, DIN, can be looked up in the table and converted into the pressure it represents, scaled so that FFH is 100 psi, VIN. To do this, let's first construct a table of pressure, voltage, converted digital word, and required linear digital word. This is shown in Table 4-1. The table entries were computed as follows:

Pressure: To have 17 entries from 0 to 100 psi means $100/16 = 6.25$ psi per entry.
Voltage: This was calculated from the equation voltage = $0.5\sqrt{P}$.
$\quad D(I)$:   These are the digital words resulting from analog-to-digital conversion of the voltages, with a 5-V reference.
$\quad\quad I$:   This simply counts the table entry.
$\quad V(I)$:   The desired, linear pressure signal is simply found by breaking 00H to FFH into 16 equal increments. In equation form this means that

$$V(I) = \left(\frac{p}{100}\right) 256 \quad \text{converted to hex}$$

In the computer, only $D(I)$ and $V(I)$ appear as the table entries. To see how this works, let's find values of VIN for two inputs.

TABLE 4-1

Pressure	Voltage	D(I)	I	V(I)
0	0	0	1	0
6.25	1.25	40	2	10
12.5	1.76777	5A	3	20
18.75	2.16506	6E	4	30
25	2.5	80	5	40
31.25	2.79509	8F	6	50
37.5	3.06186	9C	7	60
43.75	3.30719	A9	8	70
50	3.53553	B5	9	80
56.25	3.75	C0	10	90
62.5	3.95285	CA	11	A0
68.75	4.14578	D4	12	B0
75	4.33013	DD	13	C0
81.25	4.50694	E6	14	D0
87.5	4.67707	EF	15	E0
93.75	4.84123	F7	16	F0
100	5	100	17	100

Case 1: $p = 20$ psi. This will result in a voltage of $0.5\sqrt{20} = 2.236$ V and a DIN of 72H. From the tables, 72H lies between 6EH ($I = 4$) and 80H ($I = 5$), with corresponding values of $V(4) = 30H$ and $V(5) = 40H$. Thus we know VIN will lie between 30H and 40H. The interpolation formula will give a more accurate value.

(All numbers in hex)

$$VIN = 30 + \frac{40 - 30}{80 - 6E}\,(72 - 6E) = 30 + \frac{(10)(04)}{12}$$

$$= 33H$$

So the interpolation routine predicts a VIN of 33H for a pressure of 20 psi. This can be checked against the value computed directly:

$$\tfrac{20}{100}256 = 51.2$$

This converts to 33H, ignoring the fractional part. One cannot always expect such close agreement between the linearly interpolated value and the exact value.

Case 2: $p = 78$ psi, voltage $= 4.4159$ V or DIN equal to E2H. This value of DIN lies between DDH at $I = 13$ and E6H at $I = 14$. The corresponding values are $V(13) = C0H$ and $V(14) = D0H$. So we know VIN lies between C0H and D0H.

(All numbers in hex)

$$VIN = C0 + \frac{C0 - D0}{E6 - DD}\,(E2 - DD) = C0 + \frac{(10)(05)}{09}$$

$$= C8$$

So the VIN will be C8H. Let's see what a direct computation gives:

$$(\tfrac{78}{100})256 = 199.68$$

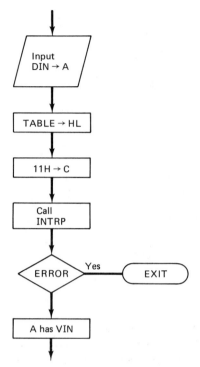

FIG. 4-20 This is the flowchart for Ex. 4-11.

This converts to C7H if truncated or C8H if rounded. Thus in this case there is an error of up to one LSB or about 0.39 psi. Figure 4-20 shows the flowchart to perform the linearization using INTRP. The input is loaded into the A register, the number of table entries (17_{10} = 11H) is loaded into the C register, and the table address (TABLE) is loaded into the HL register pair.

PROBLEMS

4-1 Construct the detailed flowchart and 8080 code to input data from the hardware system developed in Ex. 3-12.

4-2 A special data input sequence occurs as follows:

(1) Sample–hold to SAMPLE by sending b_1 low to port B3H.

(2) Wait 100 μs.

(3) Sample–hold to HOLD by sending b_1 high to port B3H.

(4) Start ADC by sending b_3 of port B3H high (b_1 must be kept high).

(5) Wait for DATA READY, indicated by b_4 of port B3H taken high by ADC. Error if wait is more than 100 μs.

(6) Input data from port B4H.

(7) Output data to mass storage by sending to port 10H.

(8) Go back to step (1).

Prepare a detailed flowchart of this process, and write the 8080 code.

4-3 Repeat Prob. 4-2 if a 6800 is used with the status on the same bits but at E000H, data input at F000H, and mass storage at FF00H.

4-4 A 16-bit ADC is started by b_0 of port 05 going high. Bit 7 of port 05 taken high indicates conversion complete. Data will be read with port 06 for the high-order byte and port 07 for the low-order byte. Write the 8080 code to start the ADC, input the data, and place it into the HL register.

4-5 Develop modifications of Ex. 4-4 so that if the timer finishes with no data interrupt an ERROR jump occurs. Also include a method of exiting the loop after the interrupt occurs.

4-6 Find the functional relation, like Eq. (4-3), between temperature and digital data for Ex. 3-12. If T is 47°C, what is the digital data word? If the digital data word is B3H, what is the temperature?

4-7 Revolutions per minute are converted linearly to a digital signal such that the range 1600 to 2200 rpm becomes 00 to FFH. Find the bias, range, and functional relation.

4-8 Displacement from 20 to 50 mm must be measured to within 0.008 mm. How many bits must the ADC have? Find the functional relation between displacement and the digital word, assuming that 20 mm produces a zero digital number.

4-9 The set point of Prob. 4-6 is 55°C. Write the 6800 instructions to find the error if the digital temperature is in the B accumulator. Find the error for temperatures of 31° and 79°C.

4-10 Develop 8080 mnemonics to find the error in Prob. 4-7, if the set point is 1950 rpm.

4-11 Use the floating-point system of Sec. 4-3.3 and Fig. 4-3 to express the following numbers, as they would appear in the floating-point words: **(a)** 2,256,000; **(b)** $-47,100$; **(c)** 0.00000502178.

4-12 Consider the problem 52171000 + 21010. Express these numbers in the floating-point format, as in Prob. 4.11. Show, by hand, what operations are necessary to perform this addition in floating point. (*Hint:* To add the mantissas, the exponents must be the same.)

4-13 Show how shifting and adding would perform the following constant operations of a number called DATA: **(a)** 5.113 * DATA; **(b)** 3.87 * DATA; **(c)** DATA/45.

4-14 A light level signal varies as shown in Fig. 4-21. Determine the proper sampling frequency to avoid sampling errors.

4-15 A system has eight variables to be measured, each of which has a maximum variation frequency of 75 Hz. A 16-bit ADC is to be used for conversion, with a conversion time of 80μs. The control algorithm requires 52 instructions to process each channel, and each instruction averages 8 μs. Determine if it will be possible to control all eight variables with one computer and still satisfy sampling rate restrictions.

4-16 A resistive transducer varies linearly from 100 to 200 Ω as force varies from 50 to 100 lb. A divider is used to convert the resistance, R_F, to voltage as

$$V = \frac{1000}{100 + R_F}$$

An ADC with a 5-V reference converts this voltage to a digital signal. Devise the software that will convert the input, DV, into a digital word that varies linearly from 00 to FFH as the force varies from 50 to 100 lb.

4-17 The thermistor of Fig. 2-6 will be used to measure temperature from 30° to 90°C. Signal

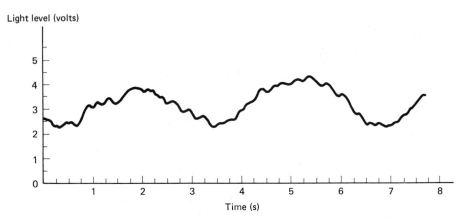

FIG. 4-21   Time signal for Prob. 4-14.

conditioning linearly converts the resistance over this temperature range to 00 to FFH. Devise a table linearization procedure such that the temperature (not resistance) from 30° to 90°C is linearly indicated by 00 to FFH.

(a) Construct a 16-term table of temperature (T), resistance (R), digitized resistance (DR), and digital temperature (DT). Thus DT varies linearly from 00 to FFH as T varies from 30° to 90°C.

(b) Write an 8080 subroutine, using INTRP, that starts with DR in the A register and returns with DT in the A register.

4-18 Construct a linearization table for light intensity measurement from 4 to 12 W/m², using the transducer with a transfer function given by Fig. 2-12. The transducer is used in the circuit of Fig. 4-22. The result of the linearization should be a digital signal that varies linearly from 00 to FFH as the light level varies from 4 to 12 W/m².

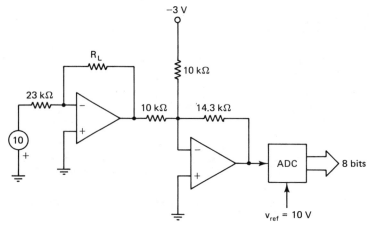

FIG. 4-22   Circuit for Prob. 4-18.

CHAPTER 5

DISCRETE-STATE CONTROL SYSTEMS

OBJECTIVES

The primary objective of this chapter is to study discrete-state systems and learn how microprocessor-based computers can be used for the control of such systems. This primary objective is accomplished by means of several secondary objectives. After studying this chapter and solving the problems at the end of the chapter, you will be able to:

1. Explain the difference between the two-state and sequential discrete systems.
2. Give an example of a noninteractive two-state system and how a computer can be used to provide control.
3. Explain the nature of an interactive two-state system, give an example of such a system, and show how a computer provides the control function.
4. Explain the difference between function-sequence and time-sequence types of sequential control systems.
5. Use an example to show how a computer can be used to provide functional sequence control.
6. Give an example of a time-sequence control process and two ways it can be accomplished using a computer.
7. Explain how a programmable controller can be used to provide discrete-state control.
8. Design the application of a computer to satisfy the control specifications of a discrete-state system.

5-1   INTRODUCTION

Control systems are used in a great range of applications in the modern world, from household appliances to the most sophisticated guided missile systems. Computers, and particularly microprocessor-based computers, are being applied in ever increasing numbers to all these areas of control. In this chapter a specialized type of control system will be studied for which all control inputs and outputs can be expressed in one of two conditions, ON or OFF. The use of computers to provide control for these types of systems will be studied. The two-value nature of the variables in such systems makes interface to the computer particularly simple, but the control operations can still become quite complex.

Discrete-State Systems.   A discrete-state system is one for which at every instant of time the *state* of the *system* is defined by the values of a set of variables, each of which can only be defined to be in one of two conditions or states. The variables themselves may be continuous in value, but insofar as the control system is concerned, their values are only required to be known relative to two states. A simple example would be in temperature control. Suppose an oven is set for 350°F. The temperature will vary continuously and smoothly over a large range, but our *description* need only be that it is "high" ($T > 350°F$) or "low" ($T < 350°F$). Thus the temperature has been defined to be in one of two conditions. The overall state of the oven may be described by defining other important two-state variables, such as door open or closed, fan on or off, light on or off. Thus the entire state of the oven is specified by discrete variables, even the temperature. This is a discrete-state system.

Discrete-State Control.   Two distinct types of control strategies are associated with discrete-state systems. One type is used to control the *value* of one or more variables in the system. This is control in the traditional definition, which has constituted most of the considerations of this text. The second type of control is *sequential* in nature and refers to the progress of the system through a defined set of discrete states, in time, to accomplish some overall objective. A sequential control system sets up each individual state of the system in a sequence depending on previous states of the system and time. In general, a discrete-state control system may involve both value control and sequential control. In an automatic oven, for example, the following sequence and associated value controls could be involved:

To Bake:

		Door	Heater	Light	Fan
State 1:	*Preheat*	CLOSED	ON	OFF	OFF
State 2:	*Loading*	OPEN	ON	ON	OFF
State 3:	*Baking*	CLOSED	ON	OFF	ON
State 3:	*Cool down*	CLOSED	OFF	OFF	ON
State 4:	*Unload*	OPEN	OFF	ON	OFF

A sequential control system will automatically step the oven system through these discrete states. A value control system will be required in state 3 to maintain the temperature within some limit of the set point. Either a continuous state or discrete-state value control system could be used for this purpose.

5-2 TWO-STATE CONTROL SYSTEMS

In this section the value control problem of discrete-state systems will be considered. We will be studying only discrete-value, ON/OFF control systems such as were introduced in Ch. 1.

5-2.1   Noninteractive Variables

In many cases a control system contains a number of variables under control that are independent of each other. These are referred to as noninteracting variables. Control operations in these instances are easier because the measurement, evaluation, and feedback procedure can go on for each variable without worrying about affecting the values of the other variables.

Single Variable.   In the simplest type of discrete-state control system there is only one input variable, with two possible states, and one output variable, also with two states. The control algorithm is based on a determination of the state of the input and using this to deduce the proper output state. In its simplest form, this can be written as

$$S_{out} = \begin{cases} ON & V_{in} > V_{sp} \\ OFF & V_{in} < V_{sp} \end{cases} \tag{5-1}$$

where S_{out} = output (feedback)
    V_{in} = intput (measurement)
    V_{sp} = limit value (set point)
ON/OFF = two possible output states.
Notice that the input variable may actually be continuous. The discrete nature of the system is based on two facts, (1) that we are only interested in the value of the input variable relative to a limit, and (2) that the output can only have two states. Of course, in some systems the input is inherently discrete in that it is only able to have two states, such as a limit switch on some machine being either on or off.

Hysteresis and Oscillation.   It was pointed out in Ch. 1 that the application of ON/OFF control to systems with a continuous controlled variable have two important practical conditions and consequences:

1. Such systems will usually always require a *deadband* or *hysteresis* about the set

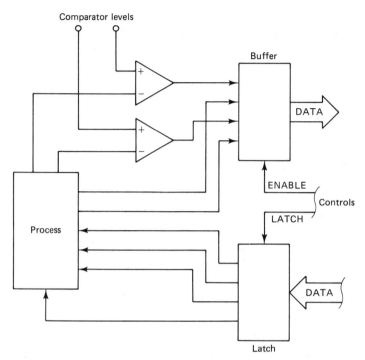

FIG. 5-1 Discrete-state systems usually require input and output of digital data.

point to prevent rapid fluctuations of the output when the input is near the set point.

2. Such systems will usually always exhibit an *oscillation* of the controlled variable within the deadband. The period of this oscillation increases with decreasing deadband width.

Multiple Variable.   Use of the computer for ON/OFF control would clearly be impractical for a single variable. For example, it would be difficult to justify using a microprocessor-based computer to turn on and off the compressor of a refrigerator. However, when there are many such independent, single variables to control in a system, it may be practical to use a computer. In such a case the control system would have a hardware configuration like that shown in Fig. 5-1. Note that the comparators are used to convert continuous variables into a two-state input, while inherently discrete variables are input directly after conversion to proper digital signals. A tristate buffer is used for interface. The output uses a latch to provide updated ON/OFF state information to the output.

The software consists of a series of decision blocks, as shown in Fig. 5-2, that evaluate the input states and update the output state. Any required hysteresis can be provided by *hysteresis* comparators, as described in Ch. 3, or by *timing loops* in the

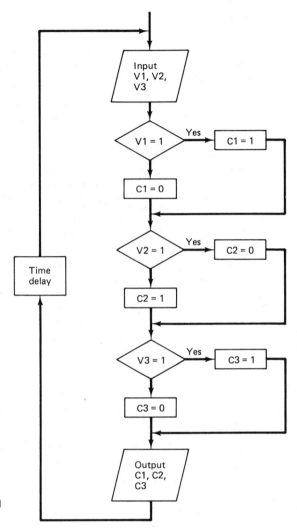

FIG. 5-2 A noninteractive discrete-state system has a flowchart consisting of individual tests and sets.

software that prevent output state changes from occurring too rapidly. Example 5-1 has been designed to illustrate many of the considerations necessary in the development of a single-variable discrete control system.

EXAMPLE 5-1   The discrete-state system shown in Fig. 5-3 controls pressure (P), temperature (T), and level (L). There are five discrete controlling outputs: input valve (VIN), output valve (VOUT), vent valve (VEN), compressor (COM), and cooler (COL). There are four discrete-state inputs provided by comparators, as shown in Fig. 5-3: temperature (T), pressure (P), critical pressure (PCR), and level (L). The following chart shows the required relationships:

Variable State	Output State		Update Time
$T = 1\ (T < TSP)$	Cooler OFF	(COL = 0)	3 min
$P = 1\ (P > PSP)$	Compressor OFF	(COM = 0)	2 min
$PCR = 1\ (P > PCRIT)$	VEN OPEN	(VEN = 0)	No delay
$L = 0\ (L < LSP)$	VIN OPEN	(VIN = 0)	2 min
	VOUT CLOSED	(VOUT = 1)	
$L = 1\ (L > LSP)$	VIN CLOSED	(VIN = 1)	2 min
	VOUT OPEN	(VOUT = 0)	

TSP is the temperature set point, *PSP* is the pressure set point, *PCRIT* is a high-pressure limit, and *LSP* is the level set point. Develop the hardware and software flowchart to provide this control, assuming an 8080-based system.

Solution: This problem can be solved by noting the relationship between the input variable states and the outputs. From the chart it is obvious that COL = $\overline{T}$, COM = $\overline{P}$, VEN = $\overline{PCR}$, VIN = $\overline{L}$, and VOUT = L. So an update of the outputs requires inputting the variables and outputting according to these relations. The general flowchart for this is shown in Fig. 5-4. Before constructing details of the software, it will be necessary to specify the hardware configuration.

Hardware.   First, time delays of 2 and 3 min are very awkward to provide using software delay loops. For this reason a 1-Hz clock will be used to drive two 8-bit binary

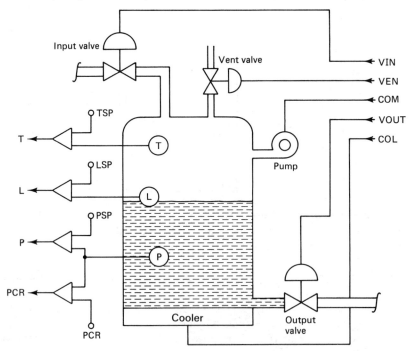

FIG. 5-3 This discrete-state system will be used for Ex. 5-1.

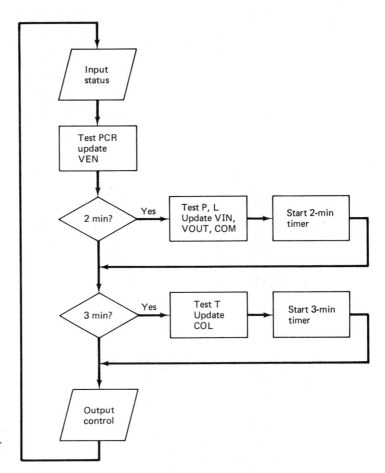

FIG. 5-4 General flowchart for Ex. 5-1 control.

counters. Two minutes will be a count of 120 or 78H, and 3 minutes will be 180 or B4H. Gates will be used to decode these count states to set F/Fs. The computer will read the F/Fs to determine when time is up and then reset them for a new time delay. Input and output of the data, controls, time state, and time reset can be handled with a single port address. After much consideration and trials, the hardware system of Fig. 5-5 emerges. An address of 04 has been chosen for the I/O port. $\overline{I/OR}$ and $\overline{I/OW}$ distinguish between input and output. The assignment of bits to inputs and outputs was made arbitrarily.

Software.   The basic plan of the software is based on the fact that an exclusive-or of 1 with a binary number will result in the complement of that number. This concept is used to change an input bit, for example *T*, into its complement, which can be used for COL. The only exception to this is VIN, which is equal to *L* and is therefore not to be complemented. Of course, the update of an output does not even occur unless the timer has timed out as indicated by the time inputs. There are many ways to code a problem such as this. Figure 5-6 shows a solution in detailed flowchart form. Extensive use is made of AND operations to mask off bits, OR operations to combine bits, and exclusive-or (XOR) operations to complement and isolate.

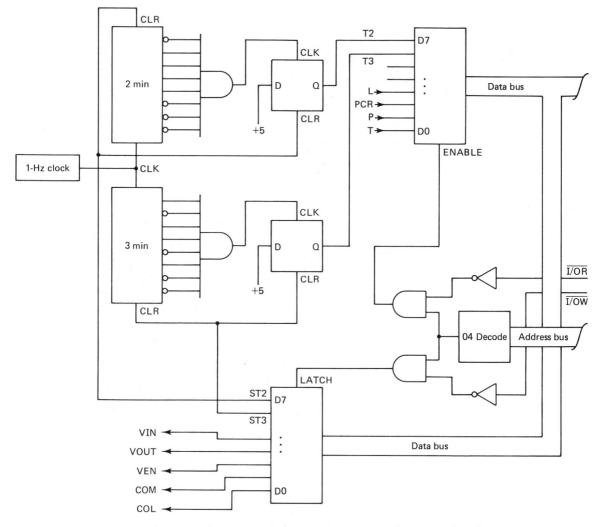

FIG. 5-5 This diagram shows the hardware design for Ex. 5-1.

5-2.2 Interactive Variables

In the previous section consideration was given to discrete-state systems that were composed of noninteractive variables, where, even though a system may consist of many variables, each is independent. Many discrete-state systems are composed of variables that interact and for which the output states are dependent on the states of several input variables. In this section the construction of control systems for such problems using the computer will be studied.

Definition. A discrete two-state system with interaction is one for which a control output is determined by the states of a number of inputs. If the inputs are all expressed in digital format (i.e., high and low), these state-dependent systems are the

Note: 1. Register D has last outputs as: 0, 0, 0, VIN, VOUT, VEN, COM, COL
2. Input is into A register as: T2, T3, 0, 0, L, PCR, P, T
3. Delay restarts are to bits 6 and 7 of D but are reset to zero after starting to avoid restarting.

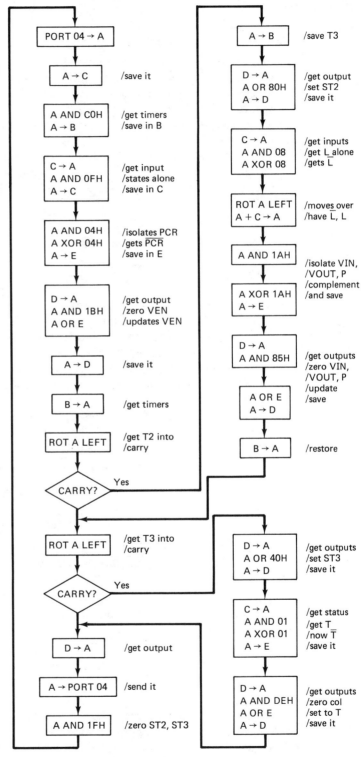

PORT 04 → A

A → C   /save it

A AND C0H   /get timers
A → B   /save in B

C → A   /get input
A AND 0FH   /states alone
A → C   /save in C

A AND 04H   /isolates PCR
A XOR 04H   /gets $\overline{PCR}$
A → E   /save in E

D → A   /get output
A AND 1BH   /zero VEN
A OR E   /updates VEN

A → D   /save it

B → A   /get timers

ROT A LEFT   /get T2 into
               /carry

CARRY? Yes

ROT A LEFT   /get T3 into
               /carry

CARRY? Yes

D → A   /get output

A → PORT 04   /send it

A AND 1FH   /zero ST2, ST3

A → B   /save T3

D → A   /get output
A OR 80H   /set ST2
A → D   /save it

C → A   /get inputs
A AND 08   /get L_alone
A XOR 08   /gets $\overline{L}$

ROT A LEFT   /moves over
A + C → A   /have $\overline{L}$, L

A AND 1AH   /isolate VIN,
               /VOUT, P
A XOR 1AH   /complement
A → E   /and save

D → A   /get outputs
A AND 85H   /zero VIN,
               /VOUT, P
A OR E   /update
A → D   /save

B → A   /restore

D → A   /get outputs
A OR 40H   /set ST3
A → D   /save it

C → A   /get status
A AND 01   /get T_
A XOR 01   /now $\overline{T}$
A → E   /save it

D → A   /get outputs
A AND DEH   /zero col
A OR E   /set to T
A → D   /save it

FIG. 5-6 The detailed flowchart, assuming an 8080, involves extensive use of logic operations.

same as combination logic systems. Generally, Boolean equations can be written by which the outputs are determined from the inputs. These equations can be solved by hardware combination logic circuits or by software in a computer. There are a number of advantages to using the computer for solving these equations. For example, changes can be easily made to accommodate new designs, it is not necessary to attempt simplification of the equations, and many such equations can be handled by one computer.

If a discrete-state system has a set of n two-state input variables and a set of m two-state control outputs, a set of Boolean equations can be written for the control:

$$C_1 = F_1(V_1, V_2, \ldots, V_n)$$
$$C_2 = F_2(V_1, V_2, \ldots, V_n)$$

$$\begin{matrix} \cdot & & \cdot \\ & & \\ \cdot & & \cdot \\ & & \\ \cdot & & \cdot \end{matrix} \tag{5-2}$$

$$C_m = F_m(V_1, V_2, \ldots, V_n)$$

where $C_1 \ldots C_m = m$ Boolean control outputs
$\quad V_1 \ldots V_n = n$ Boolean inputs
$\quad F_1 \ldots F_m = m$ functions relating inputs and outputs.

The functions will consist of Boolean equations involving the input variables and their inverses along with AND and OR operations. The control problem reduces to finding ways to implement the equations by software.

EXAMPLE 5-2   A special engine control system has two-state input varibles of rpm (R), temperature (T) and load (L). The two-state outputs are fuel feed (F), air feed (A), and spark advance (S). The outputs are required to be high under the following conditions:

Fuel feed: when the rpm is low and the load is high, or when the rpm is high and load is low.

Air feed: when the temperature is high and the rpm and load are low, or when the temperature is low and the rpm is high.

Spark advance: when the temperature is high and the rpm is low and the load is high.

Derive the Boolean equations and flowchart that will provide the required control functions.

Solution: This is done by expressing the required high states in equations using the given variable designations. The Boolean equations are:

$$F = \overline{R} \cdot L + R \cdot \overline{L}$$
$$A = T \cdot \overline{R} \cdot \overline{L} + \overline{T} \cdot R$$
$$S = T \cdot \overline{R} \cdot L$$

A general flowchart is shown in Fig. 5-7.

Specification of the control problem is often in the form of verbally stated input conditions and required output conditions, as in this example. From these statements the equations of control can then be constructed.

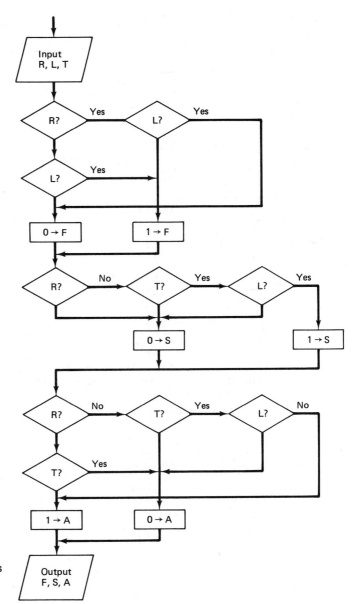

FIG. 5-7   An interactive system is like a combination logic problem. This flowchart is for Ex. 5-2.

Computer Application.   In general, the computer implements these types of systems following procedures familiar to you from digital logic problems. Instead of a set of equations, such as Eq. (5-2), a truth table is often constructed showing the required outputs for given input states. When the computer is used, the required outputs can then be deduced by using the input *states* as memory address *pointers* and the *contents* of the memory addresses as the required output states. The following example illustrates a typical state-dependent solution using a computer.

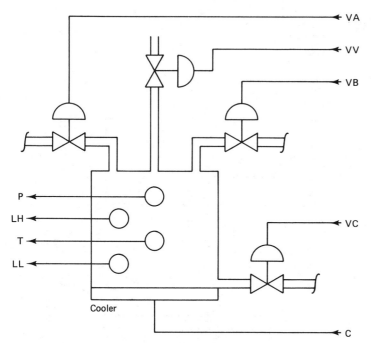

FIG. 5-8 This interactive discrete-state system is studied in Ex. 5-3.

EXAMPLE 5-3 A reaction vessel, shown in Fig. 5-8, inputs two ingredients, A and B, that react to produce an output, C. The input and output rates are controlled by valves (VA, VB, VC) with two settings each, high flow and low flow. A vent valve (VV) is used to protect against excessive conditions. Measurements are made on the system to determine

TABLE 5-1

	Input State				Output State				
	P	T	LH	LL	VA	VB	VC	VV	C
1	0	0	0	0	1	1	1	0	0
2	0	0	0	1	1	0	0	0	0
3	0	0	1	0	0	0	1	0	0
4	0	0	1	1			not possible		
5	0	1	0	0	1	1	1	0	0
6	0	1	0	1	1	1	0	0	1
7	0	1	1	0	0	1	1	0	1
8	0	1	1	1			not possible		
9	1	0	0	0	1	1	1	0	0
10	1	0	0	1	1	1	0	0	0
11	1	0	1	0	0	0	1	1	0
12	1	0	1	1			not possible		
13	1	1	0	0	1	1	1	0	1
14	1	1	0	1	1	1	0	0	1
15	1	1	1	0	0	0	1	1	1
16	1	1	1	1			not possible		

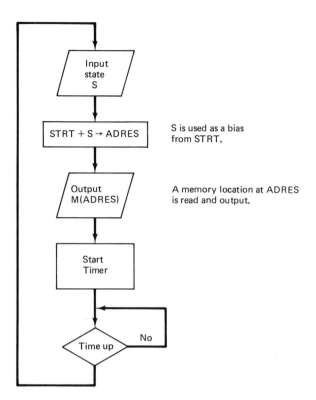

FIG. 5-9 The flowchart for Ex. 5-3.

the pressure (*P*, high or low), temperature (*T*, high or low), whether the level exceeds a high limit (*LH* high) or drops below a low limit (*LL* high). A cooler is also provided, which is turned on with a high (*C*). The truth table given in Table 5-1 relates the four input variable states to the five output states. Develop the software flow chart to provide these functions. Update should occur at 1-min intervals.

Solution: Notice that some combinations of the input states are not allowed in Table 5-1. This is because some states cannot occur. For example, *LH* cannot be high, meaning the level exceeds the high limit, and *LL* high at the same time (level below the low limit). There are many ways that this system could be provided by a computer. One way, which will be used in this example, is to use the input states as pointers to address locations. Each address location contains a byte that is the proper output state settings for the particular input states. Since there are four inputs, there will be 16 possible addresses, although we have seen that four of these cannot occur. As an example, you can see from Table 5-1 that input state 7 requires an output of 01101. This means that input state 7, given by 0110, will be used as part of the address of a memory location in which 01101 is stored. The bit assignments will be the lower-order bits, in the same sequence given in the table. Figure 5-9 shows the flowchart for the software of this problem.

Timers. In Ex. 5-3 the time function was provided by a hardware timer. This is an integrated circuit that operates in conjunction with the microprocessor to provide a measured time interval. The timer is loaded with a time-out value by the microprocessor, under program control, and started. The timer will then perform a countdown, independent of microprocessor operation. The computer can deduce time-up occurrence by either testing the timer output or by having the timer execute

149

an interrupt. In Ex. 5-3 the program goes into a loop to test the timer output for time up.

5-3   SEQUENTIAL SYSTEMS

There is a very special type of control function that does not fall strictly within the definition of control as used in previous chapters. This control concerns the sequence of operations necessary to manufacture a product. It is *control* in the sense that the sequence of operations is controlled to occur in a certain fashion. The sequence may be dependent on both satisfaction of prerequisite conditions in the process and on time. Individual steps in the sequence may involve traditional process control as required to maintain the value of some variable at a set point. In a sense, we are talking about automated manufacturing. In this section the use of the computer in sequential systems will be considered.

5-3.1   Function-Sequence Systems

Many discrete control systems require control events to occur in a sequence for which an output state *produces* a change in the input state, which then causes a change in the output state. This process of change producing change continues until some overall objective has been met. We call this a *function-sequence system*, because the present output is dependent on the sequence of previous states of the system.

A simple example would be helpful to be sure you have the idea. Consider the problem of heating up a frozen TV dinner for your supper. It is possible to define a sequence of events that must occur to accomplish the goal of having prepared supper:

1. Deduce proper heating temperature, T_{sp}.
2. Start oven heating.
3. Unpack dinner from cardboard container.
4. Make any required preparations.
5. Check for temperature, $T > T_{sp}$.
   a. If $T > T_{sp}$, go to step 6.
   b. If $T < T_{sp}$, repeat step 5.
6. Insert TV dinner into oven.
7. Set timer for proper heating time.
8. Check for time-up.
   a. If time is up, go to step 9.
   b. If not, perform other tasks such as set table, or just repeat step 8.
9. Extract TV dinner from oven and place on plate.
10. Turn off oven.
11. Eat.

Now, the significant point about this sequence is that, although it occurred *in time*, each event (with the exception of the cooking) was not really time dependent. Each event was dependent on the completion of the *previous* event. In almost every case the next event could not occur unless the previous event was successfully completed. This is a *function sequence*. Typical automated manufacturing operations will contain many such function-sequence systems.

Linear Systems.   In a linear function sequence, each sequence step depends on the completion of a single previous event. The TV dinner example was a linear system. Such a system can be programmed quite easily, since it is only necessary to keep track of one state to determine the next state of the output. From a computer implementation point of view, such a system is a linear chain of event starts and tests of completion, as shown in Fig. 5-10. The control system is nothing more than a series of outputs, inputs, and tests that lead some process through a functional sequence to a desired end result.

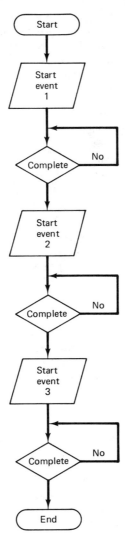

FIG. 5-10 A linear sequential system consists of events started and completed, one after the other.

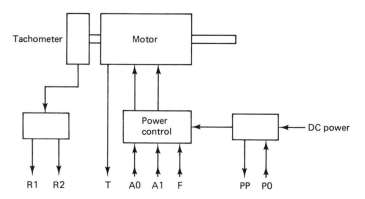

FIG. 5-11 This motor control system is an example of a linear sequence and is studied in Ex. 5-4.

EXAMPLE 5-4   A linear sequence control system will use a microprocessor-based computer for starting a dc shunt motor. The motor and electrical connections are shown in Fig. 5-11. Such a motor is started by increasing the armature current in steps until full rpm is established. In this case, current is limited by series resistors switched in and out of the armature circuit. Proper signal conditioning has provided the following input and output signals to the computer:

Signal Inputs:
1. DC power present (*PP* high)
2. Rpm > limit 1 (*R1* high)
3. Rpm > limit 2 (*R2* high)
4. Thermal overload (*T* high)

Signal Outputs:
1. Power on (*PO* high)
2. Field on (*F* high)
3. Armature position 1 (*A1* high)
4. Armature position 2 (*A2* high)
5. Dc power (OFF = red, ON = green)

The starting sequence is as follows:

1. Check that dc power is present.
   a. If not, red light on and check again.
   b. If yes, green light on and next step.
2. Check that field and all armature positions are off.
3. Check that thermal overload is off.
4. Put power on.
5. Put field on.
6. Apply armature position 1.
7. Test if rpm greater than limit 1.
   a. If yes, go to 8.
   b. If no, check for thermal overload.
      i. If yes, alarm and exit.
      ii. If no, go to step 7.
8. Apply armature position 2.
9. Test if rpm greater than limit 2.

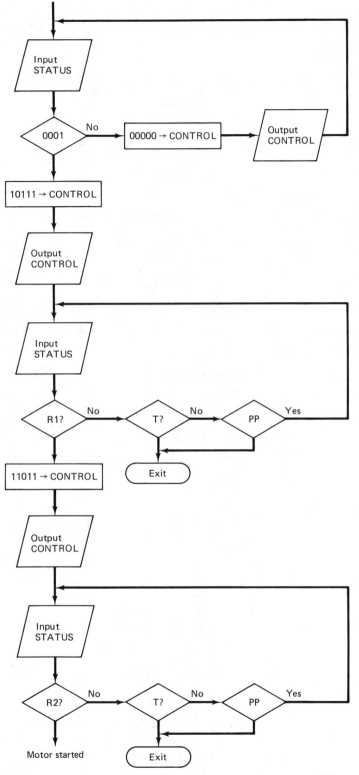

FIG. 5-12 A flowchart solution for Ex. 5-4.

        a. If yes, go to 10.

        b. If no, check for thermal overload.

            i. If yes, alarm and exit.

            ii. If no, go to step 9.

  10. Motor started.

Develop a general event flowchart for this sequence using the given inputs and outputs. Assume the inputs are provided by bits 0 through 3, in the order given, of a word called STATUS and that the outputs are initiated by bits 0 through 4 of a word called CONTROL.

Solution: The flowchart is provided by writing out the steps of the starting sequence given in flowchart symbols and using the given input and output words and variables. The first steps are provided by inputting STATUS and testing bits 0, 1, 2, and 3 for a 0001 status. Power on and field on are provided by setting bits 0 and 1 of CONTROL and outputting. The first position of the armature is selected by setting bit 2 of CONTROL and outputting. RPM is tested by examination of bit 2 of STATUS. Thus each step of sequence can be replaced by one or more flowchart steps. Figure 5-12 presents the entire flowchart. The next step would be either to convert this directly to microprocessor instructions or perhaps to a more detailed flowchart from which such code could be constructed.

Parallel Systems.   In many cases the next event in a sequence may depend on the completion of a parallel set of previous events. In this case the next event can be thought of as the result of a multiple-variable discrete-state system. An example of a parallel system can be constructed by expansion of the TV dinner problem. Suppose that in addition to the TV dinner we will have noodles. The linear sequence to produce the noodles is as follows:

1. Measure a cup of water.
2. Place in a pan.
3. Put the pan on a stove and turn on.
4. Water boiling?
   a. If yes, go to step 5.
   b. If no, repeat step 4.
5. Pour noodles into water.
6. Turn down heat.
7. Test noodles for tenderness.
   a. If tender, go to step 8.
   b. If not, wait a certain time and repeat step 7.
8. Drain off water.
9. Put noodles on plate.
10. Eat.

Now, as a linear sequence, this is no more difficult than the one used to prepare the TV dinner. The problem is that we want the TV dinner and noodles to be ready for eating *at the same time*. This means that the set of linear operations must be done at the same time (i.e., in parallel). This is a parallel-function-sequence system.

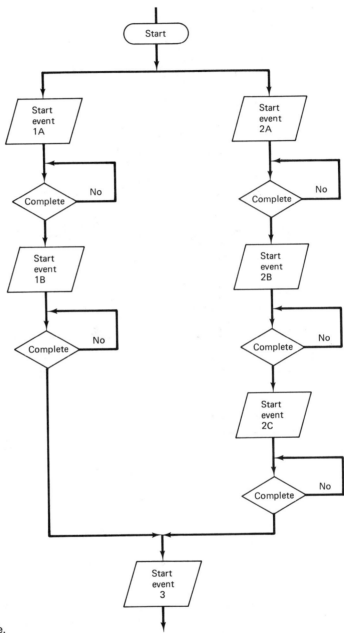

FIG. 5-13 A parallel sequence
system is like linear sequence
systems operating at the same time.

The programming of a compound system can become quite complicated; in
some cases one simply resorts to parallel computers. But it is possible in many cases to
use one computer to do the job. You must remember, however, that a computer is
essentially a *linear machine*, so parallel operations must be programmed as some kind
of simulated linear flow. In Fig. 5-13 a parallel problem has been presented pictorially

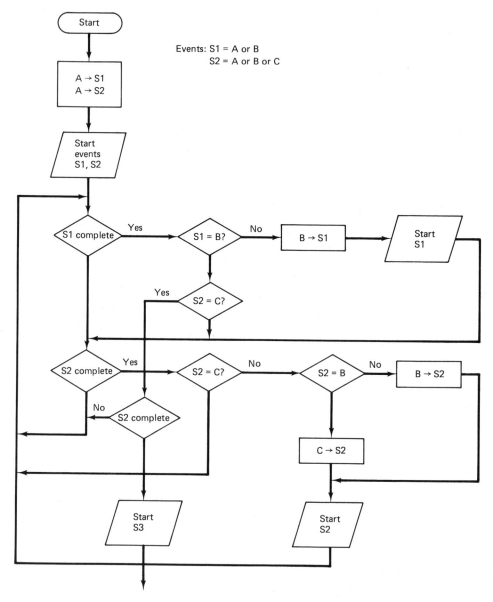

Events: S1 = A or B
S2 = A or B or C

FIG. 5-14 Since the computer is a linear machine, it must solve parallel sequence systems in an intermixed linear fashion. This flowchart solves Fig. 5-13.

as parallel operations required to produce some end result. Note that it cannot be expected that any correlation exists between event sequence 1 and event sequence 2. They don't have the same number of operations and will probably not be completed at the same time. Yet both are required before event 3 can occur.

When a program is written to implement this sequence by computer, it will be necessary to *merge* sequences 1 and 2 into a common path. A natural question to be asked is "Why not just do sequence 1 and then sequence 2, or vice versa?" If the system is truly compound, such as the TV dinner and noodle problem, the two sequences *must* be done in parallel. If it is possible to perform the sequences one after the other, we have nothing more than two linear sequences.

A compound system can be programmed in many ways. One method uses a loop that takes into account the repetitive nature of the sequence (i.e., start and test). Such a loop must keep track of which step is being performed in each sequence. The problem of Fig. 5-13 is illustrated in Fig. 5-14. Note that the sequences are really done in series, but in any one loop to test for a step completion *both* branches must be tested. Furthermore, the system must provide a test that allows either branch to be completed first.

EXAMPLE 5-5   A function-dependent sequence system is used to fill a mixing tank using the setup shown in Fig. 5-15. The sequence of operations requires the parallel achievement of two tasks, preheating of the liquid in tank A while tank B is filled to level $L1$. When the liquid in tank A is at temperature $T1$ and the level in tank B is at $L1$, then valve A is opened to let the liquid in tank A into tank B. Notice that all pertinent two-state signals have been prepared by proper signal conditioning. Prepare a flowchart showing how the control sequence is accomplished. Then write an assembly language program for the 6800 microprocessor to implement the flowchart. Use address $5\times\times\times$H for the input address with $b_0 = T$ and $b_1 = L$. *Use* $6\times\times\times$H for the output address with $b_0 = H$, $b_1 = VB$, and $b_2 = VA$.

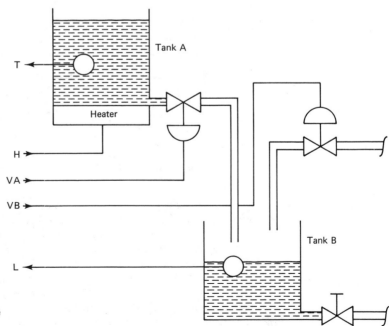

FIG. 5-15   This parallel sequence system is studied in Ex. 5-5.

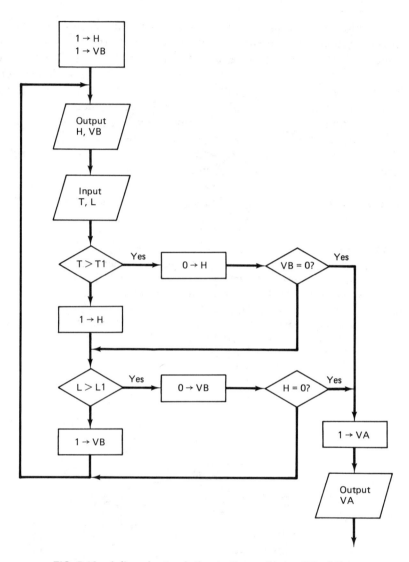

FIG. 5-16 A flowchart solution to the problem of Ex. 5-5.

Solution: The sequence consists of two parallel operations, heating tank *A* and filling tank *B*. The program must do these together but with the possibility that either can be finished first. This will involve merging the operations into one linear program. Figure 5-16 shows one way that this can be done. Note that if *T* is found to be high, meaning the temperature is OK, then the command to valve *B* is tested. If it is low, then the level must also be true and so we are finished and valve *A* can be opened. By the same logic, if the level is found to be OK, $L = 1$, then *H* is tested to see if it is 0, indicating the temperature was previously found to be OK. Again valve *VA* can then be opened. By this method, if the liquid cools off waiting for *B* to fill, the system will return to heating, and if the liquid in *B* leaks out, taking the level below *L1* while waiting for heating of *A*, filling will resume. Valve VA will not open until both $T > T1$ and $L > L1$ are satisfied. The 6800 code for this flowchart and problem are given next.

$$5000\text{H} = \text{input address,} \quad b_0 = T = 1 \text{ when } T > T1$$
$$b_1 = L = 1 \text{ when } L > L1$$
$$6000\text{H} = \text{output address,} \quad b_0 = H = 1 \text{ for heating}$$
$$b_1 = VB = 1 \text{ for open}$$
$$b_2 = VA = 1 \text{ for open}$$

Register B will be used to hold output. Register A will be used for the input.

```
            LDAB  #$03      ;set bits for heating and filling
   START:   STAB  $6000     ;send output command
            LDAA  $5000     ;read the input status
            RORA            ;get b0 = T into the carry
            BCS   HOT       ;if carry is set T = 1 and branch
            ORAB  #$01      ;if not set H = 1 to keep heating
            JMP   LEVEL     ; and go check the level
   HOT:     ANDB  #$FE      ;Hot, set b0 = 0 but keep b1 = VB
            BEQ   DONE      ;B=0 if VB=0 so jump to done
   LEVEL:   RORA            ;get b1 into carry
            BCS   FULL      ;if carry set L = 1 so branch
            ORAB  #$02      ;if not set VB = 1 and
            JMP   START     ;repeat it all
   FULL:    ANDB  #$FD      ;Full, set b1 = 1 but keep b0 = H
            BEQ   DONE      ;B=0 if b0=0 so jump to done
            JMP   START     ;otherwise repeat it all
   DONE:    LDAB  #$04      ;set b3 = 1 to open VA and
            STAB  $6000     ;send it to start flow
```

5-3.2   Time-Sequence Systems

The last category of discrete-state control systems to be considered involves a sequence depending on time. In these systems the next state of the output is determined by the lapse of time from the start of the previous state. Such a process is usually encountered as one part of an overall sequence involving functional dependence. You have already seen an example of this in the TV dinner preparation given earlier. Part of the sequence was the heating or cooking of the dinner in the oven once the proper temperature had been reached. It is a characteristic of this type of control sequence that it depends only on the passage of a fixed amount of time and not on the state of any variable in the system. Thus the TV dinner was not tested for completion of cooking. It is assumed that the correct time has been selected for the conditions of the problem.

Programmed Time Delay.   You have already seen how a simple software counter can be used to set up a time delay between events in a program. In many cases this type of timer is satisfactory. It is only necessary to determine the number of instructions that will be executed in the time loop and from this to deduce the amount of time the loop will take for each pass. This will give the number of times the loop will be processed. One problem with this type of time delay is that no other operations can be performed by the computer during the delay. This would be like requiring no activity during the time the TV dinner was heating. In simple control problems this would be satisfactory, but in more complicated, perhaps even parallel types of control problems it would not be acceptable.

Another problem with software timers is that long delay times are awkward to program. If a time on the order of several minutes is required, several million instructions must be executed. Time delays of hours are simply not practical.

Peripheral Timer.   Certain specialized integrated circuits have been developed that provide internal timers that can be used by the microprocessor for timing operations. Such timers are loaded by instruction from the microprocessor with a start count and then, typically, count down from that value. The counter can be periodically examined by the microprocessor to see if the count is up. In some cases the timer will use the microprocessor interrupt input to signal that the time is up.

An example of such a device is the 8155 (Intel Corporation). This device has a 14-bit counter that is loaded under programmed control (i.e., by an instruction). The counter counts down under control of either the computer clock or an external clock signal. The maximum count in this cases is $2^{14} = 16,384$, but the actual time depends upon the clock rate. The end of count can either be deduced by the computer reading the status of the counter or by the counter activating an interrupt line and causing the computer to service an interrupt routine. If a periodic read is required, the computer can be performing other tasks as long as a periodic read of the counter state is included. In the interrupt case the computer can be performing unrelated tasks until the timer interrupt occurs. A number of other timer modules are available.

Priority.   When time sequences are involved, the concept of priority becomes very important. Often in function-sequence operations when some function is completed the start of the next sequence can be delayed without disturbance of the overall operation. In Ex. 5-5, if one sequence was completed before the other, the end result of sequence 1 would simply wait until the other sequence was completed before the last could be started. In time-sequence problems, waiting is usually not possible. For example, when the oven timer says that the TV dinner is ready, action is required immediately to prevent burning. Thus in time sequence processing the assignment of priorities to the events is necessary when parallel operations may result in the completion of two events at the same time.

Real-Time Processing.   There are some cases in sequence control when events must occur at certain clock times (i.e., at certain times of the day or night). For this type of control problem, a real-time clock must be available that provides the computer with inputs showing clock time. Then software routines in the computer will read the clock time and determine if some event must be serviced.

5-3.3 Composite Sequential Control Systems

The most general type of sequential control system will involve every type of control strategy: simple two state, functional sequence, time sequence, and continuous variable (covered in Ch. 6). It is often possible to break down the entire control system into each of these categories and program the control system accordingly. In general, when the overall system becomes too complex, it is better to use several microprocessors, linked to a common unit, each of which performs some phase of the control.

5-4 PROGRAMMABLE CONTROLLER PRINCIPLES

No treatment of the subject of discrete-state control and sequential control would be complete without consideration of the programmable controllers. These are computer control systems designed and dedicated to the task of providing function- and time-sequence control of discrete-state systems. The concern of this text is more with how to provide control using the computer rather than how a closed system is used. Nevertheless, some discussion of this approach is beneficial to overall understanding.

5.4-1 Introduction

In nearly all industrial operations there are various sequences of operations involving the switching of 115-V, 60-Hz power to activate machinery and equipment. Examples include the start sequence for large ac or dc motors, the complex operations of conveyor systems in packaging and bottling plants, start-up and shutdown of large air handlers, and so on. In these types of operations the ac power may be used directly, may activate a relay that switches large power, or may activate solenoids that perform mechanical work on the process. All these operations are discrete.

Historically, this type of sequence was performed by banks of relays operating at 115 V ac and programmed in a logic-diagram fashion to provide the necessary switching in the correct sequence. Latching relays and time-delay relays were developed to implement more complex functions. In many cases it was found that the relays could be replaced by solid-state devices such as SCRs, and integrated-circuit logic gate systems replaced the relay logic arrays. Even so, such systems were difficult to program and often consumed large amounts of space and power.

The *programmable controller* was developed as a replacement for previous systems of providing industrial sequence control. In essence, it is a computer that has been internally configured to perform sequential, discrete-state operations on external equipment. The essential features that characterize this device can be summarized as follows and are illustrated in Fig. 5-17.

1. The device must be able to input standard ac line voltages, such as 115 V ac.
2. The device must be able to output standard ac line voltages, such as 115 V ac,

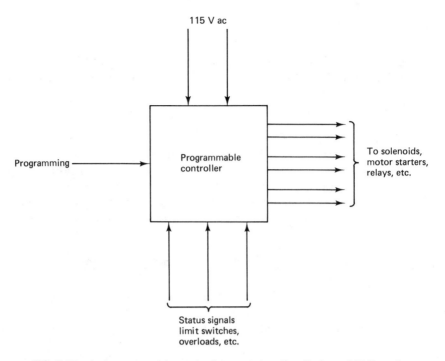

115 V ac

Programming

Programmable
controller

To solenoids,
motor starters,
relays, etc.

Status signals
limit switches,
overloads, etc.

FIG. 5-17 A programmable controller operates directly from 115-V ac signals and equipment commands.

with a 2-ampere (A) or greater current drive capability. Such a current will be sufficient to drive relays, solenoids, and motor starters.

3. The device must be programmable to perform a sequential discrete-state operation, including time delays. It must be easily reprogrammable to suit a different application or revised operation sequence.

4. The programming must be performed in easy to understand operations using the standard terminology of previously employed sequential control systems.

5. The device must be able to handle other types of electrical signals, including other ac voltages and a variety of dc voltages.

As shown in Fig. 5-17, these requirements translate into a "black box" that literally inputs 115-V ac signals from equipment to deduce the state of devices in the process and outputs 115-V ac signals to activate other devices in the process. All signal conditioning, ac-to-digital conversion, and digital-to-ac conversion are carried out in the box. In fact, in terms of connections the programmable controller is no different from the old relay switching systems.

5-4.2   Programming

The programming of the controller is carried out by inserting commands into the device via keyboards and video displays or just simple switches on a front panel. The internal computer has an executive program interpreter that converts the input commands to a series of computer instructions as necessary to perform the sequence. This is stored in memory for execution just like any program. In general, the programming uses *special* logic diagrams and *special* symbols to represent the sequential process.

Symbols.   The symbols used for the sequential diagrams are derived from those used for relays and other electromechanical devices in the historical control systems. Figure 5-18 shows some of the more common symbols and their relation to

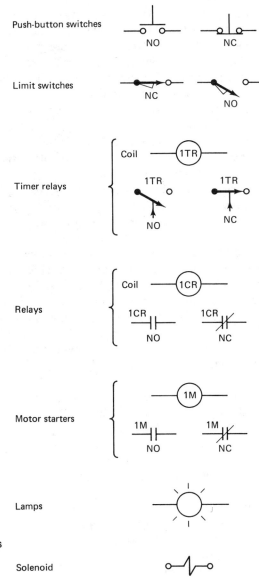

FIG. 5-18 Programmable controllers use special symbols taken from power control systems.

physical objects. Devices such as thermal contacts and limit switches represent *inputs* to the programmable controller that will be evaluated by the program. Devices such as relay coils and time delays represent outputs from the programmable controller that will be used to activate elements of the process under control. Note that timer functions are included. The following additional comments pertain to these symbols and their meaning.

1. *Push buttons.* External, momentary contact closing or opening switches used by operators.
2. *Limit switches.* Any kind of switch that is activated by part of the process. Examples are travel limit switches on machinery and thermal overload switches on motors. They are "read" by the programmable controller to be open or closed. These switches can be opened or closed by the limiting condition.
3. *Relays.* Internal operations of the programmable controller that simulate actual relay coils and contacts.
4. *Timer relays.* In the programmable controller, this is a time-delay loop in software.
5. *Motor starter.* The motor starter coil is actually an output from the controller that may go to an actual relay or other starter module that can handle large motor currents and/or voltages.
6. *Lamps.* Actual lamps or displays on an operator's console.
7. *Solenoid.* Actual outputs from the controller to solenoids that may activate mechanical operations in the process.

Ladder Diagram.   The traditional way of representing sequence operations of this type is through a ladder diagram. This diagram is the result of past application to systems operating from 115-V ac lines. These power lines are drawn as two horizontal parallel lines. The equipment to be activated and controlled is wired between the power lines, like rungs on a ladder, along with the control elements.

Let us consider an example of how such a ladder diagram is developed. Consider the problem of starting a conveyor system in a manufacturing process. The following event sequence is required:

1. With the system off, the amber light should be on.
2. Manual push-button starter causes:
    a. Motor starts if temperature limit switch is closed.
    b. Amber light off and red light on.
    c. A 30-s timer is started.
3. When the 30-s timer times out:
    a. The conveyor clutch engages.
    b. The red light goes off, and the green light goes on.
4. Manual push-button stop causes:
    a. Amber light on, all others off.
    b. Motor stops.
    c. Clutch releases.

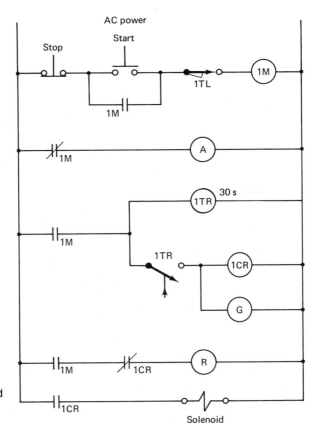

FIG. 5-19 A ladder diagram is used to draw the schematic of a programmable controller problem.

Now, the ladder diagram is constructed by taking each individual phase of this sequence and constructing the appropriate rung to perform that function. The ladder is constructed as if the system would be assembled using relays. Then, when the programmable controller is actually programmed, the "relay" functions are implemented by software instructions. Figure 5-19 shows the ladder diagram that will implement the preceding requirements.

When programmed, the only *real* inputs will probably be the push-button switch operations and the motor thermal overload switch. The real outputs will be the display (light) signals and of course signals to the motor start and clutch solenoid. Figure 5-20 shows a block diagram of how the actual system may be connected. You can see that all the control functions are contained in the controller. The actual equipment is then simply connected as required according to a wiring diagram.

PROBLEMS

5-1 Use the discrete-state-system approach to describe the operation of an automatic washing machine. Include the following states: wash fill, wash, drain, rinse fill, rinse, drain, and

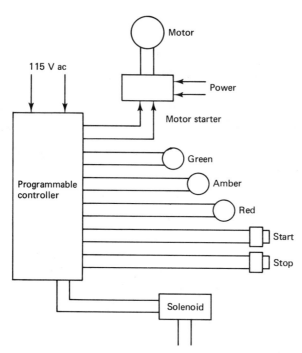

FIG. 5-20 Notice that major equipment is connected directly to the programmable controller.

spin-dry cylces. For each system state, specify the output states of the water valve, motor, agitate solenoid, spin solenoid, and drain pump solenoid.

5-2 Construct a general flowchart of the discrete-state system specified in Prob. 5-1.

5-3 A discrete-state system is shown in Fig. 5-21. The measured states are level (L), critical level (LCR), temperature (T), and critical temperature (TCR). The control ouputs are heater (H) and pump (P). A high of either input or output variables indicates a true condition. The following states are defined:

State	Condition	Control	Delay
S1	L	P (off)	1 min
S2	LCR	P (off)	None
S3	T	H (off)	2 min
S4	TCR	H (off)	None

Construct a general flowchart to describe the continuous operation.

5-4 Assume an 8080 will be used to implement the system of Prob. 5-3 and that comparators are used to set up the required inputs. Use 8212 buffer–latches for input and output. Design the hardware and 8080 mnemonic code for the solution. Use port A2H for both input and output.

5-5 A motor control has the following inputs:
    (1) $R1$ = high if rpm exceeds a low limit.
    (2) $R2$ = high if rpm exceeds a high limit.
    (3) L = high if the load is high.
Outputs to control the motor are:
    (1) $A1$ = high for armature drive 1.

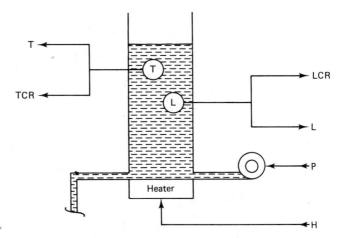

FIG. 5-21   System for Prob. 5-3.

        (2) $A2$ = high for armature drive 2.

        (3) C = high to operate clutch and connect load.

        (4) B = high to apply friction brake.

    The following conditions are to be met for control:

        (1) $A1$ if the speed is below $R1$ or if the speed is above $R1$ and the load is low.

        (2) $A2$ if the speed is above $R2$ or if the speed is below $R2$ and above $R1$ and the load is low.

        (3) C if the speed is above $R2$ or the speed is above $R1$ and the load is low.

        (4) B if the speed is above $R2$ and the load is low.

    Construct the logic equations to define the required outputs from the input states. Construct a flowchart showing how a computer would solve these equations.

5-6   Figure 5-22 shows a system for controlling liquids in a tank separated by a semipermeable

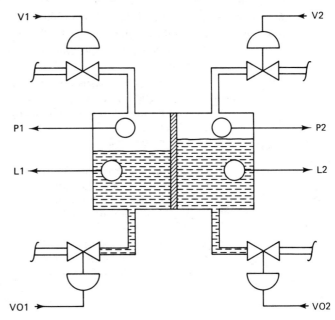

FIG. 5-22   Discrete-state system for
Prob. 5-6.

TABLE 5-2

Input State				Output State			
L1	L2	P1	P2	V1	V2	VO1	VO2
0	0	0	0	1	1	0	0
0	0	0	1	1	1	0	0
0	0	1	0	1	1	0	0
0	0	1	1	1	1	0	0
0	1	0	0	1	0	0	0
0	1	0	1	1	0	0	1
0	1	1	0	0	0	1	1
0	1	1	1	1	0	1	1
1	0	0	0	0	1	1	0
1	0	0	1	0	1	0	0
1	0	1	0	0	1	1	0
1	0	1	1	0	1	1	1
1	1	0	0	0	0	1	1
1	1	0	1	1	1	0	1
1	1	1	0	1	1	0	1
1	1	1	1	0	0	1	1

membrane. Inputs are two-state variables: level 1 ($L1$), level 2 ($L2$), pressure 1 ($P1$), and pressure 2 ($P2$). Outputs are input valves $V1$ and $V2$ and output valves $VO1$ and $VO2$. Table 5-2 gives the required relations between inputs and outputs. Construct the 8080 code that solves the control using the inputs as address pointers and the address contents as the required outputs.

5-7 Express the solution of Ex. 5-5 in 8080 code using port 6A for input and port 6B for output.

5-8 Express the solution of Prob. 5-6 in 6800 code. Use D0$\times\times$H and D1$\times\times$ for output.

5-9 Develop a general flowchart for the TV dinner sequence described in the text.

5-10 Write the 8080 or 6800 code for the problem given in Ex. 5-4. Make your own selection of ports or addresses.

5-11 Study the function-sequence system of Fig. 5-23, which fills bottles with a liquid. The following event sequence must occur:

    1. Check for bottle in position (*BP* high).
      a. No, check again.
      b. Yes, go to step 2.
    2. Stop conveyor (*CM* low).
    3. Check prefill tank level (*L* high).
      a. No, set alarm and start prefill (*VPF* high).
        i. Not filled, check again.
        ii. Filled, alarm off, prefill off and go to step 4.
      b. Yes, go to step 4.
    4. Start bottle fill (*VF* to high).
      a. Not full, check again (*BF* low).
      b. Full (*BF* high), go to step 5.

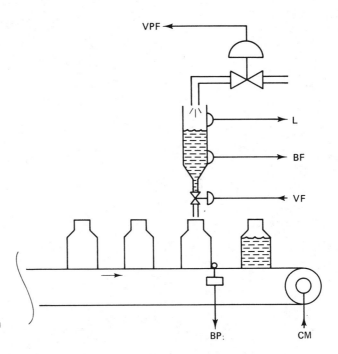

FIG. 5-23 Bottle-filling system
studied in Prob. 5-11.

        5. Bottle fill off (*VF* low).
        6. Start prefill (*VPF* high).
          a. Not full, check again.
          b. Full, go to 7.
        7. Close prefill valve.
        8. Start conveyor motor (*CM* high).
        9. Go to 1.
Construct a general flowchart for this linear system.

5-12 Modify the flowchart of Prob. 5-11 so that prefill and bottle movement occur in parallel. Account for the possibility that either event could finish first.

5-13 Construct the 8080 code or 6800 code for Prob. 5-11.

5-14 Construct the 8080 code or 6800 code for Prob. 5-12.

5-15 The system of Fig. 5-24 alternately moves material into a right bin and a left bin. A right motor (*RM*) moves the conveyor to the right and a left motor (*LM*) moves it to the left. A right limit switch (*RLS*) indicates maximum right motion, and a left limit switch (*LLS*), maximum left motion. A blue light indicates right motion, and a yellow light, left motion. The sequence is as follows:
        1. Push button to start right motion.
        2. *RM* on, *LM* off, and *V* open (on).
        3. Wait for valve switch, *VS*.
        4. *V* closed (off).
        5. Wait for *RLS*; then next step.
        6. *RM* off, *LM* on, and *V* open.

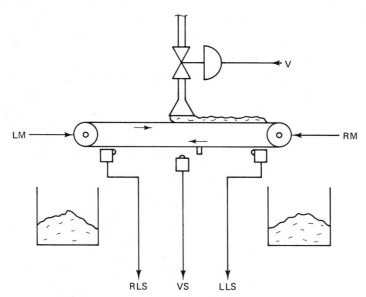

FIG. 5-24   Conveyor system for Prob. 5-15.

    7. Wait for valve switch, *VS*.
    8. *V* closed.
    9. Wait for *LLS*; then step 2.
   10. Push button to stop.
Develop a ladder diagram that solves this control with a programmable controller.

5-16 Figure 5-25 shows a system to draw material from a hopper onto a conveyor. The following conditions apply:
    1. A push button starts the conveyor and a 10-s delay.
    2. After time-out, the solenoid-operated hopper valve opens and flow starts.
   Notes: a. Hopper valve cannot open if level is low as indicated by limit switch on hopper.
           b. Solenoid cannot activate if conveyor is not operating.
Develop a ladder diagram that provides the sequence and control operations.

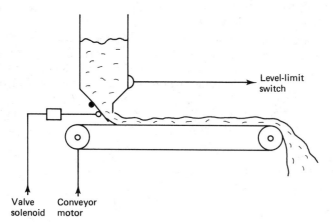

FIG. 5-25   Conveyor system for Prob. 5-16.

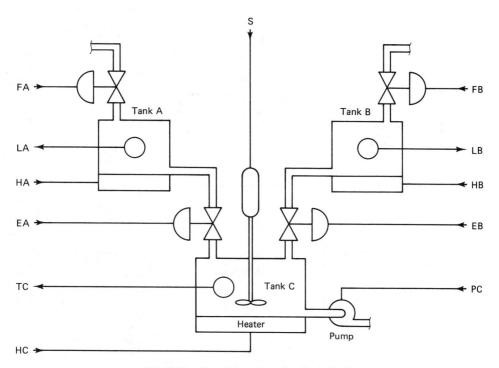

FIG. 5-26   Parallel system for Prob. 5-17.

5-17 A discrete-state, parallel mixing and heating process is shown in Fig. 5-26. The process is carried out in two phases. It is assumed that tanks A, B, and C are empty at start-up. The process phases are:

   Start-up:
   1. Fill A and B.
   2. Heat A 12 min while heating B 15 min.
   3. Empty A and B into C.

   Phase I:
   1a. Stir and heat C to T_{sp}.
   2a. Then turn off, stir, and heat.
   3a. Pump out C.
       While
   1b. Fill A and B.
   2b. Heat A 12 min while heating B 15 min.

   Phase II:
   1. Empty A and B into C.
   2. When complete, return to phase I and continue.

Prepare a general flowchart of the parallel–serial operations in start-up, phase I, and phase II.

5-18 Prepare a *serial* flowchart as necessary to implement the sequences of Prob. 5-17 using a computer.

CHAPTER 6

CONTINUOUS-STATE CONTROL SYSTEMS

OBJECTIVES

The overall goal of this chapter is to learn how continuous-state processes can be controlled by microprocessor-based computers. To accomplish this goal, a number of specific objectives can be identified. After studying this chapter and completing the problems at the end of the chapter, you will be able to:

1. Write the flowchart and microprocessor code to implement the proportional control mode.
2. Write the flowchart and microprocessor code to implement the integral control mode.
3. Write the flowchart and microprocessor code to implement the derivative control mode.
4. Describe the features and write computer codes to implement the PI, PD, and PID composite modes of control.
5. Design the hardware and software for a control system according to a given specification of a control problem.

6-1   INTRODUCTION

In Ch. 5 we considered the problem of how the computer is used to provide control of systems for which the variable data and output data are inherently discrete in nature. In this chapter the more general problem of controlling a process in which the variables are continuous will be studied. There is a slight paradox to the application of computers to the control of a continuous variable process since the representation of information in a computer is discrete. This problem is overcome by using a coded representation of such continuous data for computer processing. Chapter 3 showed how continuous-process data are converted into a digital data and coded discrete form. Nevertheless, you must remember that by using the computer we are attempting to perform continuous control using a discrete representation, and problems will occur.

The Control Equation.   The basic objective of this chapter is to show how control equations such as were introduced in Ch. 1 can be implemented by computer. This means that an *algorithm* will be found that provides a solution to the control equation. In a most general sense, then, the operations of control reduce to the equation

$$DC = F(DV) \tag{6-1}$$

where DC = digital output to the controlling variable
   DV = digital input from the controlled variable.
Equation (6-1) is a discrete representation of a continuous variation, since the computer will use a data word with a finite number of bits. For example, if the word is 8 bits, then the functions in Eq. (6-1) can only represent data with a resolution of 1 part in 256. You must be constantly aware of this limitation and its consequences on the control process.

Controlled Variable Error.   The first operation to be performed in implementation of Eq. (6-1) will be to find the error of the controlled variable, DV, from the set point established for that variable, DSP. There are many ways to express this error. For the purposes of this text, and for a general understanding of the control algorithms, it will be easier to adopt a common definition of the error, regardless of the physical variable represented. This is like converting all data in analog control systems to 4 to 20 mA of current. In the case of digital control, the *range* of the physical variable, in the computer, will always be assumed to be the full counting system of the data word. Thus for the common 8-bit machine the range is assumed to be 00H to FFH. By this choice the error can be easily expressed as the *fraction of range* using the definition of percent of range given by Eq. (1-3). First the error is defined, as usual, by the difference between the measured value and the set point:

$$DE = DV - DSP \tag{6-2}$$

This error, DE, will be a digital number in the 2's complement representation, meaning that if the number is negative it will be in 2's complement.

In accordance with the definition of Eq. (1-3), the error can be expressed by the fraction of range by dividing the error by the range:

$$DFE = \frac{DE}{RIN} \qquad (6\text{-}3)$$

where RIN = range of input variable = $DMAX - DMIN$
$\quad DFE$ = error expressed as a fraction of range.

EXAMPLE 6-1   A process variable is input in a range of 00H to FFH. The set point is 80H. Calculate the error for variable values of 90H and 70H using Eq. (6-3).

Solution: From Eqs. (6-2) and (6-3), the error is found as

$$\text{For 90H:} \quad DFE = \frac{90H - 80H}{FFH} = \frac{10H}{FFH}$$

The division is performed as follows:

```
                          00000000.00010000
             11111111 / 00010000.00000000
                          1111 1111
                          ─────────
                               10000 = remainder
```

which is a 16-bit result of 00.10H.

$$\text{For 70H:} \quad DFE = \frac{70H - 80H}{FFH} = \frac{F0H}{FFH} \quad \text{(2's comp)}$$

The division in this case gives

```
                          00000000.11110000
             11111111 / 11110000.00000000
                          1111111 1
                          ─────────
                          1111000 10
                          ─────────
                          111111 11
                          ─────────
                          110000 110
                          ─────────
                          11111 111
                          ─────────
                          10000 1110
                          ─────────
                          1111 1111
                          ─────────
                               11110000 = remainder
```

The 16-bit result of this division is the number 00.F0H. In both cases the result is a fractional binary number, as it must be since DE can never be larger than FFH. It turned out in this case that the fractional part is actually equal to DE because division by FFH simply shifts the decimal point eight places to the left. If a different range were used, this would not be the case. Of course, it is easy to show that the 2's complement of F0H is 10H so that this is actually $DE = -10H$.

In general, we will use the full range of input as FFH since this introduces some simplification into the equations *and* gives the best possible resolution. The effect of different range selections will also be considered.

Polarity of *DE*.   The value of DE calculated from Eq. (6-2) will be bipolar. This means that if $DV < DSP$ then DE will be negative and in the 2's complement representation. It is very inconvenient to use this representation of the error in subse-

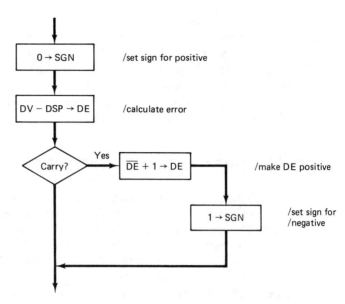

FIG. 6-1 This flowchart shows how the error DE is expressed as magnitude with a sign flag.

quent computations required to produce the output. Therefore, once DE has been calculated it will be converted to an unsigned value and the polarity will be remembered by a flag word.

The flowchart of Fig. 6-1 demonstrates the general operations necessary to do this. This routine is based on the fact that if the subtraction produces a negative result then the carry bit will be set, indicating a borrow, and the result will be a 2's complement number. In this case a flag word, SGN, is set to 1, indicating a negative, and the value of DE is converted to an unsigned integer.

To illustrate this concept, suppose DSP = 40H. Then for inputs of 45H and 3BH, the following results would occur:

$$DV = 45H \quad\quad DE = 45H - 40H = 05H \quad \text{and} \quad SGN = 0$$
$$DV = 3BH \quad\quad DE = 3BH - 40H = FBH \quad \text{(in 2's complement)}$$
$$\text{Taking the 2's complement produces:}$$
$$= 05H \quad \text{and} \quad SGN = 1$$

So in both cases DE = 05H, but one is positive (SGN = 0) and the second negative (SGN = 1).

Note that the *maximum* positive error will occur when DV = FF (for 8 bits). Then this value is FFH $- DSP$, which is just the complement of DSP. The *minimum* (negative) error will occur when DV = 00. Thus the minimum will be 00 $- DSP$ or simply DSP with SGN equal to 1. Using the DSP above:

$$DV = FFH \quad\quad DE = FFH - 40H = BFH \quad \text{and} \quad SGN = 0$$
$$DV = 00H \quad\quad DE = 00H - 40H = C0H \text{ in 2's complement, or}$$
$$= 40H \quad \text{and} \quad SGN = 1$$

Controlling Variable Output. Having defined the form of the controlled variable and its error, it remains to define the form to be used for the controlling variable output. In the controller mode representations used in Ch. 1, the controlled variable output was simply defined to be 0% to 100%. In analog process control loops, this translated into a 4- to 20-mA electric current, or a 3- to 15-psi pneumatic signal. For the digital case, we will define the range to be the full counting range of the data word. For an 8-bit computer, a solution of the controller equation will give a result, *DC*, in the range from 00H, corresponding to 0% output, to FFH, corresponding to 100% output.

6-2 PURE MODE CONTROL ALGORITHMS

This section will present the algorithms by which a computer can implement the three basic controller modes of operation: proportional, integral (reset), and derivative (rate). The algorithms will be based on an assumption that the controlling variable input and controlling variable output are expressed as described in the previous section. In each case the algorithm will be described by equation, by a general flowchart, and by examples of actual microprocessor codes. It is very common to combine these pure modes for actual applications. In the next section, composite-mode algorithm examples will be presented.

6-2.1 Proportional Mode

The proportional mode provides an output that is directly proportional to the error itself. In Ch. 1 the equation for this mode was given as

$$c = K_P e_p + c_0 \qquad (1\text{-}9)$$

The appropriate algorithm for use of this equation in microprocessor-based control has the same general form.

$$DCP = (KP * DFE * ROUT) + DC0 \qquad (6\text{-}4)$$

where *DCP* = digital controller output

  KP = digital proportional gain

  DFE = digital error as fraction of range

  DC0 = zero error controller output

  ROUT = range of output.

  If the input controlling variable is equal to the set point so that the error is zero, the controller output will be *DC0*. The digital error is determined from Eq. (6-3), and the controller output will vary over the range specified by *ROUT*. *KP* is defined as the fraction of output range change per error expressed as fraction of input range. In Ch. 1 this was expressed as a percent, but you will recognize that the only difference is multiplication by 100. Thus the product *KP* * *DFE* gives the fraction of output change specified by the error. This is multiplied times the output range, *ROUT*, to get the actual change in output. This equation can be expressed in an alternative form by writing out *DFE* using Eq. (6-3):

$$DCP = KP * DE * \frac{ROUT}{RIN} + DC0 \qquad (6\text{-}5)$$

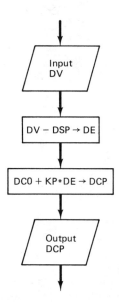

FIG. 6-2   The proportional-mode
algorithm flowchart.

Now you can see the reason for wanting to make the range of both input and output the same. If $ROUT = RIN$, then the proportional-mode equation involves only the gain, variable error, and the zero error term.

Simplified Algorithm Equation.   For the purposes of this text, it will be assumed that the ranges of input and output have been selected to be the same. Usually this choice will be the full counting range of the data word. Thus, for example, with an 8-bit microprocessor the ranges would both be FFH. In any event, these ranges cancel from the equation and leave a result:

$$DCP = (KP * DE) + DC0 \qquad (6\text{-}6)$$

where DCP = controller output
$DE = DV - DSP$ = controlled variable error
$DC0$ = zero error controller output
KP = proportional gain.

One advantage of Eq. (6-6) is that it involves no division; another is that the gain term, KP, is the same number that is determined from the designs of analog control.

Flowchart.   The general flowchart for the pure proportional mode of control is particularly simple. Figure 6-2 shows the mode algorithm expressed in flowchart format. Note that the proportional gain can be positive (direct) or negative (reverse). This means that a positive error correction may cause DCP to increase or decrease. A more detailed flowchart (Fig. 6-4) shows that other considerations are important in the practical construction of proportional control.

EXAMPLE 6-2   Proportional gain is 1.42 with direct action. Input and output ranges are 00 to FFH. The zero error ouput is 84H and the set point is 75H. Write out the control equation and construct a flowchart of the mode.

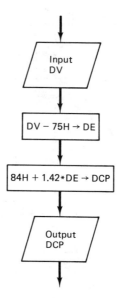

FIG. 6-3   The solution of Ex. 6-2.

Solution: The control equations are found using Eq. (6-2) for the error and Eq. (6-6) for the proportional mode, since the input and output ranges are the same. Thus $DSP = 75H$, $DC0 = 84H$, and the equations become

$$DE = DV - 75H$$
$$DCP = (1.42 * DE) + 84H$$

The flowchart is shown in Fig. 6-3. No details are given about how the input process occurs or how the calculations are to be performed.

It is usually possible to design the hardware and software of a computer-based control system so that input and output ranges are the same. In those cases when it is not possible, it will be necessary to account for this difference when the fractional quantities are computed. This can usually be done by combining the relations between input and output ranges in the constants. Example 6-3 illustrates this approach.

EXAMPLE 6-3   A control system has a proportional gain of 2.8, reverse acting. The input range is from 30H to D0H and the output range is from 47H to DFH. The set point is 80H, and the zero error output is 9EH. Construct the control equation.

Solution: You can see that the ranges are not the same. Thus it will be necesary to use Eq. (6-5) to determine the control equation. The following definitions are easily made:

$$DE = DV - 80H$$
$$RIN = D0H - 30H = A0H$$
$$ROUT = DFH - 47H = 98H$$

Then Eq. (6-5) becomes

$$DCP = \left(-2.8 * DE * \frac{98H}{A0H} \right) + 9EH$$

The numerical coefficients can be evaluated quite easily by conversion to decimal numbers:

$$\frac{2.8 * 98\text{H}}{\text{A0H}} = 2.8 * \frac{152}{160} = 2.66$$

Thus the control equation becomes

$$DCP = 9\text{EH} - (2.66 * DE)$$

Practical Application.   When actually writing programs to implement Eq. (6-6) and the proportional control mode, there are a number of practical considerations. The flowchart of Fig. 6-4 presents a more detailed account of the proportional-mode algorithm. The following issues are treated in the algorithm.

1. *Polarity of DE.* As noted in the introduction, it is convenient to use an unsigned number for DE with the sign indicated by a separate flag. The flowchart of Fig. 6-4 has incorporated this feature into the proportional algorithm.

2. *Product overflow.* When DE is multiplied by KP, it is quite possible for an overflow condition to occur. This means that the multiplication produces a number that exceeds the range of the data word. If an 8-bit number is being used, it would mean that the product with KP causes the carry bit to be set. For example, if $DE = 80\text{H}$ and $KP = 2$, the product is equivalent to a left shift of DE. This would produce 100H. But with only 8 bits, what would happen is that the carry bit would be set. As shown in Fig. 6-4, when this happens it will be necessary to set the correction factor, $KP * DE$, equal to the most negative or most positive magnitude of correction that can occur.

3. *Sum overflow and underflow.* In general, DCP will be a positive integer number with a range of $ROUT$. In fact, for the considerations of this text it is generally taken to have a range of the full counting of the digital word. Thus, if an 8-bit representation is used, DCP would vary from 00 to FFH. Corrections from errors will add to and subtract from $DC0$ to produce DCP, as shown in Eq. (6-6). An overflow occurs when the addition would cause the result to *exceed* the maximum counting of the digital word. In an 8-bit example, this would mean that the result would exceed FFH. An underflow occurs when the subtraction would cause the result to be less than the minimum value of the digital word. In an 8-bit case, this would mean that the subtraction would result in a number less than 00H. It is very important that the software detect overflow and underflow and provide corrections.

   An overflow occurs when the correction is $DC0$ is *added*, and this overflow is indicated by the carry bit being set. An underflow occurs when the correction to $DC0$ is *subtracted* and is also indicated by the carry bit being set. As shown in Fig. 6-4, the response to an underflow or overflow is to set the output to the minimum or maximum value, typically 00H and FFH.

4. *Direct or reverse action.* The polarity of KP will determine whether the action of the control is direct or reverse. Direct means that a positive error produces an increase in controlling variable output, and reverse produces a decrease in controlling variable output. From Eq. (6-6) you can see that this simply means that KP will be positive for direct and negative for reverse. Care must be taken to account for the polarity of KP in the programmed algorithm. In general, the

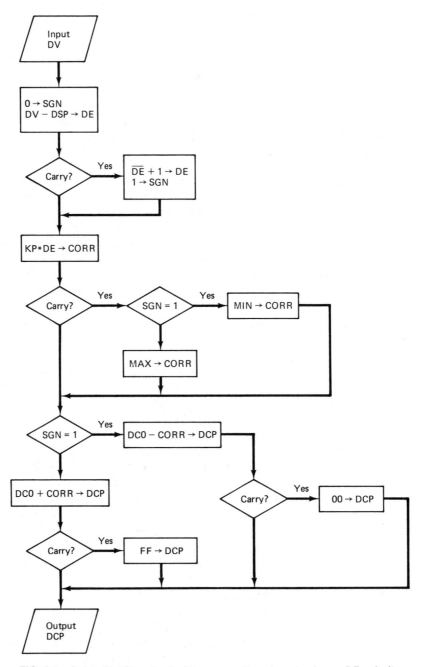

FIG. 6-4 A detailed flowchart of the proportional mode shows *DE* polarity adjustment and overflow–underflow protection.

direct or reverse action can be provided by variation of the decision block in Fig. 6-4 on whether to add or subtract the correction to $DC0$. What is shown is direct action, since a negative error (SGN = 1) causes a subtraction (reduction from $DC0$). To make this reverse action, it would merely be necessary to reverse the addition and subtraction operations.

Sample Control Problem.   To clearly demonstrate the issues involved in using a microprocessor-based computer for control, a sample design will now be presented. This should be studied in detail since many issues of importance in the practical construction of such a control system are considered.

The Problem: A microprocessor-based computer is to be used to control temperature in a system. A transducer, signal conditioning, and ADC provide the temperature as follows:

$$100°C \text{ to } 150°C \text{ becomes } 00H \text{ to } FFH$$

The controlling output is to a continuous heater that is off (no heat) for 0 V in and full on (heating) for 10 V input. This is provided by a DAC as follows:

$$00H \text{ to } FFH \text{ becomes } 0 \text{ to } 10 \text{ V}$$

The set point is 120°C. If the temperature reaches or exceeds 145°C, the heater is to be turned off and an alarm signal generated. The *proportional gain, KP,* is to be 3.5 and the action is reverse, since a temperature above the set point requires the heater to be turned down. The required zero error heater setting has been found to be 6.5 V. The system should be updated every 10 s.

Assume that an 8080 microprocessor is used and the following assignments have already been made:

Temperature input on port E0H
Heater output on port E0H
ADC start will be $b_0 = 1$ on port F0H
ADC conversion complete will be $b_1 = 1$ on port F0H
Alarm will be $b_7 = 1$ on port F0H

For the present, the following results are desired:

1. Prepare a block diagram of the required hardware.
2. Construct a detailed flowchart.
3. Construct the 8080 code that will perform the required control.

Solution: A problem such as this must be approached in a methodical manner, breaking the requirements into smaller parts and considering each separately.

For the hardware, a number of elements can be noted:

1. Address decoding will be needed for E0H and F0H.
2. A tristate buffer will be needed for input.

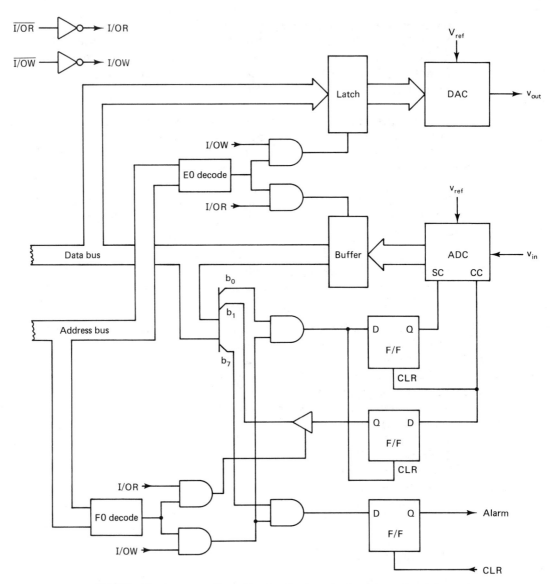

FIG. 6-5 Hardware configuration for the temperature-control problem using proportional control.

3. A latch will be needed for output.
4. F/Fs will be needed to capture the ADC start and alarm outputs.
5. A tristate buffer and F/F will be needed for the conversion complete signal.

So the next step is to get a big piece of paper and draw blocks for all these elements and the microprocessor. Then the required connections of address bus, data

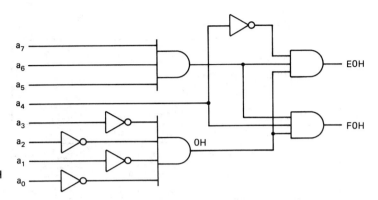

FIG. 6-6 Decoding to produce E0H and F0H signals.

bus, and control lines can be inserted. The result of this is shown in Fig. 6-5. Note that other hardware configurations would provide the same functions. You should study this diagram and understand why each element and connection is present. The E0H and F0H decodes are simply shown as blocks. One way to actually construct this is shown in Fig. 6-6. Here the lower-order nibble (nibble = 4 bits) of 0H has been decoded separately and then combined with higher-order nibble decodes of EH and FH. The next stage of hardware, which we will not do here, would be to select particular integrated circuits for the blocks shown. Often when this is done, modifications are necessary to account for peculiarities of the individual devices.

   The detailed flowchart is constructed in stages. The first step is a general flowchart showing the major operations that must occur in the control process. Such a flowchart for this problem is presented in Fig. 6-7. Each block represents a number of actual operations, which will be shown in the detailed flowchart. Before the detailed flowchart can be constructed, it will be necessary to specify how some of the required operations will be performed.

   We will use a countdown loop to provide the time delay of 10 s. Ten seconds is a long time. Probably only a few hundred microseconds will be used for actual processing, so the countdown loop should probably be designed for the full 10 s. A 16-bit decrement and jump sequence will only use 15 states, and with about 0.5 μs per state, this is only 7.5 μs. The full count of FFFFH will provide about

$$(7.5 \ \mu s)(65536) \approx 0.5 \ s$$

This means that two nested loops must be used, the inner counting from FFFFH to 0000H, and the outer repeating this enough times to make 10 s. So 10/0.5 = 20 passes in the outer loop. Thus the outer loop should count from 14H to 00H.

   The following symbolic names are selected:

$$DSP = \text{data set point } (120°C)$$
$$DC0 = \text{zero error output } (6.5 \text{ V})$$
$$ALR = \text{alarm level } (145°C)$$
$$DLY1 = 14 \text{ H} = \text{outer delay loop start count (16 bits)}$$
$$DLY2 = \text{FFFFH} = \text{inner delay loop start count}$$

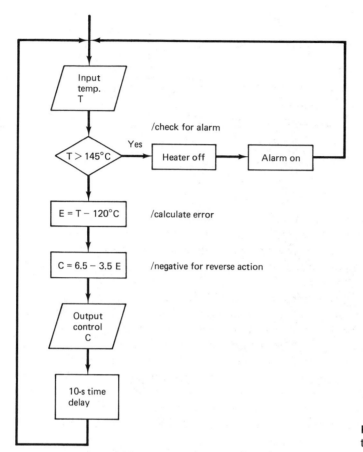

FIG. 6-7 The general flowchart for the temperature-control problem.

For the control equation, it will be necessary to decide how the multiplication is to be performed. Multiplication by 3.5 can be done quite easily by noting that

$$KP * DE = 3.5 * DE = (2 * DE) + DE + \frac{DE}{2}$$

Thus we can simply add DE to the left-shifted DE ($2 * DE$) and add this to right-shifted DE ($DE/2$). Care must be taken to look for an overflow. Note that the process is *reverse* acting since a high temperature (positive DE) will require the output to be decreased. This will be accounted for by reversing the order of addition and subtraction in calculating DCP.

Now we simply start drawing the flowchart, beginning perhaps with the input process. After many false starts, erasing, and modification, the flowchart of Fig. 6-8 results. Notes have been made on the side to indicate the operational results and purpose. The sign has been saved in the C register. You should study this flowchart carefully and understand the purpose of each operation. Many alternative methods can be used, and you may find some that are more efficient. We don't bother to assign numbers to the symbolic memory locations until the actual coding occurs.

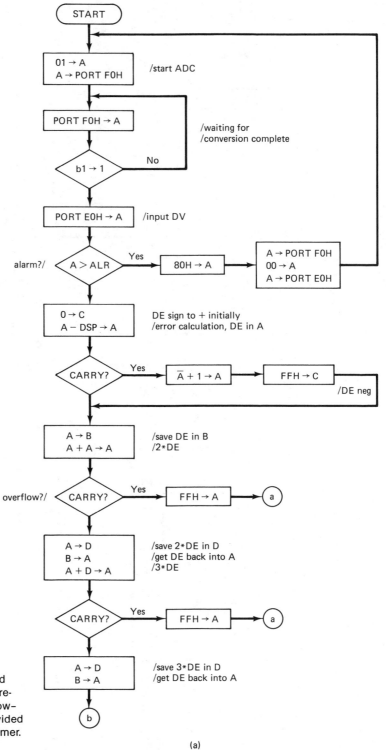

FIG. 6-8 This is the detailed flowchart for the temperature-control problem. Full overflow–underflow protection is provided with a 10-s software delay timer. (Continued on next page.)

(a)

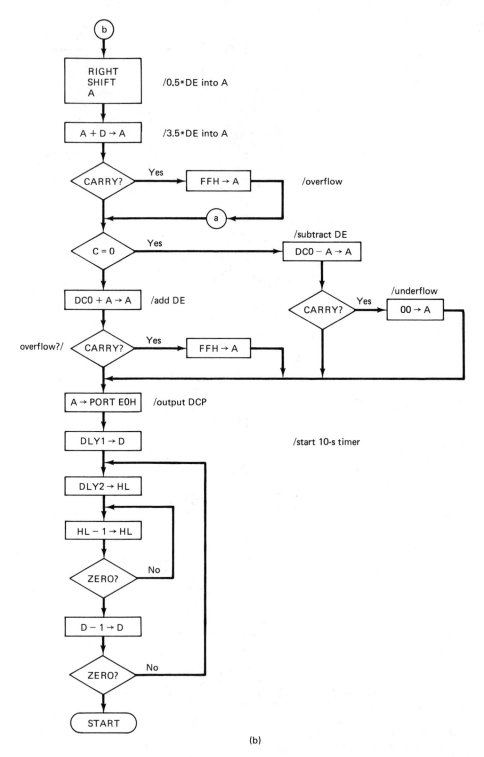

(b)

FIG. 6-8 (continued)

The actual coding can be done by simply translating the flowchart into appropriate 8080 mnemonics. In some cases, more than one instruction is required per block. In many cases, modifications are made to the flowchart during coding to make the approach fit well with the particular instructions of the computer.

The last step is to decide upon the values to be used for symbolic names. Here is where the traceability between the physical variable and digital data is important. For the temperatures, this can be done by noting that the range is $R = 150 - 100 = 50°C$ and is represented by 256 counting states from 00H to FFH. The bias is 100°C. The slope or resolution is given by $K = (50)2^{-8} = 1/5.12$. Now Eq. (4-5) can be used to relate the physical variables to the digital data. The set point of 120°C is represented by calculating $(120 - 100)(5.12) = 102.4$. The hex equivalent is easily found to be 66H. Thus $DSP = 66H$. The alarm temperature becomes $(145 - 100)(5.12) = 230.4$ or E6H, so $ALR = E6H$. The zero error output is found by noting that 10 V is distributed over 256 states. Thus for 6.5 V we have $(6.5/10)(256) = 166.4$ states. This gives $DC0 = A6H$. The 8080 assembly code for this problem, constructed from the detailed flowchart, can be written in the form shown in Fig. 6-9.

Offset Error.   When the error is zero, the proportional mode outputs a controlling variable signal given by $DC0$, which is a constant number. This means that the assumption has been made that, when the error is zero, $DC0$ is the proper output. Under the design nominal conditions this may be true, but changes in the conditions of the process may necessitate a different zero error output to keep the error zero. This is called a *load change*, and we say that the zero error controller output must be *reset*. In analog control, this amounts to a manual adjustment. In digital control, $DC0$ is a constant in the program and would require a manual insertion of a change. Either situation is poor with respect to automatic control. The inclusion of integral action will be found to eliminate this problem.

Variable KP.   The previous example constructed the product of KP times DE by programming the value of KP directly into the algorithm. This approach is fine if the value of KP will not require frequent changes. If a change is required, it will be necessary to change the coding for a different pattern of shifting and adding. In cases when changes in the value of KP are anticipated, it would be better to express KP as a number and perform the multiplication directly.

In general, KP will have an integer part and a fractional part. The multiplication will be most easily performed separately in this case and the two results added. This process is illustrated by the following example.

EXAMPLE 6-4   Show how the MULT8 routine can be used to construct control equation

$$DCP = DC0 + (3.674 * DE)$$

Solution: The required multiplication can first be written in the form

$$3.674 * DE = (3 * DE) + (0.674 * DE)$$

The first multiplication is performed by loading 3 into the multiplier register (A) and DE into the multiplicand register (E). The returned result will be 16 bits in the DE register

```
;THIS SECTION STARTS THE ADC AND WAITS FOR CONVERSION COMPLETE
START:    MVI A,01     ;LOAD A WITH ADC START BIT
          OUT 0F0H     ;START ADC
WAIT:     IN 0F0H      ;IS ADC FINISHED?
          ANI 02H      ;CHECK BIT TWO TO SEE
          JZ WAIT      ;NOT FINISHED, JUMP TO WAIT
          IN 0E0H      ;FINISHED, INPUT DATA
;NOW CHECK FOR AN ALARM OF T OVER 145 DEGREES
          CPI ALR      ;COMPARE DV TO THE ALARM VALUE
          JNC ALARM    ;NO CARRY MEANS ALARM
;CALCULATE THE ABSOLUTE ERROR AND SIGN
          MVI C,00     ;SET SIGN TO +
          SUI DSP      ;FORM DE = DV - DSP
          JNC MULT     ;NO CARRY MEANS POSITIVE
          CMA          ;CARRY MEANS NEGATIVE, GET COMPLEMENT
          ADI 01       ;ADD ONE FOR 2'S COMPLEMENT TO GET ABSOLUTE
          MVI C,0FFH   ;AND SET SIGN FOR -
;THIS SECTION CALCULATES KP*DE = 3.5*DE
MULT:     MOV B,A      ;SAVE DE IN B
          ADD A        ;GET 2*DE IN A
          JNC MULT2    ;NO CARRY MEANS NO OVERFLOW
OVER:     MVI A,0FFH   ;BUT CARRY MEANS OVERFLOW SO SET CORR TO MAX
          JMP DCP      ;AND GO ON TO FIND DCP
MULT2:    MOV D,A      ;SAVE 2*DE IN D
          MOV A,B      ;GET DE BACK IN A
          ADD D        ;NOW A HAS 3*DE=2*DE+DE
          JC OVER      ;CARRY MEANS OVERFLOW
          MOV D,A      ;PUT 3*DE BACK IN D
          MOV A,B      ;GET DE BACK IN A
          RAR          ;DIVIDE BY 2 TO GET 0.5*DE
          ADD D        ;NOW WE HAVE 3.5*DE
          JC OVER      ;CARRY MEANS OVERFLOW
;NOW THE OUTPUT IS CALCULATED DCP=DC0+KP*DE
DCP:      MOV D,A      ;SAVE CORR IN D
          MOV A,C      ;GET SIGN OF DE IN A
          ANA A        ;SET THE FLAGS TO TEST IT
          MVI A,DC0    ;GET DC0 INTO A
          JZ SUBD      ;IF DE IS POSITIVE GO SUBTRACT - REVERSE
          ADD D        ;ACTION, SO ADD IS DE IS NEGATIVE
          JNC OUT      ;CARRY MEANS OVERFLOW, IF NOT OUTPUT
          MVI A,0FFH   ;WITH CARRY SET DCP TO MAXIMUM FOR OVERFLOW
          JMP OUT      ;AND THEN OUTPUT
SUBD:     SUB D        ;FORM DCP
          JNC OUT      ;NO CARRY, GO OUTPUT IT
          MVI A,00     ;CARRY, SET DCP TO MINIMUM FOR UNDERFLOW
OUT:      OUT 0E0H     ;SEND IT TO DAC
;THIS IS THE TEN SECOND DELAY ROUTINE
          MVI D,DLY1   ;SET D FOR OUTER LOOP COUNT
          MVI A,00     ;WE WILL USE THIS FOR A COMPARISON
OUTER:    LXI H,DLY2   ;LOAD HL WITH INNER LOOP COUNT
INNER:    DCX H        ;DECREMENT THE HL REGISTER PAIR
          CMP H        ;IS UPPER BYTE ZERO?
          JNZ INNER    ;NAW, DECREMENT AGAIN
          CMP L        ;YES, IS LOWER BYTE ZERO?
          JNZ INNER    ;NOPE, DECREMENT AGAIN
          DCR D        ;YES, DECREMENT OUTER LOOP COUNTER
          JNZ OUTER    ;IF NOT ZERO START INNER AGAIN
          JMP START    ;BUT IF ZERO TIME TO GET MORE DATA
;THE FOLLOWING DEFINES ALL THE CONSTANTS
ALR:      EQU 0E6H     ;ALARM IS 145 DEGREES
DSP:      EQU 66H      ;SETPOINT IS 120 DEGREES
DC0:      EQU 0A6H     ;ZERO ERROR OUTPUT
DLY1:     EQU 14H      ;OUTER LOOP COUNT IS 20 OR 14H
DLY2:     EQU 0FFFFH   ;INNER LOOP COUNT IS FFFFH
;THIS IS THE ALARM ROUTINE
ALARM:    MVI A,80H    ;NEED THIS FOR THE ALARM F/F
          OUT 0F0H     ;SEND IT
          MVI A,00H    ;NOW WE TURN OFF HEATER
          JMP OUT      ;AND GET BACK ON LINE
          END
```

FIG. 6-9 The 8080 mnemonic code for the temperature control problem.

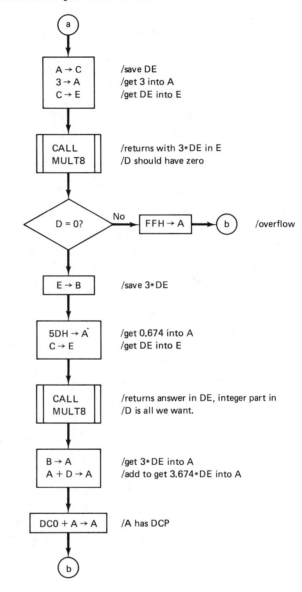

/Assume the A register has DE to start

a

A → C	/save DE
3 → A	/get 3 into A
C → E	/get DE into E

| CALL | /returns with 3*DE in E |
| MULT8 | /D should have zero |

D = 0? —No→ FFH → A → b   /overflow

E → B   /save 3*DE

| 5DH → A | /get 0.674 into A |
| C → E | /get DE into E |

| CALL | /returns answer in DE, integer part in |
| MULT8 | /D is all we want. |

| B → A | /get 3*DE into A |
| A + D → A | /add to get 3.674*DE into A |

DC0 + A → A   /A has DCP

b

FIG. 6-10 The flowchart for Ex. 6-4 shows how MULT8 can be used to multiply by *KP.*

pair. Assuming 8-bit arithmetic, only the lower byte is used. Any carry into the upper byte indicates a product overflow. The second multiplication is performed by first converting 0.674 into a binary fraction. Successive multiplication by 2 gives the result, 01011101 or 5DH. Thus 5DH is loaded into the multiplier and *DE* into the multiplicand. The returned result will be 16 bits, where the upper byte is the integer part of the result and the lower byte the fractional part. Again, assuming 8-bit arithmetic, only the upper byte would be used. The final answer is found by adding the lower byte of the integer product to the upper byte of the fractional product. The flowchart of Fig. 6-10 illustrates the process for this example.

6-2.2   Integral Mode (Reset)

In Ch. 1 the integral mode was defined as a controller response that is dependent on the history of the error rather than on the value of the error itself. This history is measured by determination of the *net* area under the error versus time curve from some starting time to the present. From a mathematical point of view, this is equivalent to finding the integral of the error, which is why this is called the integral mode. It is called *reset* because the integral mode is capable of correcting offset errors in the proportional mode by "resetting" the zero error term.

An equation for calculating the contribution of the integral mode to controller output was given in Ch. 1 as

$$c_I(t) = K_I A_e(t) + c_I(0) \qquad (1\text{-}10)$$

where K_I is the integral gain and $A_e(t)$ is the error area, which varies with time. The proper mathematical expression of this mode was also given in Ch. 1, but for our purposes the area relation is more significant. The area increases when the error is positive and decreases when the error is negative.

Area Approximation.   To implement this mode using the computer, a method must be found by which the area can be computed using the sampled input variable values. There are many approaches for doing this. For the purposes of this text, a particularly simple method, *rectangular integration*, will be used. This method is illustrated schematically in Fig. 6-11. The input to the computer consists of the samples at the indicated points of the smooth curve of controlled variable versus time. The error in each case is found by the difference of that value and the set point, as usual. Figure 6-11 also shows how each error value has been used to construct a rectangle with a base on the set point. Thus the height of the rectangle is the error, and the width is the sample time. When the variable value is above the set point, the error is positive and the rectangle will have a positive area found by the error times the sample time width. When the variable value is below the set point, the error is negative and the rectangle area will have a negative value. The *net* area will be the sum of the positive and negative areas. We use this to approximate the net area of the error versus time curve. The accuracy of the area found by this method is determined by the width, which is the time between samples. The smaller the width is, the better the

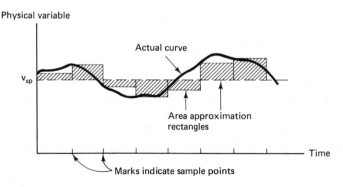

FIG. 6-11   This graph illustrates how the error-time area is approximated by construction of rectangular areas using samples of the error.

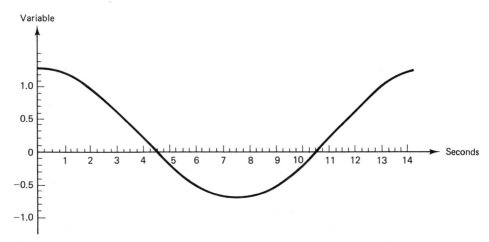

FIG. 6-12   Variable curve versus time for Ex. 6-5.

approximation of area. If the variable value changes very much during the sample time, there will be greater error.

EXAMPLE 6-5   Figure 6-12 shows a plot of a process variable versus time and the set point. The exact area of the error curve (value minus set point versus time) has been found to be 3.2289878. Compare the rectangular approximation of this area for sample times of 2, 1, and 0.5 s.

Solution: The area for each case is determined by the construction of rectangles, as shown in Fig. 6-13, for the three different sample times. Figure 6-13 shows the three cases with the appropriate rectangles drawn in. The results of adding the area of each rectangle are:

$$\begin{array}{lll} \text{2 s:} & \text{Area} = 3.36 & (3.4\% \text{ error}) \\ \text{1 s:} & \text{Area} = 3.26 & (0.9\% \text{ error}) \\ \text{0.5 s:} & \text{Area} = 3.22 & (0.3\% \text{ error}) \end{array}$$

Sample Time.   As you can see, the smallest possible sample time is desired to obtain the greatest accuracy in rectangular approximation of the area. This idea of shortest sample time was encountered before in the discussion of sampled data systems in Ch. 4. It was concluded in that case that the maximum sampling frequency, which is the smallest possible sampling time, was desired to avoid errors in data representation. A sampling time represented by a sampling frequency about 10 times the maximum signal frequency was recommended to avoid sampling error. This will be a suitable specification for area construction also, since it means that the signal will not change much in any one sampling period. Thus a rectangular approximation of area within one sample period will be quite accurate.

Algorithm.   All that remains is to specify how the area construction by rectangular areas will be performed by the computer and used in the integral-mode equation. This turns out to be quite simple. As in the proportional mode, however, we must account for the units to be used and the range of variation. In Eq. (1-10) it is

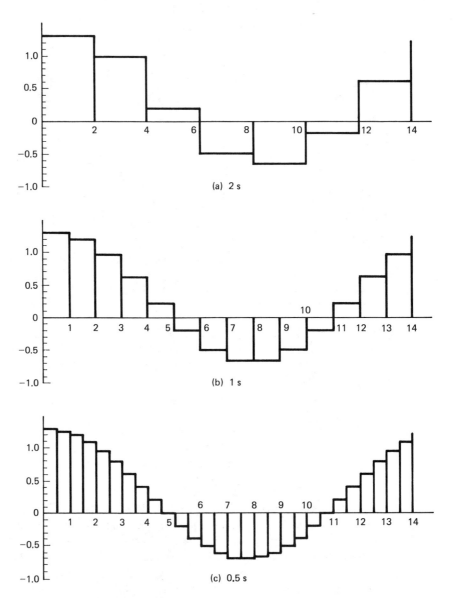

FIG. 6-13 These curves show the area approximation for three different sample times: 2, 1, and 0.5 s.

assumed that the error is expressed as percent of range and that the equation solution, c, varies from 0% to 100%, representing the output range. Thus the units of K_I are percent of output per (percent error − time). As noted before, percent is conceptually the same as fractional, so the units could just as well be fractional change in controller output per (error as fraction of range − time). The time units could be seconds, minutes, or any other time unit.

If the variable *AREA* is defined to be the net area under the error-time curve, then the appropriate integral mode equation for a digital system is

$$DCI = KI * AREA * ROUT \qquad (6\text{-}7)$$

where *DCI* = integral-mode output
       KI = integral-mode gain
   AREA = error-time curve area approximation
   ROUT = range of output variable.

Note that there is no constant added to this equation as in Eq. (1-10). This is because in the computer *DCI* will represent some register or memory location whose value is calculated and updated as each new sample changes *AREA*. If any initial value is desired, *AREA* is simply loaded with that starting value when the program starts.

Equation (6-7) assumes that the range of controller output is given by *ROUT*. Thus, *KI* * *AREA* represents the fraction of this range that results from the integral mode. If the net area is zero, this term will contribute nothing.

The area approximation, *AREA*, is calculated by summing all rectangular areas from the time the process was started, $t = 0$. This can be done by

$$AREA = AREA + (DFE * DT) \qquad (6\text{-}8)$$

where *DFE* = error as fraction of variable range [Eq. (6-3)]
       DT = time between samples.

The idea behind this equation is that the area is *updated* with each sample by adding the area represented by that sample to the previously calculated area.

Simplification. In keeping with our previous idea of using the same input and output range, the preceding equations can be simplified. To do this, let's express the equations with the ranges, *RIN* and *ROUT*, shown explicitly. Define a new variable, *SUM*, which represents the sum of all errors:

$$SUM = SUM + DE \qquad (6\text{-}9)$$

Then the area expression can be written in the form

$$AREA = \frac{SUM * DT}{RIN} \qquad (6\text{-}10)$$

If Eq. (6-10) is substituted into Eq. (6-7), the result is

$$DCI = KI * SUM * DT * \frac{ROUT}{RIN} \qquad (6\text{-}11)$$

Now, if the requirement is made that the ranges be the same, $ROUT = RIN$ (such as making both equal to the full counting range of the data word), then Eq. (6-11) is simplified. The full set of equations to define the integral mode algorithm can then be written as

$$DE = DV - DSP \qquad (6\text{-}2)$$
$$SUM = SUM + DE \qquad (6\text{-}9)$$
$$DCI = KI * SUM * DT \qquad (6\text{-}12)$$

This representation has the advantage that the value used for *KI* will be the same as that deduced for analog systems. The general flowchart for this set of equations

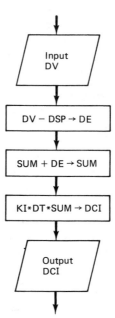

FIG. 6-14 General flowchart for the integral or rate mode of control.

is given in Fig. 6-14. This amounts to a straightforward application of the control equations.

EXAMPLE 6-6   An integral mode will be used for a system with 00 to FFH input and output ranges, a 8AH set point, and a direct gain of 0.58/min. The sample time is 5 s. Construct the control equation and give a method by which the constant multiplication can be performed.

Solution: The control-mode equation is found from Eqs. (6-12) and Eq. (6-2), with $DSP =$ 8AH. The constants become

$$KI * DT = (0.58/min)(1/60\ min/s)(5\ s)$$
$$= 0.0483$$

Then the control equations become

$$DE = DV - 8AH$$
$$SUM = SUM + DE$$
$$DCI = 0.0483 * SUM$$

The indicated constant multiplication by 0.0483 can be approximated, in 8 bits, by left shifts and adds. This is done by finding the fractional binary of 0.0483 using the method of successive multiplication by 2. The result is 00001100_2. This shows that

$$0.0483 * SUM \approx \frac{SUM}{32} + \frac{SUM}{64}$$

So the product can be formed by adding five right shifts of *SUM* to six right shifts of *SUM*. The actual product is easily seen to be 0.046875.

Detailed Flowchart.   A detailed flowchart of the integral mode must include protections against overflow and underflow, as well as keep track of the polarity of

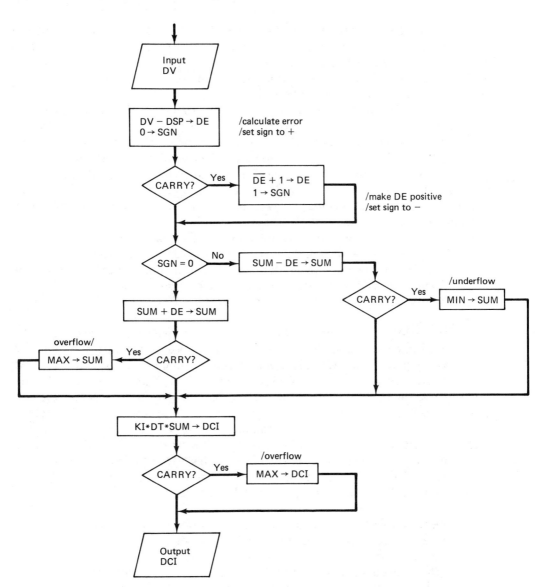

FIG. 6-15 Detailed flowchart of integral control showing the *SUM* accumulations and overflow–underflow protection.

the error. Figure 6-15 shows a flowchart that includes these facets. The polarity of *DE* is accounted for using the method introduced by Fig. 6-1 with a sign flag, SGN, and an unsigned number for *DE*.

SUM Overflow and Underflow.   In the program for using the integral mode, SUM will be one or more memory locations incremented for positive error and decremented for negative error. Since this is a continuous process, there is always the possibility that a string of positive errors will occur such that *SUM* reaches the full possible count of the number of bits used for storage. In this case the next positive error added to *SUM* will cause an *overflow*. The result of this will be that *SUM* drops to some value much lower than the maximum number representation of *SUM*. This could have serious results on the control system.

An *underflow* results when subtracting error from *SUM*. *KCI* is not typically a bipolar number; that is, it is expected to vary over the range *ROUT.* Thus *SUM* can never become a negative number; it is expected to vary from zero to the maximum count of the alloted memory space. However, if the error remains negative over an extended period of samples, it is possible for *SUM* to become very small. If a negative error sample *exceeds* the number in *SUM*, the result will be an underflow. In this case the number in *SUM* will become very large because of the way the addition of a negative number is performed.

You can see in Fig. 6-15 that an underflow is indicated by the carry bit following subtraction of *DE* from *SUM* and an overflow by a carry following addition. In either case, *SUM* must be set to the limit of the value it can hold. In general, *SUM* will be an unsigned number that varies from zero to a maximum, like FF if it is 8 bits in length. In such cases *SUMMIN* = 00H and *SUMMAX* = FFH.

SUM Size.   From a practical point of view, it may be necessary to use double precision for the accumulation of *SUM*. This is because the product of *KI* and *DT,* which will be taken times *SUM*, is often a fractional number. Thus, if *SUM* were 8 bits, then *KCI* = *KI* ∗ *DT* ∗ *SUM* could never be FFH. This would mean that the controller output could never be the maximum, assuming of course that only the integral mode is being used. If *SUM* were a double precision, 16-bit number, it would be possible to obtain the full ouput. For example, suppose *KI* ∗ *DT* = 0.5. This is equivalent to a single right shift. Then if *SUM* = FFH (as 8 bits), the maximum output would be 7FH. (Right shift *SUM* once.) However, if *SUM* = FFFFH (16 bits), a right shift would still give FFH for the output, and full output would be possible. In fact, it would remain full until *SUM* dropped to 01FDH or less.

Direct and Reverse Action.   In the form presented, it is assumed that an increasing area requires an increasing output. This is direct action. In many cases an increasing area requires a decreasing output, which is reverse action. This can be provided by the decision block for adding or subtracting the error with *SUM* in the flowchart of Fig. 6-15. It is shown for direct action since a positive error (SGN = 0) causes *SUM* to increase. Reverse action would be provided by simply reversing the decision block so that a positive error causes *DE* to be subtracted from *SUM*.

Start-up Problems.   One of the most difficult problems with the use of an integral mode is during process start-up. For example, in temperature control systems start-up involves heating of the system from some initial state. During the time when the process is being heated up to the set point, the integral term will be accumulating error area with a fixed polarity, resulting in a large overshoot from the proper zero area controller output. In such cases the integral mode can be disabled until the system is up to temperature, or loaded with a large offset initially, which will be decreased by the area accumulation.

EXAMPLE 6-7   Flow is to be controlled by a computer using the integral controller mode with an integral gain of 0.75%/ (%-min) and a sample time of 5 s. Flow is input as 00H to FFH for minimum to maximum. Output is a valve control signal with 00H being closed and FFH full open. Prepare a flowchart of the control algorithm using symbolic names for variables. The set point is 85H.

Solution: Note first that the system is *reverse* acting since an increasing flow requires a decreasing valve setting. Thus we will subtract when the error is positive. Since both KI and DT are constants, let's multiply them together ahead of time. They must have the same units:

$$KI * DT = (0.75\%/(\%\text{-min})(5 \text{ s})(\tfrac{1}{60} \text{ min/s})$$
$$= 0.0625$$

The control equations are

$$DE = DV - 85\text{H}$$
$$SUM = SUM + DE$$
$$DCI = KI * DT * SUM = 0.0625 * SUM$$

The multiplication of 0.0625 can be simply performed, because

$$0.0625 = \tfrac{1}{16} = \tfrac{1}{2}^4$$

So the multiplication is performed by shifting SUM to the right four times. Given that the valve setting is to vary from 00H to FFH, it is easy to see that SUM will have to be at least 3 bytes (12 bits). The reason is that DCI will be found from shifting SUM four times, which means that if $SUM = $ FFH, as 1 byte, the maximum DCI would be 0FH and the valve could never be open. On the other hand, if $SUM = $ FFFH, the maximum DCI would be FFH as required. A 16-bit representation would be easier from a programming point of view. The flowchart for this system is shown in Fig. 6-16 in a rather general sense. The next step would be to construct a specific flowchart for the microprocessor being used and then the code itself.

It is important to understand the accumulation process that occurs in the integral mode. This can be seen from Ex. 6-8, where actual controller operation is shown in a time sequence of variable inputs.

EXAMPLE 6-8   Use the previous control system to evaluate the response to the following time sequence of input samples (all HEX): 00, 15, 3A, 42, 5A, 7B, 92, A7, C4, DE, B3, A5, 82. Construct a table of these inputs and the corresponding values of DE, SUM, and DCI. Assume SUM is initially zero. Be careful to protect against polarity changes of DE.

Solution: The table is constructed by performing the operations of the computer on these data entries. The equations were found to be

$$DE = DV - 85\text{H}$$
$$SUM = SUM + DE \quad (\text{FFFF} = \max, 0000 = \min)$$
$$DCI = 0.0625 * SUM \quad (\text{FF} = \max, 00 = \min)$$

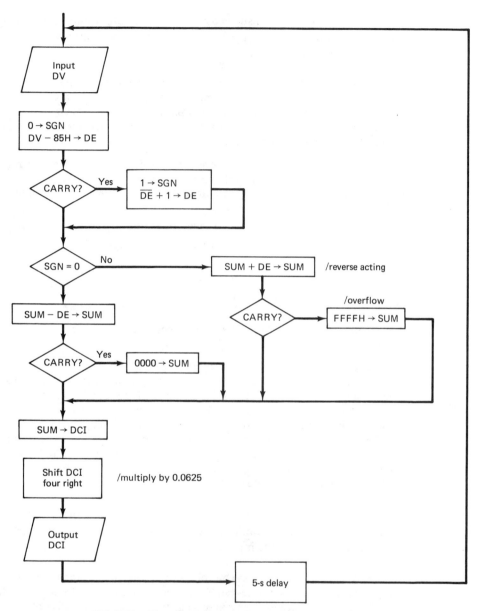

FIG. 6-16   Flowchart for solution to the control of Ex. 6-7.

The following calculations show how the first few entries are determined, using Fig. 6-16:

$$\text{For } DV = 00\text{H} \qquad DE = 00 - 85\text{H} = 85\text{H} \quad (SGN = 1)$$
$$SUM = 0000\text{H} + 85\text{H} = 0085\text{H}$$
$$DCI = 08\text{H}$$
$$\text{For } DV = 15\text{H} \qquad DE = 15\text{H} - 85\text{H} = 70\text{H} \quad (SGN = 1)$$

TABLE 6-1

DV	DE	SGN	SUM	DCI
00	85	-1	0085	08
15	70	-1	00F5	0F
3A	4B	-1	0140	14
42	43	-1	0183	18
5A	2B	-1	01AE	1A
7B	0A	-1	01B8	1B
92	0D	1	01AB	1A
A7	22	1	0189	18
C4	3F	1	014A	14
DE	59	1	00F1	0F
B3	2E	1	00C3	0C
A5	20	1	00A3	0A
82	03	-1	00A6	0A

$$SUM = 0085H + 70H = 00F5H$$
$$DCI = 0FH$$

For $DV = 3AH$
$$DE = 3AH - 85H = 4BH \quad (SGN = 1)$$
$$SUM = 00F5H + 4BH + 0140H$$
$$DCI = 14H$$

For $DV = 42H$
$$DE = 42H - 85H = 43H \quad (SGN = 1)$$
$$SUM = 0140H + 43H = 0183H$$
$$DCI = 18H$$

The rest of the entries proceed along these same lines. It might be well to see how the entries with a positive DE are handled. For example:

For $DV = C4$
$$DE = C4H - 85H = 3FH \quad (SGN = 0)$$
$$SUM = 0189H - 3Fh = 014AH$$
$$DCI = 14H$$

Table 6-1 shows the results for the entire sequence of inputs. Note that SUM increases and decreases in response to the polarity of DE.

6-2.3 Derivative Mode (Rate)

In Ch. 1 it was explained that the derivative mode of control produces a feedback that is dependent on the rate at which the error is changing. The formal definition of this mode is defined by the calculus operation of differentiation and is given by Eq. (1-13). When using the computer for control, only periodic samples of the controlled variable are available, and thus the more appropriate definition of the mode is Eq. (1-12), in terms of the change of variable value over some time period.

As pointed out in Ch. 1, the derivative mode is never used alone since no feedback is provided unless the error is changing in time. A constant error would not be corrected.

Algorithm.   In computer control applications of the derivative mode, there are a number of different algorithms by which the derivative can be estimated from samples of the variable value. The simplest, and often best, approximation is to simply use Eq. (1-12) directly. In terms of a general equation the mode would be defined as

$$DCD = \frac{KD * (DFE - DFE0) * ROUT}{DT} \tag{6-13}$$

where DCD = derivative-mode controller output
     KD = derivative-mode gain
    DFE = present error as fraction of variable range
   $DFE0$ = previous error as fraction of variable range
  $ROUT$ = range of output
     DT = sample time.

This equation uses the change in error over the sample time and the mode gain to determine what fraction of the output range, $ROUT$, should be output.

Simplification.   As in the two previous cases, it is possible to simplify the equations for this control mode if the range of input, RIN, and range of output. $ROUT$, are the same. To see this, Eq. (6-13) will be written in a fashion to show the ranges explicitly. First, $DFE = DE/RIN$ and $DFE0 = DE0/RIN$, where $DE0$ is the previous error. If these are substituted into Eq. (6-13), the result is

$$DCD = \frac{KD * (DE - DE0) * ROUT}{DT * RIN}$$

Now if $RIN = ROUT$, this equation reduces to the simpler form

$$DCD = \frac{KD * DDE}{DT} \tag{6-14}$$

$$DDE = DE - DE0 \tag{6-15}$$

A further simplification results if we write the error terms out in terms of the variable itself, $DE = DV - DSP$, $DE0 = DV0 - DSP$, where $DV0$ = previous sample of the controlled variable. Now Eq. (6-15) takes on the form

$$DDE = DV - DV0 \tag{6-16}$$

Either Eq. (6-15) or (6-16) can be used to calculate the contribution of this term. In general, it will be found easier to use Eq. (6-16) to find the derivative term. This is because when the difference between DE and $DE0$ is taken there are four possible sign combinations that must be taken into account to find the sign of DDE. On the other hand, since DV and $DV0$ are positive quantities (00 to FFH), the sign is determined by the result of the subtraction alone. The flowchart of Fig. 6-17 shows the direct application of the derivative control mode. Of course, the mode is never used alone since no feedback would be provided for a constant error. Note that it is necessary to save the previous value of DV for use in calculation of the next sample derivative.

Derivative Polarity.   When the subtraction is performed to deduce the derivative, the result will either be a positive or negative number. If negative, the number will be in the 2's complement representation. In keeping with our desire to use unsigned integer math, it will be necessary to convert the difference to a positive number

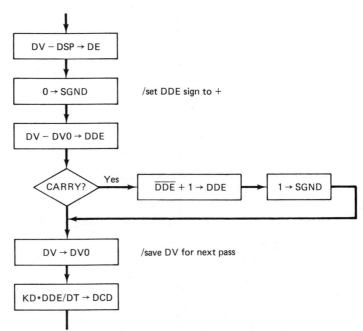

FIG. 6-17 Flowchart for the derivative mode showing how the derivative polarity must be identified.

and remember the sign of the result. This is shown in Fig. 6-17. Thus there are now two sign flags, one for DE itself and one for the derivative difference, $DE - DE0$.

Derivative Gain.   The derivative gain represents the fractional change of controller output per *rate of change* of the error as fraction of range. As such, it has a unit of time. Often when coding the equation for this mode the combination KD/DT is computed as a single constant multiplier of the difference term. It is important that the units of KD and DT agree when such a product is taken.

Direct and Reverse Action.   It is possible for the response of the derivative mode to be direct or reverse. Direct would mean that a positive rate of change of the controlled variable should produce an increasing output. Reverse means that a positive slope of variable in time should cause a reduction in the output. This can be provided by a decision on whether to add or subtract the contribution from the net controller output term. This decision is actually based upon *two* signs, the sign of the action and the sign of DDE itself. If the signs are the same, the action is addition, and if the signs are different, the action is subtraction.

EXAMPLE 6-9   A computer control system is used to regulate the rpm of a motor. For this purpose, rpm is input at $\frac{1}{3}$-s intervals. The derivative gain is 0.5% per (%/s). Construct the flowchart elements for the derivative action.

Solution: First, the derivative gain and sample time are combined:

$$\frac{KD}{DT} = (0.5)(3) = 1.5$$

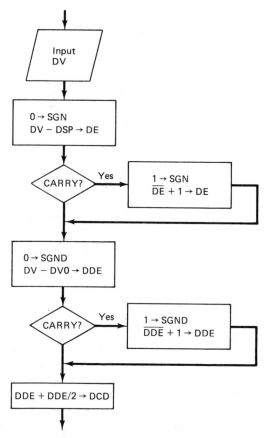

FIG. 6-18   Flowchart of Ex. 6-9.

Thus the mode equation is

$$DCD = 1.5 * (DV - DV0)$$

This can be provided by adding the difference to the difference right shifted once:

Let $$DDE = DV - DV0$$

then
$$DCD = DDE + \frac{DDE}{2}$$

The flowchart for this process is shown in Fig. 6-18. Note that SGND will be used to indicate if the derivative is positive or negative.

6-3   COMPOSITE MODES

In general, the best control of continuous-state systems is obtained when various combinations of the pure controller modes are employed. Three common combinations are used: (1) PI, a combination of proportional and integral action; (2) PD, a combination of proportional and derivative action; and (3) PID or *three mode*, a combination of all three modes, proportional, integral, and derivative.

A natural question to ask is, "Why not just use the PID composite controller action for all applications?" Indeed, any application for which the PI or PD, or even pure modes are used, could just as well be set up using the PID action. The reason this is not done is because of economy of time and effort. It is much more difficult to select the proper gains for stable control when a three-mode controller is used. Furthermore, in many processes the addition of derivative action to a PI control, for example, would not provide any improvement in control.

In the following sections the methods by which the PI and PID controller actions are programmed into a computer control system are discussed. The emphasis is on the flowcharts and gain combinations rather than on the specific techniques of coding. The examples given do not necessarily represent the most efficient coding to solve the algorithms.

6-3.1   Proportional–Integral Control Algorithm

The use of proportional action and integral action together is very common. One reason is that the integral action gives the system the capability to adjust itself to new load conditions that require changes in the zero error control output (resetting action).

The Algorithm.   In essence, the PI mode is simply a combination of the proportional and integral actions described earlier. However, it is found that proper construction of this composite mode requires the proportional gain to multiply both the error term and the error area term. Thus at any instant of time the controller output is composed of two terms. One term is due to the accumulated area of error versus time, and the other is due to the present extent of the error. It is possible to write a single equation for this mode, although the coding of this equation requires breaking of the relation into a number of parts:

$$DCPI = (KP * DE) + (KP * KI * DT * SUM) \qquad (6\text{-}17)$$

where $DCPI$ = PI controller mode output
$\qquad KP$ = proportional gain
$\qquad DE$ = error
$\qquad KI$ = integral-mode gain
$\qquad DT$ = sample time
$\qquad SUM$ = latest sum of errors, Eq. (6-11) or (6-12).

Note that if the error for any particular sample is *zero* then the output, from Eq. (6-17), will be the result of the integral term. This term is the result of the error history of the system through the SUM term. You can see then that the integral term provides the zero error response of the system.

In principle, then, the mode is simple to construct by employing Eq. (6-17) in the control output determination. In fact, however, the practical application of Eq.

(6-17) to a real problem using microprocessor-based computers creates a number of difficulties. The following issues define some of these difficulties and possible solutions.

Equations.   Equation (6-17) defines the response of the PI mode but cannot be coded directly into the computer. The coding requires breaking this equation into several steps, since the computer can perform only one mathematical operation at a time. A more practical set of equations would be

$$DE = DV - DSP \tag{6-2}$$

$$SUM = SUM + DE \tag{6-9}$$

$$DCI = KP * KI * DT * SUM \tag{6-18}$$

$$DCP = KP * DE \tag{6-19}$$

$$DCPI = DCI + DCP \tag{6-20}$$

Each of these equations can be solved by simple instructions in the computer. Of course, the constants in Eq. (6-18), $KP * KI * DT$, would be combined into one constant, say $K1$, which is used in the actual computation.

One may be tempted to combine Eqs. (6-9) and (6-18) and write the integral term as just $DCI = DCI + (KP * KI * DT * DE)$. There is a good reason why this may not be a wise choice: DE is typically a small number and the product of the constants is often a number *less* than 1. This would mean that many errors would produce no correction to DCI, since the operation of multiplying the constant times DE would leave a number smaller than can be represented by the data word. By adding DE to SUM first, the *accumulation* of many small numbers will have a finite effect on the control system. Example 6-10 illustrates this situation.

EXAMPLE 6-10   A control system is to use $KP = 2.4$, $KI = 0.8$/min, and $DT = 5$ s. Suppose in an 8-bit system the set point is 80H and successive samples are 82H, 84H, 83H, 85H, 86H, 84H, 82H, and 80H. At the start of the sample period, $DCI = 78$H and $SUM = 300$H. Compare the value of DCI at the end of the given sequence if this term is computed using the control equations given previously with that found using the combination form of DCI presented in the previous paragraph.

Solution: First, we get the errors corresponding to the given sequence of samples by subtracting 80H from the samples. Now the constants can be combined to give

$$KP * KI * DT = (2.4)(0.8)(5)(\tfrac{1}{60})$$
$$= 0.16$$

Multiplication by 0.16 can be approximated in 8 bits by the combination of $\tfrac{1}{8}$ of a number added to $\tfrac{1}{32}$ of the number. This actually gives 0.15625 instead of exactly 0.16. In this approximation the number is right shifted three times, and this is added to the number right shifted five times. The recommended sequence of equations becomes

$$SUM = SUM + DE$$
$$DCI = 0.16 * SUM \quad (\approx SUM/8 + SUM/32)$$

Using this equation sequence gives the following result as samples are accumulated:

DV	DE	SUM	DCI
82	2	302	78
84	4	306	78
83	3	309	79
85	5	30E	79
86	6	314	7A
84	4	318	7A
82	2	31A	7A
80	0	31A	7A

Notice the way *DCI* slowly increases as *SUM* accumulates error. Now suppose the direct calculation is employed where

$$DCI = DCI + (0.16 * DE) \quad \text{(using } \tfrac{1}{8} \text{ and } \tfrac{1}{32}\text{)}$$

The results are:

DV	DE	DCI
82	2	78
84	4	78
83	3	78
85	5	78
86	6	78
84	4	78
82	2	78
80	0	78

No correction is made for the error sequence! The reason is that, taken individually, each error gives zero for the result of shifting to produce an approximate product with 0.16.

You can see from this example that the order in which computations are performed can have an important effect on controller action.

Another important factor to note from Ex. 6-10 is that *SUM* required 2 bytes to keep a running track of the accumulated error. This is true because the integral term, represented by *DCI*, must be capable of a full-range output. Since the constants amounted to only 0.16, it is clear that *SUM* will have to be greater than 8 bits to be able to provide an output of FFH after multiplication by the constants. In general, enough bits must be used for *SUM* accumulations so that a full-range output of *DCI* is possible.

Overflow and Underflow.   A very serious consideration when coding the PI control mode is to provide protection against overflow and underflow of variables in the calculation. The basic idea here is that the value of *DCPI* will usually cover the integer range of the computer data word, 00H to FFH for example in an 8-bit computer. This places restrictions on the value of *DCI* to remain within this bound also, since with no error *DCPI* is equal to *DCI*. But such a restriction on *DCI* places a restriction on *SUM*, since it is this quantity that determines the value of *DCI*.

An overflow of any of these quantities occurs when an addition operation results in a number exceeding that possible in the computer, FFH for example in an

8-bit processor. When such a condition is detected, the variable must be set equal to FFH. For example, suppose *DCI* is already C5H and the feedback process provides that 52H is to be added. You can show that the proper result would be 117H, but in an 8-bit machine the result would be 17H with the carry bit set. If left undetected and uncorrected, the feedback would change from C5H to 17H! An overflow is indicated when a positive number (MSB = 0) is added and a carry bit set results.

An underflow results from subtraction that would leave *SUM*, *DCI*, or *DCPI* negative. These quantities are unsigned (positive) integers and cannot be negative. If the subtraction would make them negative, they should be set equal to zero. For example, suppose *SUM* was 27H and the error turned out to be a negative 36H. This would be E2H in 2's complement. The result of "adding" this error to *SUM* would properly give a negative 9. But, in fact, it would give F1H with no carry bit set. Thus the content would jump from 27H to F1H when the result should really have been negative. Of course, *SUM* cannot be negative, so this condition is defined as underflow and *SUM* should be set equal to zero. An underflow is indicated when a subtraction is performed and the carry bit is set.

Flowchart.   The flowchart of Fig. 6-19 shows the essential features of a PI controller algorithm. This flowchart includes some of the important features, such as overflow and underflow protection and polarity considerations. Essentially, this flowchart is simply a composite of those developed for the proportional and integral modes. You will note, however, that *KP* multiplies both terms.

Example 6-11 illustrates how the PI controller mode is applied to the problem introduced in the first section of this chapter.

EXAMPLE 6-11   Integral action is to be added to the temperature control problem presented in the proportional mode section of this chapter. The integral gain to be used is *KI* = 0.75% per %-min. Construct a general flowchart of how the integral mode will be included. Develop required modifications of the detailed flowchart and construct the 8080 mnemonic codes for including the integral action.

Solution: Let's start by construction of the equations that must be used to determine the output. From this we can work toward the detailed accounting of how the equations are to be solved. The constants involved in the control equations are:

$$KP = 3.5$$
$$KP * KI * DT = (3.5)(0.75)(10)(\tfrac{1}{60}) = 0.4375$$

where the $\tfrac{1}{60}$ was necessary to make the units agree. Now the control equations are

$$DE = DV - DSP$$
$$SUM = SUM + DE$$
$$DCI = 0.4375 * SUM$$
$$DCP = 3.5 * DE$$
$$DCPI = DCP + DCI$$

The modifications to the detailed flowchart for proportional only control of Fig. 6-8 will consist of two parts: adding the calculation of *DCI* and combining *DCI* and *DCP* to produce the output. For the first part, since *DCI* will be the output for zero error, we must be sure that *DCI* can span the entire range of 00 to FFH. This can only be possible if *SUM* is more than 10 bits, since multiplication by 0.4375 involves at least two right

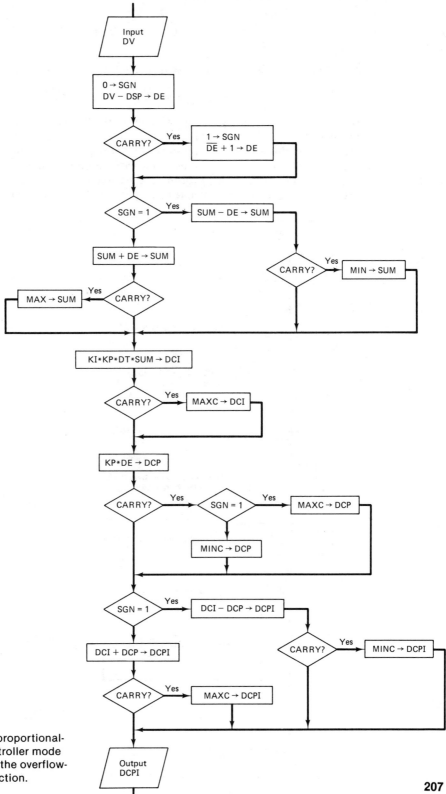

FIG. 6-19 The proportional-integral (PI) controller mode flowchart. Note the overflow-underflow protection.

shifts of *SUM*. So we will make *SUM* 16 bits in length. In fact, *DCI* can be calculated exactly by

$$0.4375 * SUM = \frac{SUM}{4} + \frac{SUM}{8} + \frac{SUM}{16}$$

This can be accomplished by adding two right shifts, three right shifts, and four right shifts of *SUM*. The 8080 does not have a 16-bit right shift operation, so a subroutine will be needed to perform these shifts. This is easily provided by performing 8-bit shifts of *SUM*, in the HL register pair, and using the carry as an intermediate bit for the shift between H and L. The flowchart for this is given in Fig. 6-20. For the rest of the flowchart, refer to Fig. 6-21. You will note that a positive *DE* is subtracted from *SUM* since

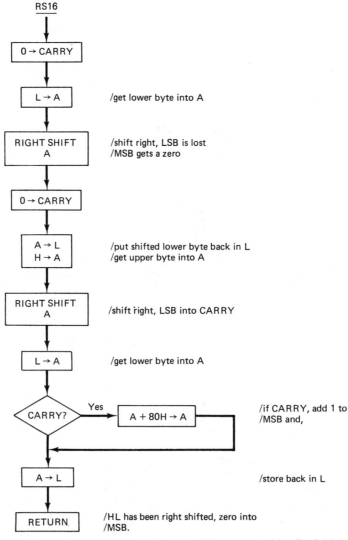

FIG. 6-20 Flowchart of a 16-bit right shift as needed for Ex. 6-11.

Initialization: 0000 → STACK   /set SUM to zero

The following routine starts after DCP = 3.5∗DE has been calculated
This is at ⓐ of Fig. 6.8

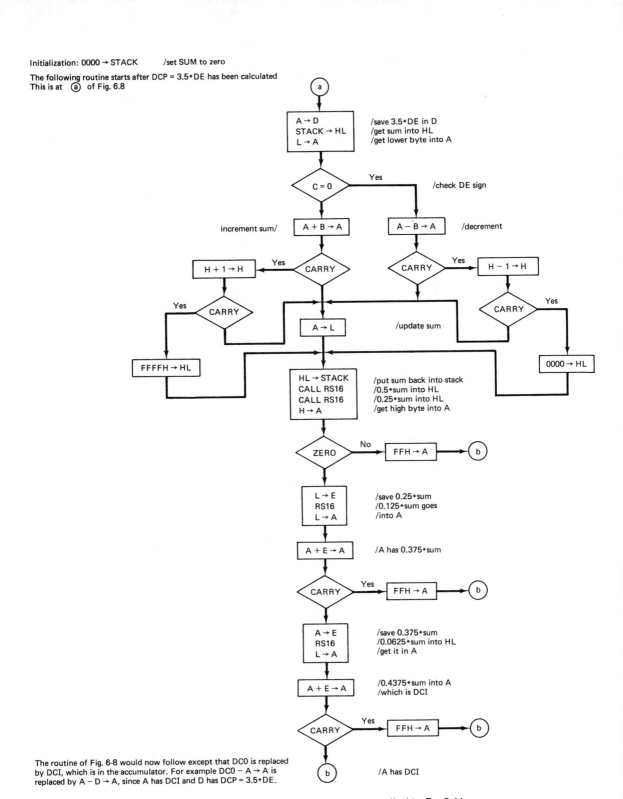

FIG. 6-21 The PI mode flowchart as applied to Ex. 6-11.

The routine of Fig. 6-8 would now follow except that DC0 is replaced
by DCI, which is in the accumulator. For example DC0 − A → A is
replaced by A − D → A, since A has DCI and D has DCP = 3.5∗DE.

```
;Initialization
            LXI  SP,STACK       ;SET UP THE STACK POINTER
            LXI  H,0000H        ;ZERO HL PAIR AND SAVE
            PUSH H              ;AS SUM
START:      MVI  A,01           ;SET BIT TO START ADC
;
;
(SAME AS THE PROPORTIONAL MODE)
;
;
            MOV  D,A            ;SAVE 3.5×DE=DSP IN D
            POP  H              ;GET SUM FROM STACK
            MOV  A,C            ;GET SIGN OF DE
            ANA  A              ;SET FLAGS TO TEST DE
            MOV  A,L            ;GET LOWER BYTE OF SUM INTO A
            JZ   SUBDE          ;IF POSITIVE WE SUBTRACT - REVERSE
            ADD  B              ;SUM + DE IS IN A
            JNC  DCI            ;NO CARRY SAYS GO CALCULATE DCI
            INR  H              ;CARRY SAYS TO INCREMENT H
            JNC  DCI            ;AND THEN GO DCI IF NO CARRY, BUT
            LXI  H,0FFFFH       ;IF SO THEN OVERFLOW AND SET SUM TO MAX
            JMP  DCI1           ;AND CONTINUE
SUBDE:      SUB  B              ;SUM - DE IS IN A
            JNC  DCI            ;IF NO CARRY THEN GO DCI
            DCR  H              ;IF CARRY DECREMENT H AND
            JNC  DCI            ;CHECK FOR CARRY SHOWING UNDERFLOW
            LXI  H,0000H        ;IF SO, SET SUM TO MINIMUM
            JMP  DCI1           ;AND CONTINUE
DCI:        MOV  L,A            ;NOW HL HAS SUM
DCI1:       PUSH H              ;SAVE SUM IN STACK, BUT STILL IN HL
            CALL RS16           ;SUM/2 INTO HL
            CALL RS16           ;SUM/4 INTO HL
            MOV  A,H            ;GET HIGH ORDER BYTE
            ANA  A              ;SET FLAGS
            JNZ  OVR1           ;IF H IS NOT ZERO THEN DCI WILL OVERFLOW
            MOV  E,L            ;IF NOT SAME SUM/4 IN E
            CALL RS16           ;SUM/8 IN HL
            MOV  A,L            ;GET SUM/8 INTO A
            ADD  E              ;AND ADD IT TO SUM/4
            JC   OVR1           ;BUT IF CARRY, THEN OVERFLOW
            MOV  E,A            ;SAVE IN E
            CALL RS16           ;FINALLY SUM/16
            MOV  A,L            ;GET IT IN A
            ADD  E              ;ADD IT TO THE REST TO GET DCI
            JNC  DCPI           ;AND JMP TO DCPI IF NO OVERFLOW
OVR1:       MVI  A,0FFH         ;FOR OVERFLOW SET A TO MAX
DCPI:       MOV  E,A            ;SAVE DCI IN E
            MOV  A,C            ;GET DE SIGN
            ANA  A              ;SET FLAGS
            MOV  A,E            ;GET DCI BACK
            JZ   SUBD           ;IF POSITIVE WE SUBTRACT - REVERSE
            ADD  D              ;THIS IS DCI+DCP IN A
            JNC  OUT            ;IF NO CARRY GO OUTPUT
            MVI  A,0FFH         ;IF SO SET A TO MAX
            JMP  OUT            ;AND GO OUTPUT
SUBD:       SUB  D              ;SO WE FORM DCI-DCP
            JNC  OUT            ;AND GO OUT IF NO UNDERFLOW
            MVI  A,00H          ;IF SO, SET A TO MIN
OUT:        OUT  0E0H           ;OUTPUT TO DAC
;
(THE REST IS THE SAME AS PROPORTIONAL

;NOW WE HAVE THE 16 BIT RIGHT SHIFT CALLED RS16
RS16:       ANA  A              ;ZERO CARRY
            MOV  A,L            ;GET LOWER ORDER BYTE IN A
            RAR                 ;ROTATE IT RIGHT, LSB INTO CARRY BUT
            ANA  A              ;ZERO CARRY, LOSE LSB, MSB IS ZERO.
            MOV  L,A            ;PUT IT BACK IN L
            MOV  A,H            ;NOW GET HIGH ORDER BYTE
            RAR                 ;ROTATE IT RIGHT, LSB TO CARRY
            MOV  H,A            ;PUT IT BACK IN H
            MOV  A,L            ;GET L BACK IN A
            JNC  RET1           ;NOW TEST THAT CARRY BIT FROM H
            ADI  80H            ;IT WAS SET SO MAKE L MSB = 1
RET1:       MOV  L,A            ;AND PUT A BACK IN L
            RET                 ;GO BACK
```

FIG. 6-22 Code in 8080 mnemonics for the temperature-control problem using PI described in Ex. 6-11.

the control is reverse acting. *SUM* overflow is corrected by placing FFFFH into *SUM*. Actually, instead of this, we could have used any number greater than 247H, so that the product 0.4375 ∗ *DE* can allow *DCI* to equal the maximum, FFH. An underflow of *SUM* is resolved by setting *SUM* equal to 0000H. An overflow of *DCI* is indicated if the shifting does not leave H empty. In this case, *DCI* is set equal to the maximum, FFH. The second part, combining *DCI* and *DCP*, is provided by replacing *DC*0 by *DCI* in the flow chart of Fig. 6-8. Note that *SUM* is saved in the stack when not being used. Figure 6-22 shows the assembly language code for the modifications and for the 16-bit right shift algorithm, RS16. The main routine is designed to be merged with that given in Fig. 6-9 for proportional only control.

6-3.2 PID Controller Action

The three-mode controller represents the ultimate in control of continuous process for which a specific system transfer function cannot be written. The tuning of such a control system is more complicated simply because there are more terms to consider, but the control that can be achieved is substantially greater in many applications. In this section the PID control mode implementation by computer is shown.

   The Algorithm.   Actually, all we are going to do is introduce derivative action into the PI controller action discussed in the previous section. As in that case, it becomes necessary to use the proportional gain to multiply the derivative term as well as the derivative gain. The resulting control equation has three terms: one directly proportional to the error, one dependent on the error history, and one dependent on the present rate of change of the error:

$$DCPID = (KP * DE) + (KP * KI * DT * SUM) + \frac{KP * KD * DDE}{DT} \qquad (6\text{-}21)$$

where $DCPID$ = controller output
   KP = proportional gain
   DE = variable error = $DV - DSP$
   KI = integral gain
   DT = sample time
   SUM = error running sum
   KD = derivative gain
   DDE = $DV - DV0$ = error change from last sample.

Note that if the error is zero the output is determined by both the accumulation in *SUM* and by the change of the error from the last sample.

   The actual programming of Eq. (6-21) requires that the equation be broken into a number of individual parts. The following sections describe some practical considerations in the application of this control mode.

   The Equations.   The practical application of PID control requires that the control equation, Eq. (6-21), be broken into a number of parts since the computer can perform only one operation at a time. The typical control equations consist of the set:

$$
\left.\begin{aligned}
DE &= DV - DSP \\
SUM &= SUM + DE \\
DDE &= DV - DV0 \\
DV0 &= DV \\
DCI &= KP * KI * DT * SUM \\
DCD &= \frac{KP * KD * DDE}{DT} \\
DCP &= KP * DE \\
DCPID &= DCP + DCI + DCD
\end{aligned}\right\} \quad (6\text{-}22)
$$

The constants are combined in actual implementation of the equations. As usual, a number of important practical considerations are necessary in the coding of these equations into an actual application. Most of these are just a repeat of those mentioned earlier for the derivative and PI controller action. Those that are specific to the inclusion of the derivative mode are given next.

Polarity of *DDE*.   *DDE* is a polarity dependent term and so the decision to actually add or subtract *DCD* from *DCI* + *DCP* must be based upon an evaluation of that polarity. Note that if the action is direct ($KP > 0$) then a positive rate of change ($DDE > 0$) means that *DCD* would be added, while if the action were reverse, *DCD* would be subtracted for $DDE > 0$.

Overflow.   If the constants that multiply *DDE* are greater than 1, it will be possible for *DCD* to overflow. For this reason, overflow detection must also be provided.

Example 6-12 shows the modifications required in the temperature problem to include derivative action in the control.

EXAMPLE 6-12   Develop the flow diagram and coding necessary to modify the PI control of the previous section to include derivative action. The derivative gain is given to be $KD = 0.08\%$ per %/min.

Solution: This can be done by specifying what additional calculations are required to provide the derivative control. First, the equation for derivative control will be developed. The constant is found as

$$
\frac{KP * KD}{DT} = (3.5)(0.08)(\tfrac{1}{10})(60) = 1.68
$$

Then the equations become

$$
DDE = DV - DV0 \quad (DV0 = \text{previous } DE)
$$
$$
DCD = 1.68 * DDE
$$

The product of 1.68 times *DDE* can be performed by the following construction:

$$
1.68 * DDE \approx DDE + \frac{DDE}{2} + \frac{DDE}{8} + \frac{DDE}{32} + \frac{DDE}{64} + \frac{DDE}{128}
$$

The initialization must zero the first three STACK locations.
Then the following derivative routine starts just after the alarm
test. The conditions are A has DV, the STACK has SUM, DCD and sign,
DV0 (previous DV), in that order.

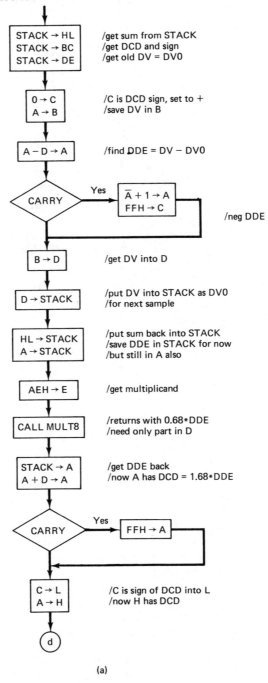

STACK → HL STACK → BC STACK → DE	/get sum from STACK /get DCD and sign /get old DV = DV0
0 → C A → B	/C is DCD sign, set to + /save DV in B
A − D → A	/find DDE = DV − DV0
CARRY — Yes — $\overline{A}$ + 1 → A / FFH → C	/neg DDE
B → D	/get DV into D
D → STACK	/put DV into STACK as DV0 /for next sample
HL → STACK A → STACK	/put sum back into STACK /save DDE in STACK for now /but still in A also
AEH → E	/get multiplicand
CALL MULT8	/returns with 0.68*DDE /need only part in D
STACK → A A + D → A	/get DDE back /now A has DCD = 1.68*DDE
CARRY — Yes — FFH → A	
C → L A → H	/C is sign of DCD into L /now H has DCD

d

(a)

FIG. 6-23 Modifications of the flowchart of temperature control to include
derivative action. (Continued on next page.)

213

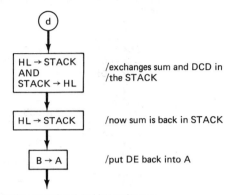

Now continue with proportional and integral terms.

DCD is combined with DCPI from Fig. 6-23.
A has DCPI = DCI + DCP

(b)

FIG. 6-23 (continued)

However, this shift and add operation is complicated enough that it might be easier to use a multiplication routine. In this case we can use MULT8, which multiplies two 8-bit numbers and gets a 16-bit result. If the multiplier is taken to be 0.68, the 16-bit result will consist of a whole part in the upper 8 bits and a fractional part in the lower 8 bits. Thus we need only include the upper 8 bits since only the whole number part is needed. The multiplicand is to be *DDE* and the multiplier is AEH (≈ 0.68). When actually trying to construct the flowchart for adding derivative action, it becomes clear that the stack will have to be used to pass the new variables. In particular, we now must save *DV*0, *DCD*, and its sign. To accomplish this, the stack will be used. The stack order will be *SUM*, *DCD*, and sign, *DV*0. The flowchart of Fig. 6-23 shows how the derivative action is included. Calculation of *DCD* is accomplished right after the alarm check in Fig. 6-8.

```
;INITIALIZATION
            LXI SP,STACK            ;SET UP THE STACK POINTER
            LXI H,0000H             ;ZERO THE HL REGISTER PAIR
            PUSH H                  ;AND THEN ZERO
            PUSH H                  ;THE NEXT THREE
            PUSH H                  ;STACK CONTENTS
START:      MVI A,01H               ;SET BIT TO START ADC
;
(SAME AS PI EXCEPT THAT RIGHT AFTER THE ALARM TEST THE
FOLLOWING IS INSERTED)
;
            POP H                   ;GET SUM INTO HL
            POP B                   ;GET PREVIOUS DCD AND SIGN
            MVI C,00                ;SET SIGND TO + INITIALLY
            POP D                   ;GET PREVIOUS DV, NOW DV0 INTO D
            MOV B,A                 ;MOVE DV INTO B TO SAVE
            SUB D                   ;NOW FORM DDE = DV - DV0
            JNC DCD                 ;IF NO CARRY GO CALCULATE DCD
            CMA                     ;IF CARRY SET DDE TO ABSOLUTE
            ADI 01                  ;BY 2'S COMPLEMENT AND
            MVI C,0FFH              ;SET SIGN OF DDE TO -
DCD:        MOV D,B                 ;GET DV BACK
            PUSH D                  ;SAVE IT TO BE DV0 ON NEXT PASS
            PUSH H                  ;PUT SUM BACK IN STACK FOR NOW
            PUSH PSW                ;SAVE DDE FOR THE MOMENT
            MOV E,0AEH              ;NOW TO MULTIPLY BY 0.68 LOAD E
            CALL MULT8              ;AND GO MULTIPLY TIMES DDE
            POP PSW                 ;GET DDE BACK
            ADD D                   ;AND ADD IT TO 0.68XDDE TO GET DCD
            JNC SAVE                ;IF NO CARRY OVERFLOW GO TO SAVE
            MVI A,0FFH              ;IF CARRY SET DCD TO MAX
SAVE:       MOV L,C                 ;MOVE SIGN OF DCD (DDE) TO L
            MOV H,A                 ;MOVE DCD TO H
            XTHL                    ;EXCHANGE HL WITH STACK
            PUSH H                  ;THEN PUSH IT BACK TO GET ORDER RIGHT
            MOV A,B                 ;GET DV BACK TO START PROPORTIONAL
;
;THE REMAINING ROUTINES ARE THE SAME AS DCPI, EXCEPT WHEN THE OUTPUT
COMES INSTEAD OF JNC OUT AND JMP OUT, WE JNC DCPID AND JMP DCPID
THEN:
;
DCPID:      POP H                   ;GET SUM
            POP B                   ;GET DCD AND SIGN INTO B AND C
            MOV E,A                 ;MOVE DCPI INTO E
            MOV A,C                 ;GET SIGN OF DCD INTO A
            ANA A                   ;SET FLAGS TO TEST IT
            MOV A,E                 ;GET DCPI BACK
            JZ SUBD                 ;IF POSITIVE GO SUBTRACT - REVERSE
            ADD B                   ;FORM DCPID=DCPI + DCD
            JNC RESTO               ;NO CARRY GO RESTORE STACK AND OUTPUT
            MVI A,0FFH              ;CARRY, OVERFLOW, SET DCPID TO MAX
            JMP RESTO               ;AND GO RESTORE AND OUTPUT
SUBD:       SUB D                   ;FORM DCPID = DCPI - DCD
            JNC RESTO               ;NO CARRY GO RESTORE STACK AND OUTPUT
            MVI A,00                ;CARRY, UNDERFLOW, SET DCPID TO MIN
RESTO:      PUSH B                  ;RESTORE DCD AND SIGN
            PUSH H                  ;RESTORE SUM
            OUT 0E0H                ;OUTPUT TO DAC
;
(REST IS THE SAME AS PI CONTROL)
```

FIG. 6-24 Modifications of the code to include derivative action in the
temperature-control problem.

The result is stored in the stack along with the sign. This term is included in the output by
adding a routine immediately after *DCPI* has been calculated, as shown in the flowchart
of Fig. 6-23. Since the action is reverse, a positive *DCD* is subtracted from *DCPI* to get
the output. The 8080 code for this example is shown in Fig. 6-24. Note the use of the
stack to retain and pass variables within the program.

PROBLEMS

6-1 A computer control system has a set point of $DSP = 7AH$. The input range is 00 to FFH and the error will be an 8-bit word. Find the error, DE, and fractional error, DFE, for inputs of $DV = 07H$, 28H, 6EH, C4H, and EDH.

6-2 Repeat Prob. 6-1 if the input range is given by 23H to EBH.

6-3 A digital controller output varies over the range 00 to FFH. Control equations predict the output to be 0.681 of the range. Find the output in hex.

6-4 A proportional mode controller has a gain of 3.75, direct acting. Input and output ranges are 00 to FFH, the set point is A4H, and the zero error output is 7BH. Sample time is 1.5 s. Write out the simplified control equation and construct a general flowchart for the control.

6-5 Assume DV is already in the accumulator of an 8080-based computer. Develop a detailed flowchart of Prob. 6-4.

6-6 Assuming an 8080, port E5 for input, and port E6 for output, develop the machine language code to implement the flowchart of Prob. 6-5.

6-7 A proportional control has a gain of 4, reverse acting. The set point is 81H and the zero error output is D4H. If the input range is 2AH to E5H and the output range is 80H to FFH, find the control equations.

6-8 A flow control system has the following specifications:

$$\begin{aligned}
\text{Flow:} \quad & 20 \text{ to } 80 \text{ gal/min} \rightarrow 00 \text{ to FFH} \\
\text{Control valve:} \quad & \text{closed to open} \rightarrow 00 \text{ to FFH} \\
\text{Set point:} \quad & 58 \text{ gal/min} \\
\text{Zero error output:} \quad & \text{valve } 44\% \text{ open} \\
\text{Proportional gain:} \quad & 3.55, \text{ reverse acting} \\
\text{Update delay:} \quad & 5 \text{ s}
\end{aligned}$$

(a) Develop the control equations.

(b) Construct a flowchart of the control system.

6-9 Assume an 8080 processor with the following conditions:

01H to port E7 starts ADC
80H from port E7 signals data ready
Input data from port E8
Output data to port E9

Write the 8080 menmonic code for Prob. 6-8.

6-10 Assume a 6800 processor with the following conditions:

01 to E700H starts ADC
80 from E700H signals data ready
Input data from E800H
Output data to E900H

Write the mnemonic code for Prob. 6-8.

6-11 The input and output ranges of a direct-acting integral-control system are 00 to FFH. The integral gain is 0.64 % per %-min and the sample time is 2.5 s. Construct the control equation (set point = 85H).

6-12 Given sample hex inputs for DV of 00, 24, 5A, 7B, 82, 91, B4, Cb, D4, E9, C3, AA, and 8E, an integral controller operates by

$$DE = 80H - DV$$
$$SUM = SUM + DE \quad \text{(16 bit)}$$
$$DCI = 0.285 * SUM$$

Construct a table of *DE*, *SUM*, and *DCI* for these samples. Include overflow and under-flow and polarity protection in your hand calculations.

6-13 Construct the 6800 or 8080 code to implement the flowchart of Ex. 6-7. Assume memory-mapped I/O and use:

> Main program starts at 2000H
> 01H to 5000H starts ADC
> An interrupt vectored to 1000H signals data ready
> Input data from 6800H
> Ouput data to 7000H

(Allow a maximum of 200 μs for conversion; then signal an error by writing FFH to 8000H.)

6-14 A derivative control mode has $KD = 0.8\%$ per %/min and a 1.5-min sample time. Find the derivative-mode output for the following sequence (hex): 83, 85, 91, AE, 9C, 94, 82, 83.

6-15 Pressure will be controlled with a PI composite mode. The specifications are:

> Input: 150 to 280 psi $\rightarrow$ 00 to FFH
> Control valve: open to closed $\rightarrow$ FFH to 00H
>
> $KP = 3.45$ (direct)
> $KI = 0.75\%$ per %-min
> $DT = 5$ s
> set point $= 200$ psi

(a) Develop the control equations.
(b) Develop a flowchart.
(c) Develop the 8080 menmonic code assuming:

> 01 to port A0 starts converter
> 80 from port A0 signals conversion complete
> Input from port A1
> Output to port A1

6-16 A type J TC with a 0°C reference is used with signal conditioning that provides 0 V at 500°C and 10 V at 700°C. This voltage becomes 00 to FFH for input to a computer. The set point is 600°C. A PI control mode has a 3-s sample time, proportional gain of 5.5 (reverse), and an integral gain of 0.21/min. Output will be 00 to FFH. Construct the control equations and flowchart. If necessary, include linearization of the input voltage so that 500° to 700°C is linearly represented by 00 to FFH.

6-17 Modify Prob. 6-15 to include derivative action with a gain of 0.08% per %/min.

THERMOCOUPLE TABLE

Table A-1 gives the voltage generated by a type J thermocouple with the reference junctions at 0°C. The materials are iron and constantan. The voltages are given in millivolts and are measured with the iron as positive and the constantan as negative. When the temperature of the measurement junction is less than the reference, the polarity will be reversed, as the table shows. The table gives the millivolts produced for every 5°C increment in temperature.

TABLE A-1
Type J: Iron–Constantan

T(°C)	0	5	10	15	20	25	30	35	40	45
					°C →					
−150	−6.50	−6.66	−6.82	−6.97	−7.12	−7.27	−7.40	−7.54	−7.66	−7.78
−100	−4.63	−4.83	−5.03	−5.23	−5.42	−5.61	−5.80	−5.98	−6.16	−6.33
− 50	−2.43	−2.66	−2.89	−3.12	−3.34	−3.56	−3.78	−4.00	−4.21	−4.42
− 0	0.00	−0.25	−0.50	−0.75	−1.00	−1.24	−1.48	−1.72	−1.96	−2.20
+ 0	0.00	0.25	0.50	0.76	1.02	1.28	1.54	1.80	2.06	2.32
50	2.58	2.85	3.11	3.38	3.65	3.92	4.19	4.46	4.73	5.00
100	5.27	5.54	5.81	6.08	6.36	6.63	6.90	7.18	7.45	7.73
150	8.00	8.28	8.56	8.84	9.11	9.39	9.67	9.95	10.22	10.50
200	10.78	11.06	11.34	11.62	11.89	12.17	12.45	12.73	13.01	13.28
250	13.56	13.84	14.12	14.39	14.67	14.94	15.22	15.50	15.77	16.05
300	16.33	16.60	16.88	17.15	17.43	17.71	17.98	18.26	18.54	18.81
350	19.09	19.37	19.64	19.92	20.20	20.47	20.75	21.02	21.30	21.57
400	21.85	22.13	22.40	22.68	22.95	23.23	23.50	23.78	24.06	24.33
450	24.61	24.88	25.16	25.44	25.72	25.99	26.27	26.55	26.83	27.11
500	27.39	27.67	27.95	28.23	28.52	28.80	29.08	29.37	29.65	29.94
550	30.22	30.51	30.80	31.08	31.37	31.66	31.95	32.24	32.53	32.82
600	33.11	33.41	33.70	33.99	34.29	34.58	34.88	35.18	35.48	35.78
650	36.08	36.38	36.69	36.99	37.30	37.60	37.91	38.22	38.53	38.84
700	39.15	39.47	39.78	40.10	40.41	40.73	41.05	41.36	41.68	42.00

°C
↓

SPECIAL SUBROUTINES

The following subroutines are used in this text to demonstrate how control algorithms can be coded. For each subroutine is given a flowchart and the 8080 mnemonic code to program the flowchart. The programs are referred to in several examples in the text and can be used to solve a number of the problems given at the end of the chapters. Of course, the routine algorithms are general in nature and may be of value for actual software design problems.

B-1 MULT8

The MULT8 subroutine multiplies two 8-bit binary numbers together and gets a 16-bit result. The routine can be used to multiply two integer digits, in which case the result is a 16-bit integer. If used to multiply an 8-bit fraction times an integer, the result is a 16-bit number composed of an 8-bit integer part and an 8-bit fractional part.

Use Conditions. The conditions under which this subroutine is used can be summarized as follows:

Input:	Multiplier in A register (destroyed)
	Multiplicand in E register (destroyed)
Uses:	HL register pair
Output:	Product in DE register pair

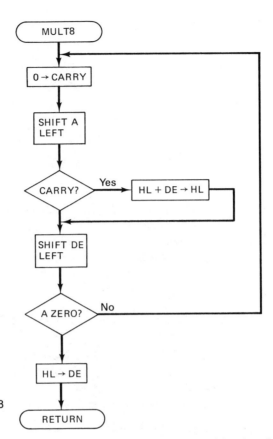

FIG. B-1 Flowchart for the MULT8 subroutine.

Note that both the multiplier and multiplicand are destroyed by the algorithm. This means that if either or both will be needed again they must be saved by the calling program. This is also true of the HL register pair. Although not used for input, this pair is used for intermediate stages of the calculation.

Flowchart.   The flowchart of this subroutine is shown in Fig. B-1. The basic idea is to shift each bit of the multiplier, which is in A, into the carry. If the carry is not set, the answer register is simply shifted left, which is equivalent to adding zero in the multiplication process. If the carry is set, multiplicand is added to the answer before the shift occurs.

Code.   The 8080 code for this subroutine is as follows:

```
MULT8:    LXI H,00H        ;ZERO HL PAIR

          MVI D,00H        ;ZERO D REGISTER

NEXT:     ANA A            ;ZERO CARRY

          JZ DONE          ;QUIT IF A ZERO LEFT IN A

          RAR              ;GET LSB OF A INTO CARRY

          JNC NOADD        ;IF NO CARRY THE NO ADD
```

```
                DAD D           ;CARRY SO ADD DE TO HL
      NOADD:    XCHG            ;EXCHANGE DE AND HL FOR SHIFTING
                DAD H           ;THIS SHIFTS LEFT
                XCHG            ;EXCHANGE THEM BACK NOW
                JMP NEXT        ;GO GET ANOTHER BIT
      DONE:     XCHG            ;GET ANSWER FROM HL INTO DE
                RET             ;AND RETURN
```

B-2   DIV16

The DIV16 subroutine is used to divide a 16-bit binary number by an 8-bit binary number. The result is returned as a 16-bit number. Any remainder is lost by this process, although it would be easy to modify the routine to keep the remainder. Essentially, if a 16-bit integer is divided by an 8-bit integer, the result will consist of a 16-bit integer also. If the 16-bit number consists of an 8-bit integer part and an 8-bit fractional part, the answer will consist of the same format.

Use Conditions.   The conditions that occur when this subroutine is used can be summarized as follows:

Input: Divisor in the C register (destroyed)
            Dividend in the HL register pair (destroyed)
Uses: A, BC, DE, HL registers
Output: Quotient is in the DE register

Since the divisor and dividend are both destroyed, they must be saved before calling this subroutine if they will be needed again. In fact, since all registers are used by the routine, any critical data must be saved prior to a call.

Flowchart.   The flowchart for this subroutine is shown in Fig. B-2. Note that the basic idea is to perform the division like long division by hand. In this case it is done by starting with just one bit of the dividend and then increasing the number of bits considered until a combination is found that is greater than the divisor. Then the subtraction occurs.

Code.   The 8080 code for this subroutine is as follows:

```
      DIV16:    LXI D,0000H     ;ZERO DE REGISTER PAIR
                MVI B,10H       ;SET B FOR NUMBER OF PASSES = 16
                MVI A,00H       ;ZERO THE A REGISTER
      MORE:     XCHG            ;EXCHANGE THE DE AND HL REGISTER
                DAD H           ;SHIFT THE HL LEFT MSB TO CARRY
                XCHG            ;EXCHANGE THEM BACK
                JC SUB          ;IF THE MSB IS SET, GO SUBTRACT
                DAD H           ;NOW SHIFT THE ANSWER LEFT
```

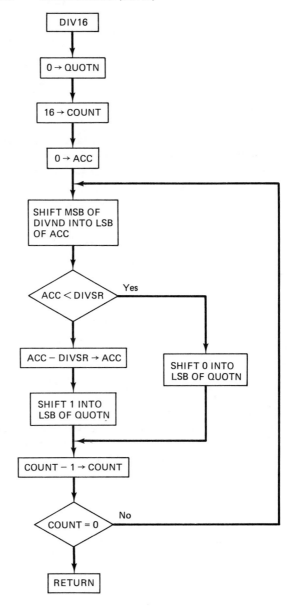

DIVSR = DIVISOR (8 BITS)
DIVND = DIVIDEND (16 BITS)
QUOTN = QUOTIENT (16 BITS)
ACC   = ACCUMULATOR (8 BITS)

DIV16

0 → QUOTN

16 → COUNT

0 → ACC

SHIFT MSB OF DIVND INTO LSB OF ACC

ACC < DIVSR

Yes

ACC − DIVSR → ACC

SHIFT 0 INTO LSB OF QUOTN

SHIFT 1 INTO LSB OF QUOTN

COUNT − 1 → COUNT

COUNT = 0

No

RETURN

FIG. B-2   Flowchart for the DIV16 subroutine.

223

```
            RAL                ;GET DIVISOR MSB INTO CARRY

            CMP C              ;COMPARE DIVISOR TO SHIFTED NUMBER

            JM ZERO            ;IF LESS DO NOT SUBTRACT

SUB:        SUB C              ;SUBTRACT DIVISOR

            INX H              ;AND ONE TO ANSWER REGISTER PAIR

ZERO:       DCR B              ;DECREMENT COUNTER

            JNZ MORE           ;NOT DONE GO BACK FOR MORE

            RET                ;DONE GO BACK TO CALLING PROGRAM
```

B-3   INTRP

The INTRP subroutine is used in table linearization of input data. The input data values and corresponding variable data are contained in a table in memory. The subroutine finds the table values that bracket the input data and then performs linear interpolation to deduce a best estimate of the physical variable data. The linearization process is described in Ch. 4. For the purposes of this subroutine calculation, the following interpolation formula is used:

$$DV = DT(I - 1) + \frac{[DT(I) - DT(I - 1)]}{[VT(I) - VT(I - 1)]} [V - VT(I - 1)]$$

where DT = table linearized value

$\quad\quad V$ = input data

$\quad VT$ = table input data values

$\quad DV$ = linearized data output

$\quad\quad I$ = table pointer to pair just larger than input

$I - 1$ = table pointer to pair just smaller than input.

Use Conditions.   Subroutine INTRP is used with the following conditions on input, output, and registers employed:

Inputs: Data input in register A

Number of table entries in register C

Starting address of table in HL register pair

Uses: Subroutine DIV16

Subroutine MULT8

Stack

All registers

Outputs: Interpolated variable value in register A.

ERROR from DIV16 is indicated by 0000 in HL pair.

If the data input is less than the least table value, C is returned with 00H. If the data input is greater than the largest table value, C is returned with FFH.

Table: The table consists of N entry pairs of input data and variable data. The table is arranged serially in memory. The first N entries are input data values and the next N entries are variable data values.

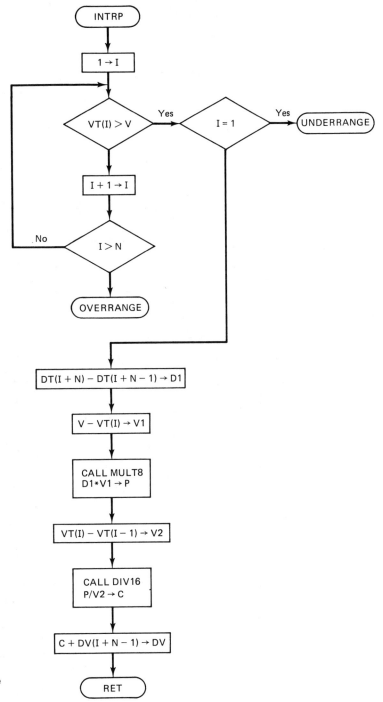

FIG. B-3 General flowchart for the INTRP subroutine.

Flowchart. The general flowchart for INTRP is shown in Fig. B-3. The routine consists of two separate parts, the table search and the interpolation. Table search finds the data values that bracket the input value by identifying number, I, that points to the table value just greater than the input. The $I - 1$ points to the value just less than the input data. $I + N$ and $I + N - 1$ bracket the value on the variable side of the table. Overrange and underrange protection is also provided. The interpolation

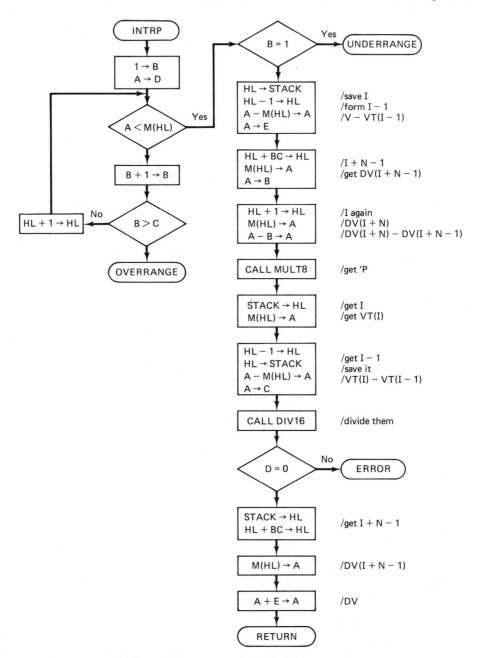

FIG. B-4   Detailed flowchart for the INTRP subroutine.

routine simply solves the given interpolation equation. A detailed flowchart is presented in Fig. B-4.

Code.   The 8080 code for this routine is presented next as constructed from the detailed flowchart of Fig. B-4.

```
INTRP:  MVI B,01        ;B WILL COUNT PASSES THROUGH THE TABLE

        MOV D,A         ;SAVE INPUT DATA, V, IN D

CMPAR:  CMP M           ;COMPARE V TO V(I) IN M(HL)

        JM MORE         ;IF V LESS KEEP LOOKING

        MOV A,B         ;IF NOT BRING IN TABLE COUNTER

        CPI 01          ;IS THE COUNTER 1?

        JZ UNDER        ;IF YES WE HAVE AN UNDERFLOW

        JMP CALC        :IF NOT LETS GO INTERPOLATE

MORE:   INR B           ;INCREMENT TABLE COUNTER TO LOOK SOME MORE

        MOV A,B         ;LETS CHECK THE COUNTER VALUE

        CMP C           ;ARE WE AT THE END OF THE TABLE?

        JM AGAIN        ;NO, SO LOOK AT NEXT ENTRY

        JZ AGAIN        ;DITTO IF THE LAST ENTRY

        JMP OVER        ;LAST ENTRY WE HAVE AN OVERFLOW

AGAIN:  INX H           ;INCREMENT THE TABLE POINTER

        MOV A,D         ;GET THE INPUT DATA BACK

        JMP CMPAR       ;AND GO LOOK AT THE NEXT VALUE

;NOTE THAT HL POINTS TO THE I TABLE LOCATION DATA

CALC:   MVI B,00        ;NOW WE WILL USE B FOR STORAGE

        PUSH H          ;SAVE THE TABLE POINTER IN STACK

        DCX H           ;DECREMENT IT TO GET I-1

        MOV A,D         ;GET V

        SUB M           ;FORM V - VT(I-1)

        MOV E,A         ;SAVE IT IN E

        DAD B           ;FORM I+N-1

        MOV A,M         ;GET DT(I+N-1) INTO A

        MOV B,A         ;SAVE IT IN B

        INX H           ;FOR I+N

        MOV A,M         ;GET DT(I+N) INTO A

        SUB B           ;FORM DT(I+N) - DT(I+N-1)

        CALL MULT8      ;FIND PRODUCT OF NUMERATOR TERMS
```

```
            POP H              ;GET I BACK FROM STACK
            MOV A,M            ;GET VT(I) INTO A
            DCX H              ;FORM I-1
            PUSH H             ;SAVE THIS IN STACK
            SUB M              ;FORM VT(I) - VT(I-1)
            PUSH B             ;SAVE BC IN STACK SO WE CAN USE THEM
            MOV C,A            ;SAVE IT IN C
            CALL DIV16         ;NOW DIVIDE
            JZ ERROR           ;IF A RETURNS ZERO THERE IS AN ERROR
            POP B              ;GET BC BACK
            POP H              ;GET I BACK
            MVI B,00           ;ZERO B REGISTER SO WE CAN DOUBLE ADD
            DAD B              ;ADDS
            MOV A,M            ;GET DT(I-1)
            ADD E              ;THIS IS THE ANSWER
            RET
OVER:       MVI C,0FFH         ;OVERFLOW ERROR, SET C TO FFH
            RET
UNDER:      MVI C,00H          ;UNDERFLOW ERROR, SET C TO 00
            RET
ERROR:      LXI H,0000         ;DIVIDE ERROR OCCURED
            RET
            END
```

MICROPROCESSOR INSTRUCTION SETS AND ASSEMBLY LANGUAGE

The following sections present a brief summary of the instruction sets and assembly language structure for the 8080 and 6800 microprocessors.

C-1 8080

Instruction Set. Table C-1 presents the 8080 instruction set in mnemonic form. The number of system cycles per instruction is also given. When two values are given, as return on carry (RC) with 5/11 cycles, the first assumes the condition is not met and the second that the condition is met. In general, the execution time of a program can be approximately accounted for by adding the number of clock cycles and knowing the clock time. The flags affected by the instruction are denoted by the letter combinations: Z (zero), S (sign), P (parity), C (carry), AC (auxiliary carry).

Assembly Language. The key features of the assembly language can be summarized as follows:

1. The mnemonics of the instructions are used for reference to the specific instructions.
2. A register reference instruction will use any of A, B, C, D, E, H, L or *r* in the mnemonic.

3. Memory reference instructions are referred to using M for the memory notation, where the actual 16-bit address is contained in the HL register pair.
4. Hex numbers are written with a trailing H, octal with a trailing O, binary with a trailing B, and decimal with no trailing indicator.
5. Hex numbers beginning with a letter must be preceded by a zero.

TABLE C-1
8080 Instruction Set

Mnemonic*	Description	Flags	Cycles
MOV r1,r2	Move between registers	none	5
MOV r,M	Move from memory	none	7
Mov M,r	Move to memory	none	7
MVI r,data8	Move immediate to register	none	7
MVI M,data8	Move immediate to memory	none	10
LXI rp,data16	Load immediate register pair	none	10
LDA addr	Load accumulator direct	none	13
STA addr	Store accumulator direct	none	13
LHLD addr	Load HL pair direct	none	16
SHLD addr	Store HL pair direct	none	16
LDAX rp	Load accumulator indirect	none	7
STAX rp	Store accumulator indirect	none	7
XCHG	Exchange HL with DE	none	4
ADD r	Add register	ZSPCYAC	4
ADD M	Add memory	ZSPCYAC	7
ADI data8	Add immediate	ZSPCYAC	7
ADC r	Add register with carry	ZSPCYAC	4
ADC M	Add memory with carry	ZSPCYAC	7
ACI data8	Add immediate with carry	ZSPCYAC	7
SUB r	Subtract register	ZSPCYAC	4
SUB M	Subtract memory	ZSPCYAC	7
SUI data8	Subtract immediate	ZSPCYAC	7
SBB r	Subtract register with borrow	ZSPCYAC	4
SBB M	Subtract memory with borrow	ZSPCYAC	7
SBI data8	Subtract immediate with borrow	ZSPCYAC	7
INR r	Increment register	ZSPAC	5

*See Notes on p. 233.

TABLE C-1 (cont.)
8080 Instruction Set

Mnemonic	Description	Flags	Cycles
INR M	Increment memory	ZSPAC	10
DCR r	Decrement register	ZSPAC	5
DCR M	Decrement memory	ZSPAC	10
INX rp	Increment register pair	none	5
DCX rp	Decrement register pair	none	5
DAD rp	Add register pair to HL	none	10
DAA	Decimal adjust accumulator	ZSPCYAC	4
ANA r	AND register	ZSPCYAC	4
ANA M	AND memory	ZSPCYAC	7
ANI data8	AND immediate	ZSPCYAC	7
XRA r	Exclusive OR register	ZSPCYAC	4
XRA M	Exclusive OR memory	ZSPCYAC	7
XRI data8	Exclusive OR immediate	ZSPCYAC	7
ORA r	OR register	ZSPCYAC	4
ORA M	OR memory	ZSPCYAC	7
ORI data8	OR immediate	ZSPCYAC	7
CMP r	Compare register	ZSPCYAC	4
CMP M	Compare memory	ZSPCYAC	7
CPI data8	Compare immediate	ZSPCYAC	7
RLC	Rotate left, A7 → CY	CY	4
RRC	Rotate right, A0 → CY	CY	4
RAL	Rotate left through carry	CY	4
RAR	Rotate right through carry	CY	4
CMA	Complement accumulator	none	4
CMC	Complement carry	CY	4
STC	Set carry	CY	4
JMP addr	Unconditional jump	none	10
JC addr	Jump on carry	none	10
JNC addr	Jump on no carry	none	10
JZ addr	Jump on zero	none	10
JNZ addr	Jump on no zero	none	10
JM addr	Jump on minus	none	10

TABLE C-1 (cont.)
8080 Instruction Set

Mnemonic	Description	Flags	Cycles
JP addr	Jump on positive	none	10
JPE addr	Jump on parity even	none	10
JPO addr	Jump on parity odd	none	10
CALL addr	Call subroutine	none	17
CC addr	Call on carry	none	11/17
CNC addr	Call on no carry	none	11/17
CZ addr	Call on zero	none	11/17
CNZ addr	Call on no zero	none	11/17
CM addr	Call on minus	none	11/17
CP addr	Call on positive	none	11/17
CPE addr	Call on parity even	none	11/17
CPO addr	Call on parity odd	none	11/17
RET	Return from subroutine	none	10
RC	Return on carry	none	5/11
RNC	Return on no carry	none	5/11
RZ	Return on zero	none	5/11
RNZ	Return on no zero	none	5/11
RM	Return on minus	none	5/11
RP	Return on positive	none	5/11
RPE	Return on parity even	none	5/11
RPO	Return on parity odd	none	5/11
RST n	Restart (n=0,1,2,3,4,5,6,7)	none	11
PCHL	HL to program counter	none	5
PUSH rp	Push register pair	none	11
PUSH PSW	Push accumulator and flags	none	11
POP rp	Pop register pair	none	10
POP PSW	Pop accumulator and flags	none	10
XTHL	Exchange top of stack with HL	none	18
SPHL	HL to stack pointer	none	5
IN port	Input from port	none	10
OUT port	Output to port	none	10
EI	Enable interrupts	none	4

TABLE C-1 (cont.)
8080 Instruction Set

Mnemonic	Description	Flags	Cycles
DI	Disable interrupts	none	4
HLT	Halt	none	4
NOP	No operation	none	4

Notes: data8 = 8-bit number

data16 = 16-bit number

addr   = 16-bit address

port   = 8-bit port address

r   = 8-bit register:A,B,C,D,E,H,L

rp   = 16-bit register pair: BC, DE, HL, SP

C-2   6800

Instruction Set.   Table C-2 presents the 6800 instruction set. For each basic instruction the mnemonic is given as well as the op code, cycles, and bytes for different forms of the instruction. Addressing may be carried out in one of several forms (immediate, direct, indexed, extended, or implied) as given by the form of the mnemonic noted in the next section. Any effect of the instruction on condition codes is given by the letters of the conditions: H (half-carry), I (interrupt), N (negative), Z (zero), V (overflow), C (carry).

Assembly Language.   The key features of the 6800 assembly language are as follows:

1. Hex numbers are noted by a *preceding* $, binary by %, octal by @, and decimal by no preceding indicator.
2. Addressing mode is indicated as follows:
    a. *Immediate:* a # precedes the number.
    b. *Direct:* the number alone but in the range from 0 to FFH or its equivalent in other number systems.
    c. *Indexed:* indicated by ZZ,X, where ZZ is a number from zero to FFH or its equivalent in other number systems.
    d. *Extended:* a number from 0000H to FFFFH or its equivalent in other number systems, with leading zeros if necessary.
    e. *Implied:* given by the instruction.

TABLE C-2
6800 Instruction Set

OPERATIONS	MNEMONIC	IMMED OP	~	#	DIRECT OP	~	#	INDEX OP	~	#	EXTND OP	~	#	IMPLIED OP	~	#	BOOLEAN/ARITHMETIC OPERATION (All register labels refer to contents)	5 H	4 I	3 N	2 Z	1 V	0 C
Add	ADDA	8B	2	2	9B	3	2	AB	5	2	BB	4	3				A + M → A	↕	•	↕	↕	↕	↕
	ADDB	CB	2	2	DB	3	2	EB	5	2	FB	4	3				B + M → B	↕	•	↕	↕	↕	↕
Add Acmltrs	ABA													1B	2	1	A + B → A	↕	•	↕	↕	↕	↕
Add with Carry	ADCA	89	2	2	99	3	2	A9	5	2	B9	4	3				A + M + C → A	↕	•	↕	↕	↕	↕
	ADCB	C9	2	2	D9	3	2	E9	5	2	F9	4	3				B + M + C → B	↕	•	↕	↕	↕	↕
And	ANDA	84	2	2	94	3	2	A4	5	2	B4	4	3				A · M → A	•	•	↕	↕	R	•
	ANDB	C4	2	2	D4	3	2	E4	5	2	F4	4	3				B · M → B	•	•	↕	↕	R	•
Bit Test	BITA	85	2	2	95	3	2	A5	5	2	B5	4	3				A · M	•	•	↕	↕	R	•
	BITB	C5	2	2	D5	3	2	E5	5	2	F5	4	3				B · M	•	•	↕	↕	R	•
Clear	CLR							6F	7	2	7F	6	3				00 → M	•	•	R	S	R	R
	CLRA													4F	2	1	00 → A	•	•	R	S	R	R
	CLRB													5F	2	1	00 → B	•	•	R	S	R	R
Compare	CMPA	81	2	2	91	3	2	A1	5	2	B1	4	3				A − M	•	•	↕	↕	↕	↕
	CMPB	C1	2	2	D1	3	2	E1	5	2	F1	4	3				B − M	•	•	↕	↕	↕	↕
Compare Acmltrs	CBA													11	2	1	A − B	•	•	↕	↕	↕	↕
Complement, 1's	COM							63	7	2	73	6	3				M̄ → M	•	•	↕	↕	R	S
	COMA													43	2	1	Ā → A	•	•	↕	↕	R	S
	COMB													53	2	1	B̄ → B	•	•	↕	↕	R	S
Complement, 2's	NEG							60	7	2	70	6	3				00 − M → M	•	•	↕	↕	①	②
	NEGA													40	2	1	00 − A → A	•	•	↕	↕	①	②
	NEGB													50	2	1	00 − B → B	•	•	↕	↕	①	②
Decimal Adjust, A	DAA													19	2	1	Converts Binary Add. of BCD Characters into BCD Format	•	•	↕	↕	①	③
Decrement	DEC							6A	7	2	7A	6	3				M − 1 → M	•	•	↕	↕	④	•
	DECA													4A	2	1	A − 1 → A	•	•	↕	↕	④	•
	DECB													5A	2	1	B − 1 → B	•	•	↕	↕	④	•
Exclusive OR	EORA	88	2	2	98	3	2	A8	5	2	B8	4	3				A ⊕ M → A	•	•	↕	↕	R	•
	EORB	C8	2	2	D8	3	2	E8	5	2	F8	4	3				B ⊕ M → B	•	•	↕	↕	R	•
Increment	INC							6C	7	2	7C	6	3				M + 1 → M	•	•	↕	↕	⑤	•
	INCA													4C	2	1	A + 1 → A	•	•	↕	↕	⑤	•
	INCB													5C	2	1	B + 1 → B	•	•	↕	↕	⑤	•
Load Acmltr	LDAA	86	2	2	96	3	2	A6	5	2	B6	4	3				M → A	•	•	↕	↕	R	•
	LDAB	C6	2	2	D6	3	2	E6	5	2	F6	4	3				M → B	•	•	↕	↕	R	•

COND. CODE REG.

ADDRESSING MODELS

TABLE C-2 (cont.)
6800 Instruction Set

OPERATIONS	MNEMONIC	IMMED OP	~	#	DIRECT OP	~	#	INDEX OP	~	#	EXTND OP	~	#	IMPLIED OP	~	#	BOOLEAN/ARITHMETIC OPERATION (All register labels refer to contents)	H	I	N	Z	V	C
OR, Inclusive	ORAA	8A	2	2	9A	3	2	AA	5	2	BA	4	3				A + M → A	•	•	↕	↕	R	•
	ORAB	CA	2	2	DA	3	2	EA	5	2	FA	4	3				B + M → B	•	•	↕	↕	R	•
Push Data	PSHA													36	4	1	A → M_SP, SP − 1 → SP	•	•	•	•	•	•
	PSHB													37	4	1	B → M_SP, SP − 1 → SP	•	•	•	•	•	•
Pull Data	PULA													32	4	1	SP + 1 → SP, M_SP → A	•	•	•	•	•	•
	PULB													33	4	1	SP + 1 → SP, M_SP → B	•	•	•	•	•	•
Rotate Left	ROL							69	7	2	79	6	3				M	•	•	↕	↕	⑥	↕
	ROLA													49	2	1	A	•	•	↕	↕	⑥	↕
	ROLB													59	2	1	B	•	•	↕	↕	⑥	↕
Rotate Right	ROR							66	7	2	76	6	3				M	•	•	↕	↕	⑥	↕
	RORA													46	2	1	A	•	•	↕	↕	⑥	↕
	RORB													56	2	1	B	•	•	↕	↕	⑥	↕
Shift Left, Arithmetic	ASL							68	7	2	78	6	3				M	•	•	↕	↕	⑥	↕
	ASLA													48	2	1	A	•	•	↕	↕	⑥	↕
	ASLB													58	2	1	B	•	•	↕	↕	⑥	↕
Shift Right, Arithmetic	ASR							67	7	2	77	6	3				M	•	•	↕	↕	⑥	↕
	ASRA													47	2	1	A	•	•	↕	↕	⑥	↕
	ASRB													57	2	1	B	•	•	↕	↕	⑥	↕
Shift Right, Logic	LSR							64	7	2	74	6	3				M	•	•	R	↕	⑥	↕
	LSRA													44	2	1	A	•	•	R	↕	⑥	↕
	LSRB													54	2	1	B	•	•	R	↕	⑥	↕
Store Acmltr.	STAA				97	4	2	A7	6	2	B7	5	3				A → M	•	•	↕	↕	R	•
	STAB				D7	4	2	E7	6	2	F7	5	3				B → M	•	•	↕	↕	R	•
Subtract	SUBA	80	2	2	90	3	2	A0	5	2	B0	4	3				A − M → A	•	•	↕	↕	↕	↕
	SUBB	C0	2	2	D0	3	2	E0	5	2	F0	4	3				B − M → B	•	•	↕	↕	↕	↕
Subtract Acmltrs.	SBA													10	2	1	A − B → A	•	•	↕	↕	↕	↕
Subtr. with Carry	SBCA	82	2	2	92	3	2	A2	5	2	B2	4	3				A − M − C → A	•	•	↕	↕	↕	↕
	SBCB	C2	2	2	D2	3	2	E2	5	2	F2	4	3				B − M − C → B	•	•	↕	↕	↕	↕
Transfer Acmltrs.	TAB													16	2	1	A → B	•	•	↕	↕	R	•
	TBA													17	2	1	B → A	•	•	↕	↕	R	•
Test, Zero or Minus	TST							6D	7	2	7D	6	3				M − 00	•	•	↕	↕	R	R
	TSTA													4D	2	1	A − 00	•	•	↕	↕	R	R
	TSTB													5D	2	1	B − 00	•	•	↕	↕	R	R

Column headings under COND. CODE REG.: 5 H, 4 I, 3 N, 2 Z, 1 V, 0 C.

235

TABLE C-2 (cont.)
6800 Instruction Set

Index Register and Stack Manipulation Instructions

POINTER OPERATIONS	MNEMONIC	IMMED OP	IMMED ~	IMMED #	DIRECT OP	DIRECT ~	DIRECT #	INDEX OP	INDEX ~	INDEX #	EXTND OP	EXTND ~	EXTND #	IMPLIED OP	IMPLIED ~	IMPLIED #	BOOLEAN/ARITHMETIC OPERATIONS	5 H	4 I	3 N	2 Z	1 V	0 C
Compare Index Reg	CPX	8C	3	3	9C	4	2	AC	6	2	BC	5	3				$X_H - M, X_L - (M+1)$	•	•	⑦	↕	⑧	•
Decrement Index Reg	DEX													09	4	1	$X - 1 \rightarrow X$	•	•	↕	↕	•	•
Decrement Stack Pntr	DES													34	4	1	$SP - 1 \rightarrow SP$	•	•	•	•	•	•
Increment Index Reg	INX													08	4	1	$X + 1 \rightarrow X$	•	•	↕	↕	•	•
Increment Stack Pntr	INS													31	4	1	$SP + 1 \rightarrow SP$	•	•	•	•	•	•
Load Index Reg	LDX	CE	3	3	DE	4	2	EE	6	2	FE	5	3				$M \rightarrow X_H, (M+1) \rightarrow X_L$	•	•	⑨	↕	R	•
Load Stack Pntr	LDS	8E	3	3	9E	4	2	AE	6	2	BE	5	3				$M \rightarrow SP_H, (M+1) \rightarrow SP_L$	•	•	⑨	↕	R	•
Store Index Reg	STX				DF	5	2	EF	7	2	FF	6	3				$X_H \rightarrow M, X_L \rightarrow (M+1)$	•	•	⑨	↕	R	•
Store Stack Pntr	STS				9F	5	2	AF	7	2	BF	6	3				$SP_H \rightarrow M, SP_L \rightarrow (M+1)$	•	•	⑨	↕	R	•
Index Reg → Stack Pntr	TXS													35	4	1	$X - 1 \rightarrow SP$	•	•	•	•	•	•
Stack Pntr → Index Reg	TSX													30	4	1	$SP + 1 \rightarrow X$	•	•	•	•	•	•

COND. CODE REG.

Jump and Branch Instructions

OPERATIONS	MNEMONIC	RELATIVE OP	RELATIVE ~	RELATIVE #	INDEX OP	INDEX ~	INDEX #	EXTND OP	EXTND ~	EXTND #	IMPLIED OP	IMPLIED ~	IMPLIED #	BRANCH TEST	5 H	4 I	3 N	2 Z	1 V	0 C
Branch Always	BRA	20	4	2										None	•	•	•	•	•	•
Branch If Carry Clear	BCC	24	4	2										$C = 0$	•	•	•	•	•	•
Branch If Carry Set	BCS	25	4	2										$C = 1$	•	•	•	•	•	•
Branch If = Zero	BEQ	27	4	2										$Z = 1$	•	•	•	•	•	•
Branch If ≥ Zero	BGE	2C	4	2										$N \oplus V = 0$	•	•	•	•	•	•
Branch If > Zero	BGT	2E	4	2										$Z + (N \oplus V) = 0$	•	•	•	•	•	•
Branch If Higher	BHI	22	4	2										$C + Z = 0$	•	•	•	•	•	•
Branch If ≤ Zero	BLE	2F	4	2										$Z + (M \oplus V) = 1$	•	•	•	•	•	•
Branch If Lower Or Same	BLS	23	4	2										$C + Z = 1$	•	•	•	•	•	•
Branch If < Zero	BLT	2D	4	2										$N \oplus V = 1$	•	•	•	•	•	•
Branch If Minus	BMI	2B	4	2										$N = 1$	•	•	•	•	•	•
Branch If Not Equal Zero	BNE	26	4	2										$Z = 0$	•	•	•	•	•	•
Branch If Overflow Clear	BVC	28	4	2										$V = 0$	•	•	•	•	•	•
Branch If Overflow Set	BVS	29	4	2										$V = 1$	•	•	•	•	•	•
Branch If Plus	BPL	2A	4	2										$N = 0$	•	•	•	•	•	•
Branch To Subroutine	BSR	8D	8	2										} See Special Operations	•	•	•	•	•	•
Jump	JMP				6E	4	2	7E	3	3					•	•	•	•	•	•
Jump To Subroutine	JSR				AD	8	2	BD	9	3					•	•	•	•	•	•
No Operation	NOP										01	2	1	Advances Prog. Cntr. Only	•	•	•	•	•	•
Return From Interrupt	RTI										3B	10	1	} See Special Operations	•	•	⑩			
Return From Subroutine	RTS										39	5	1		•	•	•	•	•	•
Software Interrupt	SWI										3F	12	1		•	•	•	•	•	•
Wait for Interrupt*	WAI										3E	9	1		•	⑪	•	•	•	•

COND. CODE REG.

*WAI puts Address Bus, R/W, and Data Bus in the three-state mode while VMA is held low.

TABLE C-2 (cont.)
6800 Instruction Set

Condition Code Register Manipulation Instructions

OPERATIONS	MNEMONIC	IMPLIED			BOOLEAN OPERATION	COND. CODE REG.					
		OP	~	#		5 H	4 I	3 N	2 Z	1 V	0 C
Clear Carry	CLC	0C	2	1	0 → C	•	•	•	•	•	R
Clear Interrupt Mask	CLI	0E	2	1	0 → 1	•	R	•	•	•	•
Clear Overflow	CLV	0A	2	1	0 → V	•	•	•	•	R	•
Set Carry	SEC	0D	2	1	1 → C	•	•	•	•	•	S
Set Interrupt Mask	SEI	0F	2	1	1 → 1	•	S	•	•	•	•
Set Overflow	SEV	0B	2	1	1 → V	•	•	•	•	S	•
Acmltr A → CCR	TAP	06	2	1	A → CCR	⑫					
CCR → Acmltr A	TPA	07	2	1	CCR → A	•	•	•	•	•	•

CONDITION CODE SYMBOLS:

H	Half-carry from bit 3;
I	Interrupt mask
N	Negative (sign bit)
Z	Zero (byte)
V	Overflow, 2's complement
C	Carry from bit 7
R	Reset Always
S	Set Always
↕	Test and set if true, cleared otherwise
•	Not Affected

LEGEND:

OP	Operation Code (Hexadecimal)
~	Number of MPU Cycles
#	Number of Program Bytes
+	Arithmetic Plus
−	Arithmetic Minus
M$_{SP}$	Contents of memory location pointed to be Stack Pointer

+	Boolean Inclusive OR
⊕	Boolean Exclusive OR
$\overline{M}$	Complement of M
→	Transfer Into
0	Bit = Zero
00	Byte = Zero

Note—Accumulator addressing mode instructions are included in the column for IMPLIED addressing

237

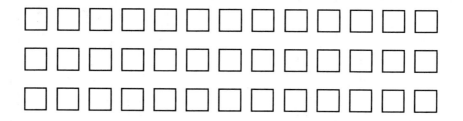

CHAPTER 1

1-7 $Q = 67.2 \ \text{m}^3/\text{h}$

1-9 Underdamped, duration = 6.5 min
Maximum positive = 30 psi or 50%
Maximum negative = -12 psi or -20%

1-11 Error as flow = 30.8%
Error as voltage = 36.4%
Cannot use voltage because of nonlinearity

1-13 Period = 2.133 min

1-15 Plot shown in Fig. S-1

1-17 $c = 5e_p + 7.5 \int e_p \, dt + 2.5 \dfrac{de_p}{dt} + 45$
Plot shown in Fig. S-2

CHAPTER 2

2-1 $v(0.5) = 4.24$ V, $v(2) = 5.36$ V, $v(3) = 5.88$ V, $v(5) = 6.56$ V

2-3 $\tau = 1.15$ s

2-5 50 K is $-233.15°$C or $-369.7°$F
320 K is $46.9°$C or $116.3°$F
757 K is $483.9°$C or $902.9°$F

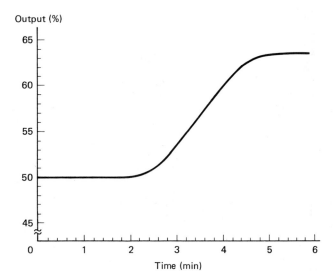

FIG. S-1 Plot for Problem 1-15.

2-7 $R(0°) = 89.5 \ \Omega$, $R(87°C) = 126 \ \Omega$
2-9 $i_{max} = 7.07 \ mA$
2-11 For 20°C the error is 1.7°C
         For 50°C the error is 6.1°C
         For 100°C the error is 30.5°C
2-13 $T(37.73 \ mV) = 676.77°C$, $T(22.44 \ mV) = 410.71°C$
2-15 $T(37.71 \ mV) = 655.81°C$, $T(22.44 \ mV) = 387.5°C$
2-17 $\Delta T = 0.28°C$

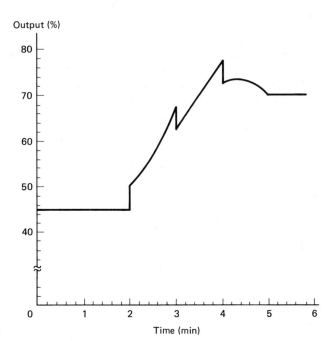

FIG. S-2 Plot for Problem 1-17.

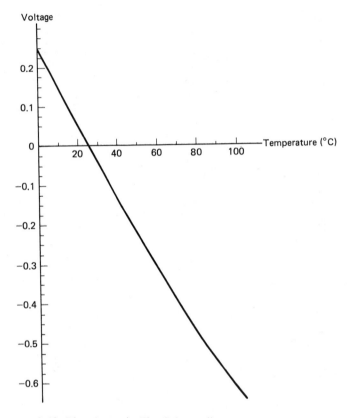

FIG. S-3 Plot for Problem 2-19.

2-19 Plot shown in Fig. S-3, nonlinear
2-21 Figure 2-16a: $R = 5$ kΩ, $C = 636$ pF (among many solutions)
Attenuation at 500 Hz is by 0.99995 (almost none)
2-23 Fig. 2-16b; $R = 10$ kΩ, $C = 0.0159$ μF (one of many)
Attenuation at 120 Hz is 0.119; at 12 kHz the attenuation is 0.997

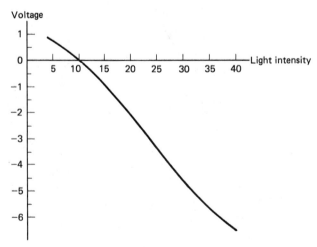

FIG. S-4 Plot for Problem 2-25.

2-25 Plot shown in Fig. S-4
2-27 Figure 2-22 with $R_1 = 1 \text{ k}\Omega$ and $R_2 = 480 \text{ k}\Omega$, for example

CHAPTER 3

3-1 Circuit shown in Fig. S-5
3-3 Circuit shown in Fig. S-6

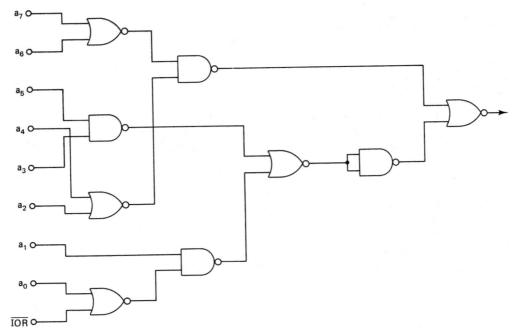

FIG. S-5   Circuit for Problem 3-1.

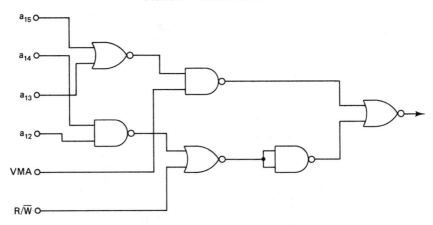

FIG. S-6   Circuit for Problem 3-3.

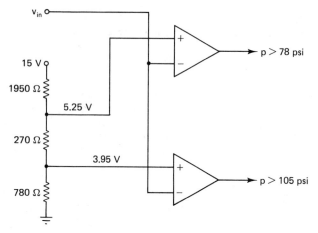

FIG. S-7   Circuit for Problem 3-13.

3-5 4095_{10} locations
3-7   0.410 V, 1.035 V, 2.852 V, 3.184 V, and 4.825 V
3-9   Output = 101111101011_2 with an error of -0.00012695 V
3-11 For 2.2 V: 1100011001_2 with an error of 0.0046875 V
          For -3.15 V: 0001101100_2 with an error of -0.00625 V
3-13 Circuit shown in Fig. S-7
3-15 Figure 3-19 with $R_1 = 1$ kΩ and $R_2 = 71.43$ kΩ will work
          ON for 595 lumen, OFF for 590.3 lumen
3-17 $V_{ref} = 8.127$ V
3-19 For 3.49 V: 1011001_2
          For -2.24 V: 01000110_2
3-21 Temperature = 76.56°C; output for 73°C = A9H

CHAPTER 4

4-3
```
              LDAA  #$00

              STAA  $E000

              LDX   #$XXXX        ;100 µs counter
      DELAY:  DEX

              BNE DELAY

              LDAA  #$02

              STAA  $E000

              LDAA  #$06

              STAA  $E000

              LDX   #$XXXX        ;100 µs counter
      WAIT:   LDAA  $E000

              ANDA  #$10
```

```
                    BNE DATA

                    DEX

                    BEQ ERROR

                    BRA WAIT
         DATA:      LDAA $F000

                    STAA $FF00
```

4-5
```
                         LDAB #$1B

                         LDAA #$00

                         STAA $0301

                         LDAA #$80

                         STAA $F100
            WAIT:        LDAA $0301

                         BNE DATA

                         DECB

                         BNE WAIT

                         JMP ERROR
            DATA:        LDAA $0300

                           .

                           .

    Interrupt routine:

                         LDAA $F101

                         STAA $0300

                         LDAA #$FF

                         RTS
```

4-7 $V = 2.34375N + 1600$

4-9 SUBB #$70
Error for 31°C is EBH or -15H
Error for 79°C is 4CH

4-11 For 2,256,000:   Byte 1 = 00100010
                         Byte 2 = 01101100
                         Byte 3 = 00011000

For $-47,100$:   Byte 1 = 10110111
                         Byte 2 = 11111100
                         Byte 3 = 10010000

For 0.00000502178:   Byte 1 = 10101000
                         Byte 2 = 10000000
                         Byte 3 = 01010001

4-13 5.113 * DATA =   DATA
                          + DATA left shifted twice
                          + DATA right shifted four times
                          + DATA right shifted five times
                          + DATA right shifted six times
      3.87 * DATA =   DATA
                          + DATA left shifted once
                          + DATA right shifted once, twice, four times, five times, six times, and seven times
      DATA/45 =   DATA right shifted six times + DATA right shifted eight times

4-15 Maximum computer sample frequency is 252 Hz, but sampling theory requires 750 Hz, so it cannot be done with one computer.

4-17

T	R	DR	DT
30	3950	00	00
34	3340	2CH	11H
38	2800	54H	22H
42	2400	71H	33H
46	2050	8AH	44H
50	1750	A0H	55H
54	1525	B1H	66H
58	1325	C0H	77H
62	1150	CCH	88H
66	1000	D7H	99H
70	875	E0H	AAH
74	775	E8H	BBH
78	675	EFH	CCH
82	600	F5H	DDH
86	525	FAH	EEH
90	450	FFH	FFH

CHAPTER 5

5-1

	Variable				
State	Water	Motor	Agitate	Spin	Drain
1. Fill	on	off	off	off	off
2. Wash	off	on	on	off	off
3. Drain	off	on	off	off	on
4. Fill	on	off	off	off	off
5. Rinse	off	on	on	off	off
6. Drain	off	on	off	off	on
7. Spin	off	on	off	on	on

5-3   See Fig. S-8

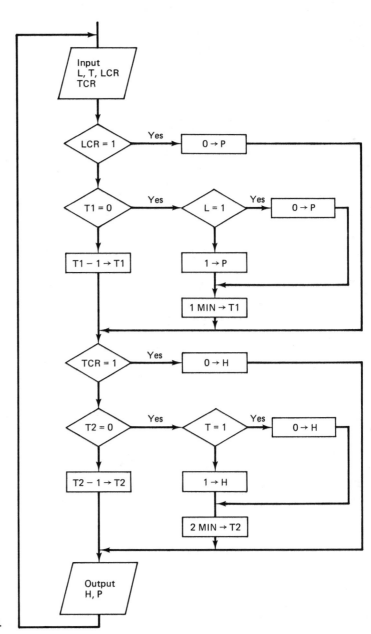

FIG. S-8 Flowchart for Problem 5-3.

5-5 $A1 = \overline{R1} + R1 \cdot \overline{L}$, $A2 = R2 + \overline{R2} \cdot R1 \cdot \overline{L}$, $C = R2 + R1 \cdot \overline{L}$,
$B = R2 \cdot \overline{L}$
See Fig. S-9

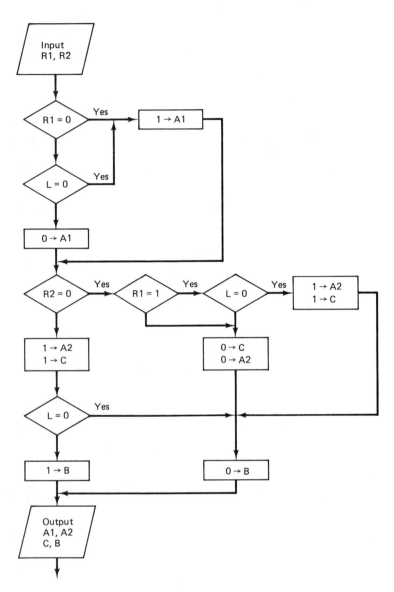

FIG. S-9 Flowchart for Problem 5-5.

```
5-7              MVI  A,03H
        OUT1:    OUT  6BH
                 IN   6AH
                 RAR
                 MOV  C,A
                 MOV  A,B
```

```
                    JC HOFF

                    ORA 01H

                    JMP LEVEL

        HOFF:       ANI 0FEH

                    MOV B,A

                    RAR

                    RAR

                    JNC OUT2

        LEVEL:      MOV A,C

                    MOV A,B

                    JC VBOFF

                    ORA 02H

                    JMP OUT1

        VBOFF:      ANI 0FDH

                    MOV B,A

                    RAR

                    JNC OUT2

                    MOV A,B

                    JMP OUT1

        OUT2:       MVI A,04H

                    OUT 6B
```

5-9   See Fig. S-10
5-11 See Fig. S-11
5-15 See Fig. S-12
5-17 See Fig. S-13

CHAPTER 6

6-1

DV	DE	DFE
07	− 73(8D)	− 00.73
28	− 52(AE)	− 00.52
6E	− 0C(F4)	− 00.0C
C4	4A	00.4A
ED	73	00.73

6-3   AEH
6-5   See Fig. S-14

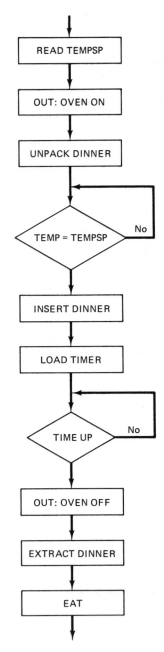

FIG. S-10 Flowchart for Problem 5-9.

6-7 $DE = DV - 81H$
$DCP = -4.13 * DE + D4H$

6-11 $DE = DV - 85H$
$SUM = SUM + DE$
$DCI = 0.0267 * SUM$

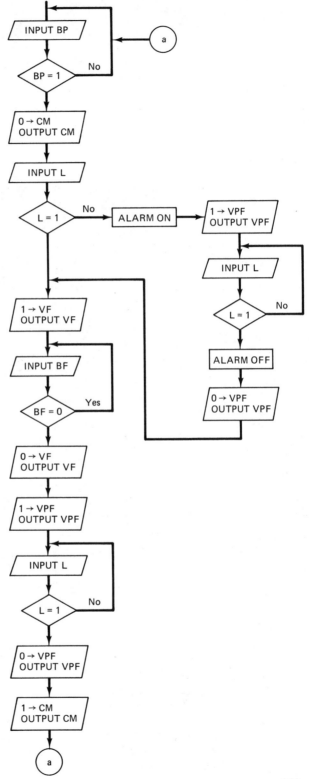

FIG. S-11 Flowchart for Problem 5-11.

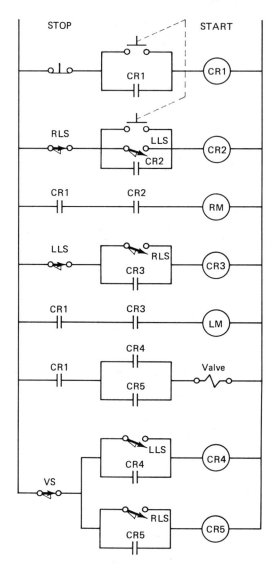

FIG. S-12 Flowchart for Problem 5-15.

6-15 $DE = DV - 62H$
$SUM = SUM + DE$
$DCI = 0.215625 * SUM$
$DCP = 3.45 * DE$
$DCPI = DCP + DCI$
6-17 $DCD = 3.312 * DDE$
$DDE = DV - DV0$

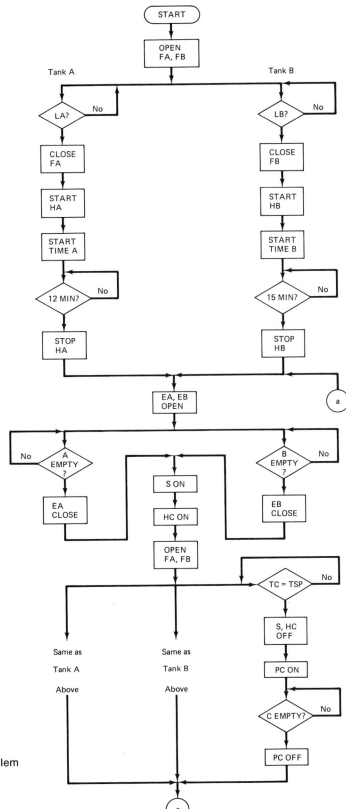

FIG. S-13 Flowchart for Problem 5-17.

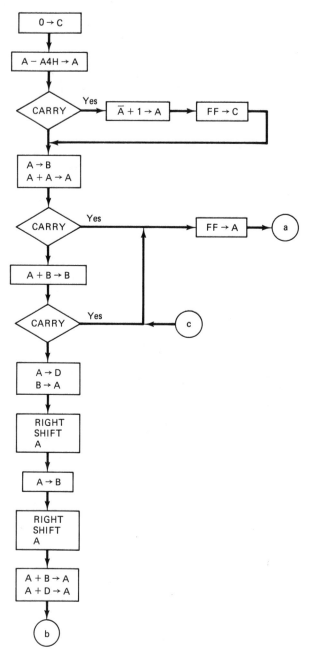

FIG. S-14 Flowchart for Problem 6-5. (Continued on next page.)

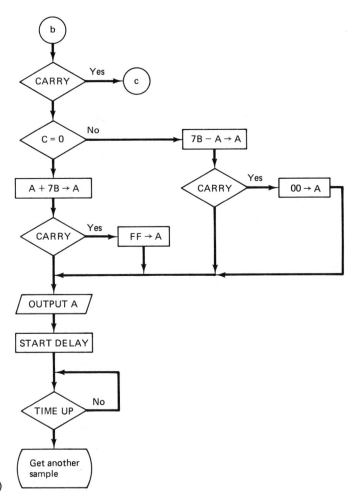

FIG. S-14   (continued)

INDEX